Wyoming
in Profile

Wyoming
in Profile

Jean Mead

PRUETT *P* PUBLISHING COMPANY
Boulder, Colorado

For my husband, Bill, whose patience, support and encouragement made this book possible; and for my children — Terry, Lynda, Lisa, Susie and Billy.

Library of Congress Cataloging in Publication Data

Mead, Jean, 1936–
  Wyoming in profile.

  Includes index.
  1. Wyoming—Biography.   2. Interviews—Wyoming.
I. Title.
CT269.M4   1982   920'.0787   82-12230
ISBN 0-87108-600-X
ISBN 0-87108-601-8 (pbk.)

First Edition

1 2 3 4 5 6 7 8 9

Printed in the United States of America

FOREWORD

Jean Mead's love affair with Wyoming started less than a dozen years ago, but, Oh!, how it has blossomed. And this collection of biographies offers plenty of testimony to her deep feeling for the Equality State and its neighborly people. Ruggedness and beauty, freedom and openness, more opportunity and less restrictions, high education levels—these are some of the things Jean Mead found as she traveled the state, interviewing ranchers, cowboys, politicians, sportsmen, all those "just plain people," soaking up high country friendliness and paving the way for her "Wyoming in Profile."

Her ability to write is unchallenged, as is her perception of the people who make up the Cowboy State. Her style is interesting and fast-moving, yet cautious and careful to the point of simplicity at its best. After all, an uncomplicated writing style is suited very well to the uncomplicated, beautiful people she has chosen to write about.

Carl Skiff
The Denver Post
Former editor, *Empire Magazine*

CONTENTS

INTRODUCTION

Wyoming is not only the richest state per capita in the nation, it's also rich in people; the most unpretentious, candid, talented people I've ever met. While traveling around my adoptive state to interview more than fifty of its well-known residents, I found that three-fourths of them—those who have left their imprint on Wyoming's social and cultural landscape—have migrated from various parts of the country. They are linked by a common bond: "The Wyoming State of Mind," a condition first revealed to me in 1971 by Emmie Mygatt, a transplanted easterner.

Literally thousands of Wyomingites should be profiled here, but only a small random sampling could be produced between these covers. I want to thank those who took the time from their busy schedules to share their life histories. I thoroughly enjoyed meeting and interviewing each of them because they are all truly unique individuals who love Wyoming as much as I do.

My purpose in writing this book is to share these biographies, achievements, tragedies and dreams as well as providing an outlet for those who have received unfavorable publicity and have not had the opportunity to tell their sides of the "story." Although the book is primarily intended to entertain and inform, there are a number of themes and currents throughout the text that I will leave to the reader to interpret.

Jean Mead,
a devout Wyomingite

Darrell Winfield, the "Marlboro Man"—*courtesy Leo Burnett Advertising Agency*

DARREL WINFIELD

"What kind of man is he?"

Darrell Winfield, Marlboro's macho cowboy, spends half his time working on location and the rest relaxing at his forty-acre Riverton, Wyoming, ranch where he buys, rides and trades quarter horses. Volumes have been written about his habits, some of it untrue or inaccurate, but most attest to his innate sense of humor which often embarrasses his charming wife, Lennie.

"People who know him personally understand that he likes to joke around," she says, "but other people who read [newspaper and magazine articles] about him say 'What kind of man is he?'" The Marlboro man was once quoted as saying he choked his wife the night before an interview when the reporter noted Lennie's hoarse voice. As a result of a number of unflattering articles stemming from his humorous quips, Winfield gives few interviews and is cautious and brief with his answers to questions until a particular subject such as "equal rights" provokes a spontaneous response. Then he launches into a humorous tirade on male superiority which fortifies his macho image.

"Deep down you know we're right," he says from his leather recliner. "Men are superior to women in most respects. But I can't talk too loud because I have a wife and five daughters. And when you leave, I'll be in trouble." Everyone laughs, but a nagging suspicion lingers on that he just might be serious. His quip that "women have it made" compounds the feeling that Winfield is a not-so-closet chauvinist, although a chivalrous one. And his background typifies the western macho image he represents.

The ruggedly handsome, almost six-foot, once lanky cowboy was born in the northeastern section of Oklahoma in 1929; the eldest of six children born to Marion and Dapalean Caywood Winfield. His father "did everything" including farming, hay baling, cotton ginning, and millwrighting before moving his family to California's central valley. Winfield's son, Darrell, attended Hanford schools in the San Joaquin Valley, milked cows at his father's dairy, raised some livestock, did a little "rodeoing," and quit high school as a sophomore because his main interests were "gettin' out of school" and becoming a cowboy. Two years later he married Lennie Spring, a sixteen-year-old Hanford High School student, and in 1948 they moved to Kerman, California, where he worked as a ranch hand until 1960, specializing in horses and cattle. Winfield next ran a feedlot for the Eastside Ranch in Firebaugh until 1968, when he was offered the job of cattle foreman for the Quarter Circle Five Ranch in Pinedale, Wyoming.

Lennie resisted the move to Wyoming three years earlier because she feared the cold weather and didn't want to leave their eldest daughter who had recently married. But her husband was determined to relocate after flying to Pinedale to see the ranch. "I love it out there," he told his wife upon his return and asked if she would be ready to move within two weeks. During the following week, however, Winfield's current boss committed suicide, and he stayed on for another month to pave the way for a new manager. The cowboy convinced his wife to make the move to Wyoming during that time, telling her that he "might become rich and famous."

Ironically, three months later in June of 1968, the Leo Burnett Advertising Agency was filming commercials for the Phillip Morris Tobacco Company at the Quarter Circle Five Ranch in Pinedale when the "Marlboro" photographer spotted cattle foreman Darrell Winfield and took pictures of him. A number of professional models were on location for the advertising "takes" but Winfield, he decided, looked more like a true Wyoming cowboy.

"Darrell always wore a big hat and the big mustache and all," Lennie says, "so they seen him and they wanted to know who he was. They thought he was a real 'Wyomian.' They didn't believe that he was a Californian and only out here for a few months." That fall Winfield became the original "Marlboro man with a mustache" and has been seen on more billboards and magazine ads than probably any other model in the world.

"I was pretty happy about it," he says, although they photographed him very little at first. He continued to work as cattle foreman in Pinedale for the next six and a half years while taking occasional "location" trips to Colorado, Texas and every western state—with the exception of Washington—to be photographed on a horse. Winfield herded cattle and horses across the television screen for Marlboro until the early '70s when cigarette commercials were banned from broadcasting. He continued to "cowboy" on film for billboards and the print media until it began to occupy at least half of his time in 1980. His location trips have taken him all over the West and as far south as Venezuela.

The Marlboro man, a photographer and a couple of assistants settle into a bunkhouse or main building of a working ranch on location, and he's in the saddle at daybreak. "They pretty well have the storyboard written out, and they want you to ride across this little knoll or whatever," he says. "That's about all. Or you gather this little bunch of cattle or chase this horse. It's fairly simple." Depending on weather and light conditions for photographing the action, "the commercials can take only an hour to film. Others may take a week."

A few regular, lesser-known cowboys usually serve as background for Winfield, and he says that the Phillip Morris Company uses him to "portray an individual that does as he pleases and owns the world." Someone who "does as he wants to do." He also feels that the Leo Burnett Advertising Agency is "very well read and they probably know more about the West—the cowboying end of it—than ninety percent of the cowboys do. They're very authentic and sincere," he insists. "And they really go all out to study and research the West." The sorrel-haired, blue-eyed cowboy can't recall any unusual happenings while on location because he says "we work with professional cowboys and with

3

professional men on the other end. It's really not a hell of a lot different than everyday ranching life. They just try to take inserts out of everyday living and portray it." Only the glamorous side of ranching is portrayed, he admits. You'll never see the Marlboro man shoveling manure or clearing a ditch.

Winfield refuses to discuss the pros and cons of smoking, saying that it's up to the individual to decide for himself. And as most cowboys have traditionally done on the job for safety reasons, he chews tobacco. While working on location, however, he lights up two or three packs of Marlboros during a sunup to sundown shooting schedule, although they're tossed away and a fresh one lighted for each "take." He averages ten takes for each scene filmed, "but if everything goes well, if myself or one of the other cowboys or the cameraman don't goof up, it will just snap right along," he says.

The cowboy changes clothes often during a day's filming. Shirts and coats are changed frequently according to the season and different colors of clothing are worn in each setting. During the summer months the crew spends some nights out on the range, rising early to help a rancher actually move a herd of cattle or horses. Winfield takes his own horses on location whenever possible. His favorite is Olen, a sorrel quarter horse that he once traded but regained shortly thereafter.

When the Marlboro man is home at his forty-acre ranch near Riverton, he likes to "lie around the house"; do some team roping with his partner, Bill Young, at the Old Timer's Rodeo; trade some horses; ride everyday, weather permitting, and he collects old saddles, bits and spurs. Winfield and Young have won at least three of six team-roping championships at the Old Timer's Rodeo, competing with as many as 50–100 teams, but he calls himself "an average roper." He rides a modified association saddle made in Montana and began collecting antique saddles recently. The oldest dates back to 1906.

The Winfields bought their small ranch in Riverton in 1974, a year before they moved into it, and brought his parents to live there as caretakers from their previous home in Oregon. When the Marlboro advertising campaign became lucrative enough for him to quit his cattle foreman's job a year later, they moved into the rustic log ranch house northwest of Riverton and found it a better location from which to commute. From Pinedale, Lennie had to drive him to Rock Springs and was "just getting started back on the 100 miles to Pinedale when he was arriving in Denver," she laughs. "Now he can fly out of Riverton to Denver, so it's a lot easier." Her husband is gone from four days to three weeks at a time of late, and she occupies her time with grand-children who live nearby—they have eight now—as well as a few ranch chores. "I know it's his job, and I'm just about to get used to his being gone so much," she says. "I pack his clothes and send him off with a hug and a kiss, and he calls often so we always know where he is."

The Winfields were invited to a Marlboro company party in Chicago shortly after he became their cowboy model in 1968, and Lennie was taken by surprise by a huge picture of her husband that stretched across four lanes of traffic on Ohio Street. "It just sort of takes your heart away," she says. When asked how she felt to see her husband's picture plastered all over the country, she replied: "It's kind of exciting to know that it's him, and I know him and he's mine—at least part of the time. They keep him away from me a lot."

The Winfield's daughters are scattered from California to Pine-dale, next door and a teenager still at home. Their only son works for the city of Riverton as a heavy equipment operator. Most of the neighbors are aware of the Winfield-Marlboro man con-nection but he's not exactly a celebrity in his own community, nor does he want to be. The best part of being the Marlboro man is "the money and getting to go to different parts of the country to see how different ranches operate, and the many, many good friends that I've made over the years," he says. He earns "a very comfortable living." Recent guesstimates published of his annual income vary from $50,000–$100,000 with a large share reportedly set aside for his retirement. But he drives "an old Dodge pickup" and lives "pretty much the same way I always have."

Seeing his face staring back at him from billboards and maga-zine ads fills him with "pride. And that's because I'm working for a first-class outfit," he says. "And they, in turn, portray you as a pretty good-looking and macho guy. I think something would be wrong with you if you didn't feel a little bit proud."

5

Curt Gowdy, super sportscaster—*courtesy Curt Gowdy*

CURT GOWDY

*"I'm lucky for a boy who grew up in Wyoming
loving the outdoors"*

It's been a long haul from "soap box" broadcasting of the early
'40s to the 1981 "Sportscasters and Sports Writers Hall of Fame,"
but he accomplished the feat with "a lot of hard work, determination and luck." He also credits his "very strict mother" and a ruptured disk with his success. The silver-haired announcer has
amassed a fortune by doing what comes naturally for him: fishing, world traveling with famous sportsmen, announcing and ana-
lyzing sports events and operating five of his own radio stations.
Along the way he's racked up some impressive broadcasting records as well as gaining himself a reputation as a leading sports
authority.

His own private "super bowl" occurred during the early '70s
when Governor Stan Hathaway rewarded his efforts by naming
an 11,000-acre state park after him, between Laramie and Cheyenne, and proclaimed "Curt Gowdy Day."

No other sportscaster can match Gowdy's record of announcing fourteen World Series; twelve Rose Bowls; seven Super Bowls; six Olympic games; twelve National Collegiate Basketball Championships; thousands of baseball, basketball, and football games; special events; and radio shows during his more than thirty-five years in the business.

The prize catch in his creel has been an outdoorsman's dream, "The American Sportsman," an Emmy Award-winning television show he has hosted and participated in for nineteen consecutive years. Gowdy has taken his television crew of eight all over the world to film segments for the popular program. He fished with Jack Lemmon for Atlantic salmon in Iceland, hunted for grouse in Scotland with champion race car driver Jackie Stewart, and angled for tiger fish in Africa with Peter O'Toole, among many others. He produced three of the fourteen shows annually and spent twelve to fourteen weeks on program narration.

Fly fishing is his passion. He's considered one of America's foremost fishermen and was inducted into the "International Fishing Hall of Fame" several years ago. But then, fishing came naturally to the boy from Green River, Wyoming. Born the son of a railroad chief dispatcher, he was an only child until the age of nine when his sister, Margaret, was born. The Gowdys had left Green River three years earlier when his father was transferred to Cheyenne. As Ed Gowdy worked his way up to superintendent of the Wyoming branch of the Union Pacific, his wife made sure that their young son received the most from his education.

"My mother was a very unusual gal," he says. "She made me take typing in high school, and I was the only boy in the class. She also made me take elocution lessons, and all the things that most young, vigorous American boys wouldn't want. I used to get so mad at her, but I had to do it or she'd shut everything off." That included basketball, the love of his high school years. The All-State athlete and uncontested high scorer was taken off the squad because his mother felt his English grades were too low. "I was furious at her, but she wouldn't budge an inch. So I got my grade up in about a week and was back on the team," he laughs.

The average-sized youth graduated from Cheyenne High School and continued to play ball for the University of Wyoming (UW) where he majored in business and earned his B.S. degree in 1942, "right after Pearl Harbor." Gowdy was active in ROTC and graduated with a second lieutenant's commission which he hoped would qualify him for "Flight Officer Grade." He wanted to fly, but he reasoned, if he flunked out, he could still hang on to his commission. Just before graduation, however, he began experiencing agonizing back pain, "and I went into the service like that," he says. "I was assigned to Maxwell Field in Alabama to take flight training, and I couldn't bend over or do calisthenics, and I was limping."

He was placed in a military hospital for a year before being transferred to Fitzsimmons Hospital in Denver for discharge. The army diagnosed the twenty-one-year-old officer's ailment as "spinal arthritis." But the doctors at Mayo Clinic in Minnesota found that he had a ruptured disk. They operated.

"I should have had good results from the surgery," he says, "but they put me to sleep in the army and stretched me. I imagine that they drove the disk into the nerve and damaged it beyond repair, so I had a very rough time during my early broadcasting days."

Following surgery, he was sent home with orders not to work for six months. During the fourth month, he received a call from the manager of the local radio station, KFBC in Cheyenne, asking him to announce a six-man football game between two high schools. The manager was desperate. Everyone had enlisted or been drafted into the service, but he had remembered Gowdy from his basketball-playing days at the university.

"I said, 'Sure,' I'd go down there and take a crack at it, and my mother made me wear my long underwear and take a thermos of hot soup." Cheyenne's Novembers are notoriously cold, but he sat through the game on a soapbox, doing play-by-play announcing, sans yard lines or numbers on the players' backs.

Two years later, Ken Brown, manager of 50,000-watt radio station KOMA in Oklahoma City, was driving through Cheyenne one night when he heard Gowdy announcing a basketball game. Impressed, he called the station and was given the sportscaster's home phone number. He called after the game to invite him to breakfast the next morning, but Gowdy thought it was a gag, "another fake offer from one of my buddies." Brown persisted in his offer, however, and they met the following morning. He told Gowdy that he was having problems with his current sports director and asked if he would be interested in moving to Oklahoma City. Several months later, Gowdy began broadcasting two sports shows a night from KOMA.

"It was probably one of the best moves I ever made," he grins. He broadcast both the University of Oklahoma games and Oklahoma A&M (now called Oklahoma State). A&M won the national basketball championship the first year he was there, and Gowdy traveled all over the country with the team, including the national championship games at Madison Square Garden. By 1948, he was announcing two championship teams following Bud Wilkinson's arrival at Oklahoma as head coach, the beginning of his football dynasty. Gowdy's chance encounter with KOMA manager Ken Brown was, indeed, a lucky break, he says.

Another lucky break was meeting his future wife, Jerre Dawkins, a broadcasting student at the University of Oklahoma. Gowdy married her the following year while he was Mel Allen's assistant announcer for the New York Yankees baseball games. More than 300 announcers were auditioned for the job and Gowdy got it.

"I rode the train up there and was scared to death," he says. "I had lunch with Mel Allen, and he took me to the Yankee offices. . . . I'll never forget what George Weiss said to me: 'Curt, what kind of money do you want?' And I said, 'Mr. Weiss, who's kidding who? I'm just lucky to be here. I'm in no position to be demanding anything. I've never even seen a big league baseball game in my life.' "

Gowdy's salary as Allen's assistant was $15,000 in 1949, "which could be compared to $50–$75,000 now," he says. The 27-year-old rookie announcer joined the Yankees in St. Petersburg, Florida, for spring training where he met Joe DiMaggio and all the other well-known players he had heard about. He worked the Yankee broadcasts for three seasons until he left to become "The Voice of the Red Sox" in 1951. The year before, he had also begun broadcasting all the basketball games from Madison Square Garden.

Gowdy broadcast the Red Sox games for the next fifteen years. He also started freelancing in 1945 when NBC offered him a network job announcing basketball. He was then offered the "Game of the Week" with Paul Christman, so he left the Red Sox for network sports which then included baseball, the "Top Pro Game" and football.

The sportscaster traveled 250,000 miles for half the year. He left home on Friday to do the Saturday "Game of the Week" and returned on Tuesday when NBC began broadcasting "Monday Night Football." His wife, Jerre, traveled with him to all the bowl games and Olympics but found that packing for short trips wasn't worth the effort. To occupy her time while her husband was gone, she worked "behind the scenes" at their radio station in Lawrence, Massachusetts.

The Gowdy's eldest offspring, Cheryl, works as program director for their 50,000-watt FM station, WCGY in Boston. She also puts in a daily four-hour stint as a disc jockey. "She's good," her father says, "and not just because she's my daughter." Cheryl Ann Gowdy graduated from college in Colorado Springs with a degree in communications.

Curt Gowdy, Jr., is an executive producer with ABC sports and is married to Karen Morris who portrays "Faith" on the soap opera, "Ryan's Hope." He met his future wife, a Wyoming native, in 1978 while he and his father were filming the Cheyenne "Frontier Days" rodeo for "Wide World of Sports." Gowdy's youngest son, Trevor, majored in communications at Ithaca College in New York and is selling stocks and bonds. He hopes to get into television producing.

The senior Gowdy's contract with CBS features twenty-six events, including NFL football, seven sports spectaculars and his favorite show—"The American Sportsman." He also tapes his sports commentaries at his radio stations: WCCM-AM in his city of residence, Lawrence, Massachusetts; WCGY-FM in Boston; WEAT-AM&FM in Palm Beach, Florida, where the Gowdys maintain a second home; and KOWB in Laramie.

Gowdy was inducted into the 1981 "Sportscasters and Sports Writers Hall of Fame" in Salisbury, North Carolina, where he joined the ranks of ten other famous announcers such as Dizzy

Dean, Red Barber, Bill Stern, Lindsey Nelson, Ted Husing and his former broadcasting partner, Mel Allen. In the years preceding the honor, he was named "Sportscaster of the Year" seven times, and he received the coveted Peabody Award, the first sportscaster to do so.

He is also president of the "Basketball Hall of Fame" in Springfield, Massachusetts, where he was enshrined in 1973. Five years later, he received the John W. Bunn Award as the man who contributed most to basketball.

In retrospect, he says, "I've been lucky for a boy who grew up in Wyoming loving the outdoors. If you had told me that someday I'd be in television, and that somebody would be paying me to travel around the world, I would have said, 'Ah, come on, you gotta be crazy.' "

Lynn Simons, Superintendent of Public Instruction—*courtesy Casper Star-Tribune*

LYNN SIMONS

"We cannot live our dreams"

Vibrant, outspoken, aware, informed: adjectives that only begin to describe Lynn Simons, Wyoming's superintendent of public instruction. Whatever Simons says is backed with constant research and sage quotations.

As a child she read incessantly, checking out three books a day from the library when she was eleven, which amounted to well over 500 books that year. Her father later told her, "We were scared you were going to become a hermit." She even read books under the covers with a flashlight. "As a consequence," she says with a laugh, "I've never objected to my own kids reading in bed, but they don't have to use a flashlight." Her sons, Clay and Bill, are also avid readers.

Lynn, the eldest child of Robert and Dorothy Briggs Osborn, was accustomed to mothering boys since she had three younger brothers. The former teacher was born in Havre, Montana, and moved to Flint, Michigan, at the age of eight when World War II began. Her mother, who had been forced to give up her teaching career during the depression because "two married people could not maintain their jobs within the school system," became a salesperson and credit manager. But four years of Michigan weather were too much for the Osborns and they moved again; this time to Golden, Colorado, where her father spent the rest of his career as a mathematics professor at the Colorado School of Mines.

"Looking back on my childhood," she says, "I had a certain degree of precocity. . . . I was an A and B student, not a genius by any means, and never the best student in the class." She graduated tenth in a class of ninety-two students from high school in Golden and enrolled at the University of Colorado. "I spent an awful lot of time in the library reading, but I didn't spend a lot of time on my studies. There's a lot of things going on in students' lives when they're that age," she explains. Lynn returned to graduate school two years later and was "an eager and good student. But between the ages of eighteen and twenty-two, I didn't excel at all."

Her fiancé was a geologist with the Union Pacific Railroad and was stationed in Las Vegas, Nevada, when she graduated from college, but she wasn't able to find a teaching position there. She did get a job in Salt Lake City, however, and taught junior high school math, English and American history from February until January of the following year when they were married. "I quit my job, and we lived ·off and on in Rock Springs, Las Vegas, Rawlins, Evanston and then in Laramie," she recalls. In Laramie she went back to school for a year and a half where she continued her general English-social studies course and became a candidate for her master's degree in American Studies. "That's English and American studies and one other field," she explains. "In my case, I was interested in political science. And when I finished with my course work and was starting on my thesis, I got a job teaching at the university school of education."

The Simons traveled extensively during the next few years via passes from the Union Pacific, and Lynn became a skier. "Then we decided to have a family; my husband left the railroad and we moved to Casper," she says. Their first son, Clay, was born in Casper, and a short time later her husband, John, was offered a job in Mexico as a mining geologist. They subsequently moved to Mexico City for a year "and that led to him becoming professionally involved in mineral development in Mexico," she says. When the year was up, they moved back to Casper "and at that time we made a choice that was really critical. I was willing, since it looked as if his career was going to be Mexican-based, to establish a home in Mexico. He was very opposed to living in Mexico— there are hazards to living there—and we finally decided together that we didn't want our children growing up to be expatriates," she laughs. "So we went back to Casper."

Lynn maintained a home in Wyoming while her husband worked in northern Mexico; their two sons, born four years apart, grew up in Casper. "The wife of a mining geologist learns to fend for herself because her husband is gone a great deal, so I think that those years when the kids were little, I needed to have some outside activities. It's very hard for women with small children to maintain their sanity without something else to do." So she became active in the League of Women Voters in Casper and in educational matters through the league. She was also involved in the Casper Symphony Orchestra Guild and in an art gallery with some friends. Then, during the early 1970s, she was appointed by Governor Stan Hathaway to the State Board of Education as a result of her involvement with the league. She served on the board for six years. "That was when I decided to go into education politically," she says.

Lynn decided to run for superintendent of public instruction, the top educational post in Wyoming, in 1978. To her family "it seemed like a lark that Mama was going on," she recalls, "until I was successful. And then it was very difficult for the move to be made. I'm probably one of the few women who could move and the household could move, without great dislocation. As a matter of fact, it's more convenient for my husband to live in Cheyenne than it was in Casper. He still does a lot of work in Mexico, but he's more oriented to the Rocky Mountain region in the past few years." Her sons who were teenagers, however, were upset by the move because they had always lived in Casper and had many friends in the area. She told her son Clay that he would "go to Cheyenne and make some of the best friends you'll ever have in your life. And that's proven to be prophetic," she says.

The attractive educator quotes Oliver Wendell Holmes when

17

asked about her accomplishments in office: " 'We cannot live our dreams. . . .' I've thought of that many times," she says, "because while I've had my dreams, things move very slowly. Innovatively, I wanted to institute a system of educators sharing their own practices with one another. We've instituted it, but it has not become something that has taken off yet. At the time I took office, there was a great deal of dissension in the educational community. That is, teachers against administrators, administrators against boards, boards against the public, and a lot of acrimony in many cases; a lot of bickering and I think that has been allayed. It will never be a completely harmonious atmosphere because we cannot agree. We have different interests in the case of teachers and school boards. And we're dealing in a labor-management kind of setting. But when I took office, I said that I would never work exclusively with one educational group.

"Franklin said that 'We will all hang together or we will all hang separately.' And I think that's an important concept for educators in an era of declining resources nationally, but not necessarily statewide. We must join in that battle together for declining funds because there are lots of demands on what's available."

Wyoming students fare quite well when compared scholastically with others, she says. "They consistently do above the national and regional averages, and there are a variety of reasons for that. We are well funded and the pupil-teacher ratio is relatively small, around 20 to 1. Also, I think that Wyoming parents have aspirations for their children. The level of adult education is high, and until recently, it was over high school, between twelfth and thirteenth grades, although it declined slightly within the last ten years because of the state's phenomenal growth."

Despite her openness, Lynn has encountered discrimination while in office, "not in terms of opportunity, but in attitude," she says. "For instance, every single superintendent in the forty-nine school districts of Wyoming, with one exception [in 1981], has been a man. And there is an 'Old Boy's Network' firmly entrenched in the state's educational system which excludes women, regardless of their experience or abilities.

"There is a power structure in not only government, but in Wyoming, that is very definitely masculine. But the discrimination is not overt. It has more to do with being taken seriously, or pro-

18

posals being rejected with the consensus that 'if it comes from a woman, it's not worthwhile.' It's very frustrating to cope with, and I think that when that happens, a woman becomes harder and tougher. And the tougher you get, the more likely you are to overcome it. 'Discrimination is obscene,'" she says, quoting a women's rights activist, "for reasons that cannot be controlled, such as race, sex or national origin. And the more subtle the discrimination, the more obscene it can be."

The administrator is excited about the coming "revolution" of the computer and its effects upon the classroom. Its impact "will be greater than radio or television or anything that we've yet experienced," she says. "I think that by 1984 there will be 500,000 homes in the United States with computers. By 1990, there will be more home computers than television sets. And we already know that there are more television sets than bathtubs in this country."

The superintendent feels that computers in the classroom can be a liberator of teachers, "and a wonderful teaching tool. If we don't do what we can to help teachers use this wonderful teaching device, education is going to be set back badly. All those things that have been routine matters—that don't demand personal intervention—teachers can provide for students with a machine. So the things that are really innovative and creative about teaching, that make you feel buoyant at the end of the day, are the things teachers are going to be freed for. It will be a remarkable change if handled properly."

Lynn Simons would like to be remembered as a person "who stood up and mattered for something. I'd like to have some major accomplishment in education," she says. "We talk about integrity in this department constantly. 'What is the honorable way to go with integrity?' I suppose that there are lessons, the things that you learn like the integrity of being in public office, the importance of separation of powers and the slow dawning of understanding of things. What they mean affect your personal behavior along those lines of being honest and full of integrity."

Harold McCracken, author

HAROLD McCRACKEN

"The most gratifying thing I've ever done"

Alaskan grizzly bear hunter, biplane stunt cameraman, author, cinematographer, producer, museum director: Harold McCracken has done them all and more. His friendship with Amelia Earhart and scores of other successful and renowned people have filled his social cup, but his most gratifying accomplishment has been the phenomenal success of the Buffalo Bill Historical Center in Cody, Wyoming.

McCracken was persuaded to single-handedly transform the empty building, donated by Gertrude Vanderbilt-Whitney in 1959, into a western art museum within three and a half months. The lanky, cigar-puffing New York writer had been completing his George Catlin biography at the Creative Valley Ranch on Southfork and was ready to board a plane for the East Coast when members of the proposed museum's board talked him into taking over the project. "I had turned it down before," he says, "and I told them that it was hopeless for there was no acquisition money available. But in a weak moment I said I would."

21

McCracken returned to Cody a few months later and surveyed the museum which looked like "Grand Central Station. There wasn't a calendar, chair or anything at all in it," he says, shaking his head. "I wouldn't undertake it again for all the tea in China, but I was always interested in challenges, and I had friends in New York art galleries, and I knew a lot of collectors because of my interest in western art." He contacted a number of them, including Bill Davidson, a leading art dealer who had been stockpiling western art for years in the hope that it would eventually become popular. Davidson sent his friend a truckload of paintings in time for the May 1 opening, a date insisted upon by Sonny Whitney (Gertrude's husband). Thus, the director was able to fill his new museum with borrowed art and continued to do so for the next few years. Ninety-five percent of all the art on display was loaned by galleries and private collectors for several years until McCracken acquired some acquisition funds and was able to persuade wealthy patrons to donate artwork in exchange for tax deductions.

Because the museum was located on the route leading to Yellowstone Park, McCracken reasoned that tourists stopping for the night would be interested in seeing the display. So he insisted on personally opening each morning at seven o'clock, running two shifts, and staying open until ten o'clock at night to accommodate them. "The board laughed at me," he says, "but it worked. Sometimes there would be seventy-five people outside waiting for me to open in the mornings."

Since that time, additional wings have been added to the Whitney Gallery: the Buffalo Bill Museum, the Winchester collection, the Plains Indian exhibit, and the Natural History Museum. Thousands of visitors tour the historical center each year from all over the world.

Although McCracken lived for years on Long Island, he's a surefooted westerner. Born in Colorado Springs in 1894, he was the son of James Owen McCracken, a crusading newspaper publisher and reporter. With $400 between them the elder McCracken with his brother George and another partner, created the *Des Moines* (Iowa) *Daily News*, "the first penny newspaper west of Chicago." George McCracken had plenty of business savvy, according to his nephew, which James lacked although he was a remarkable interviewer who pursued notorious characters of the

West for his exclusive newspaper articles. McCracken wrote the first interview with Geronimo when the Indian chief was imprisoned at Fort Sill, Oklahoma; and spent a week getting Calamity Jane's biography, among many others. "He spent so much time away from Des Moines that my Uncle George told him he ought to buy a newspaper out West where his interests were. So he sold his interest and bought into the Colorado *Gazette* where he worked when I was born," he says. "Uncle George also sold his interest and bought into Minneapolis and Kansas City newspapers."

George McCracken then went to New York where he instigated new advertising methods and invested in the New York Stock Exchange; his business flourished, while James' floundered. "My father went bankrupt in Cripple Creek, Colorado," he says, due to a mining venture that "ran out of ore." He then took his family to Montana in search of a newspaper job, was unsuccessful, but bought two ranches in Idaho, sight unseen. "One was sagebrush and the other was sagebrush for miles with some buildings on it. He traded the first one for half-interest in a grocery store so we wouldn't starve to death," he says. Young Harold grew up on the banks of the Snake River where he ran into a black bear among the sagebrush when he was eight. The experience made him decide to become a bear hunter when he grew up, but not black bear. He decided on grizzly because his father teased him about his fear.

James McCracken then bought the Salt Lake City *Herald* while it was in financial trouble, and the family moved to Utah's capital city. Harold's maid accompanied them to their new residence, which became a family joke, because the neighbors thought they were Mormons with two wives. His younger sister, Haddie Lee, died in Salt Lake City, making him an only child; and his mother, Laura Crapsey McCracken, a successful artist and "highly educated person," continued to teach him the "three R's" at home. "Father then got involved in a silver mine in Mexico, sold the ranch and took mother and me as far as Dallas, Texas, because there was a yellow fever epidemic where he was going. Then he came back and took us to Woodward, just outside of Des Moines" in 1903. There, Harold went to school for the first time in his life at age nine.

"I was a tall, skinny kid, and they didn't know where to put me," he says. "So they started me in the first grade to let me work my way up. I could hardly get my legs under the desk and the other kids gave me a bad time, so I developed a strong antipathy for schools, which I never got over." He elaborates no further on his childhood, except to say that "we were vagabonds." They next moved to Philadelphia where his father was "involved in gasoline pumps for filling stations in 1910, right at the beginning. If he had stuck with that, he probably would have made a fortune," he speculates, "but Dad never stuck with anything."

Harold McCracken quit high school because he was "bored, but my mother instilled in me, very solidly and deeply, a determination to get an education and try to become someone out of the ordinary," he says. "And I became a high school dropout to get my education in the field that I wanted to spend my life in—writing books." He had corresponded with author Jack London as a teenager and still has the letters tucked away in London's books. The exchange led to McCracken's later sojourn into British Columbia and Alaska where he hunted the largest carnivorous animal on earth, the grizzly bear.

Before his ambitious ventures, however, he enrolled at Ohio State University as a "special student" with no possibility of obtaining a degree. "I had inherited an interest in writing from my father," he says, "but I guess I was pretty dumb because I was literally kicked out of the school of journalism. The dean told me that I was wasting my time trying to be a writer. But it was a blessing in disguise." The author of thirty-one books was "terribly hurt" and didn't tell his parents for some time, but he was determined to "show that S.O.B. that I could be a writer."

Between high school and college, his Uncle George had arranged for him to receive an education "in the ways of animal life" by living with a Cree Indian on the North Thompson River in British Columbia. "He taught me to be a hunter, and he would never let me shoot until I got close enough to hit them over the head with the butt of my rifle," he laughs.

While at the university, McCracken persuaded the school to finance a one-man, two-year, natural-history-collecting expedition to Alaska. His money ran out, however, while he was hunting Dall Mountain sheep on the Alaskan slopes, and he wrote to

Harold McCracken with his world-record grizzly bear (1,600 pounds) in 1916 on Alaska's western peninsula—*courtesy Harold McCracken*

a friend who was publisher of *Hunter, Trader, Trapper* magazine in Des Moines, asking $200 for two articles he planned to write. When the check arrived, however, he was out on the western Alaskan peninsula hunting grizzly bears some 800 miles from the nearest bank on Kodiak Island. He had meanwhile made an "alliance with a fur trader" and travelled with him on his small schooner as a one-man crew in exchange for periodic hunting forays. McCracken was thus able to collect his 1,600-pound male grizzly with twelve shots from his .30/40 rifle (which set a world's weight record in 1916) as well as a 1,000-pound female and three yearling cubs. He then spent the winter in an Eskimo village with the Aleuts where he studied the mummification techniques of their ancestors. During his second trip to Alaska in 1928, he exhumed a number of "mummies" and continued his study of the burial process along the Pacific coast into Chile on a number of occasions. He also unearthed a Wyoming "mummy" in a cave near the Northfork of the Shoshone River in the Absaroka Range.

McCracken's adventures were not limited to hunting. During World War I, he enlisted in the air force and was trained as a cinematographer. He used his training to become a stunt cameraman during the depression and earned $150 a day by strapping himself to the wings of biplanes to film all manner of aerial stunts and events happening on the ground. He spent part of his wages on antique furniture and books from auctions while formerly successful businessmen were "out on the streets selling apples." He worked for Pathe News in New York filming newsreels for movie theatres and received the first slow-motion camera imported from France, which he used to film acrobats and other novelty acts before producing his own one-reelers of broadway shows and musical comedies during the period of silent movies. One of his movie "shorts" won him a silver medal, the forerunner of the "Oscar."

He also worked as associate editor of *Field and Stream* magazine; was assistant to publisher George Putnam; wrote thirty-one books about Alaska, western artists, natural history, juvenile books and others which have been translated into a number of foreign languages. McCracken holds the distinction of escorting Amelia Earhart from her Tenth Street social worker's settlement house in New York City to have lunch for the first time with

George Putnam, her future husband. Since then, the writer's friends and acquaintances have read like *Who's Who in America*.

McCracken retired as director of the Buffalo Bill Historical Center in 1974. He and his wife, Angelyn Conrad McCracken, their daughter, son-in-law and five granddaughters continue to live in Cody within sight of the impressive museum he created. Despite his various successes, he maintains that establishing the museum was "the most gratifying thing I have ever done in my life."

Conrad Schwiering, artist—*courtesy Conrad Schwiering*

CONRAD SCHWIERING

"The only way I can live"

"**A**rt is a harsh mistress. If she ever gets you, she'll never let you go." Conrad "Connie" Schwiering has repeated that phrase many times during his long career "because it's the truth," he insists. "It wouldn't matter if I was starving to death, I would still paint, somehow, if I had to dig ditches or sell insurance because that's the only way I can live."

Schwiering, renowned for his western scenes and landscapes, works seven days a week from nine until five "and later," regardless of weather conditions. He paints primarily out-of-doors, often in subzero temperatures because his work becomes "more succinct and direct" due to pressures he forces himself to work under.

"You have to be determined, but you also capture things that can't be achieved any other way," he explains. "I have to admit that cleaning up is an awful task (below zero) because my fingers won't close around the brush to wipe off the paint, but painting is very exciting when I do it that way."

As a fledgling artist he learned the techniques necessary to paint in cold weather from Belmore Brown, a noted Alaskan landscape artist, while the two were working at the Museum of Natural History in New York City—Schwiering as an assistant background artist following his training at the "League."

Now, he wears knit woodchopper's mitts and a "johnny hand warmer" on each wrist, inserting his brush through the knit material so that his entire hand grips the brush as he paints. He leaves his car motor running with the heater on so that when the paint on his pallet becomes stiff, he can thaw it and himself at regular intervals. He also keeps food and a thermos of hot coffee handy.

Schwiering's paintings now earn him "in the neighborhood of $2,000 each," and his one-man shows have led him up to the gallery of the "Cowboy Hall of Fame" in Oklahoma City during the winter of 1981–82, one of only five artists to be so honored. He was also the subject of a thirty-minute documentary, the prestigious "Profiles in Art" television series in January of 1982 on Public Broadcasting. A charter member of the National Academy of Western Art, he and thirty-one other artists from seventeen western states, Canada and Mexico produce juried art shows of high standards—"the very best in western art."

But success has not come easily to the Wyoming native. His "starving artist" days began in Jackson Hole in 1946 following college and almost six years in the army. He and his wife, Mary Ethel, bought an eight-by-twenty-eight-foot mobile home, "probably the first trailer in Jackson" and moved into it one block off the "square" on Broadway. Schwiering painted all summer before selling two oils, western scenes, for thirty-five dollars each.

"I was really the first artist in Jackson who stuck," he says. "There were other artists who came for the summer, but they would paint a little while and leave, or they just couldn't make a go of it. But Mary Ethel was trained as a teacher and she got a job teaching school so I went right on painting." The budding artist was offered various jobs from local merchants which he declined because he was determined to succeed at his craft.

"I painted western scenes, horses, the kind of a picture where a guy on a ranch is mending a fence. I could always use a horse, but my models were usually young kids who would pose for me on the square because it was fun, and they had interesting horses

I could paint." Many of his former models are now ranchers in the Jackson area.

Not long after the Schwierings arrived in the "nice little cow town," a tailor shop on one corner of the square closed, and the young couple wasted little time turning it into an art gallery. "I contracted with [the landlord] to pay him fifty dollars a month for the shop which was more than we had. Then we went the whole darn summer before we had a sale," he remembers. "We had some success, but not a great deal."

Schwiering then opened a gallery in the mezzanine of the famed Wort Hotel during the winter of '48, where his business gradually flourished over the next fifteen years. During that period, he and his wife lived in the small trailer off the square, and they added a "painting porch" and storage building to their residence. "It didn't cost much to live in the trailer, and we were saving for our house," he says. In 1952, the Schwierings bought five acres in Antelope Flats, a twenty-minute drive from Jackson, just off the route to Yellowstone Park. They planned to build a house and studio but found that traditional financing was not available to artists.

"We undertook a tremendously big house for someone who didn't have any money," he says. "And we couldn't borrow from anybody. The bank wouldn't loan us money because artists were considered deadbeats. We couldn't qualify for an FHA loan because we didn't have a steady income, but I was finally lucky enough to find a private investor who would lend me the money to get started on the house. And I built it with the help of my friends. I had a lot of swell friends who helped with the engineering, and they let me think big about what I wanted to do. And believe me, I think big. Artists don't think little."

Five years later, in the early '60s, the house was ready for occupancy—a large frame house just off the beaten path, surrounded by natural flora with a magnificent, unframed landscape of the Tetons in its backyard. The artist can set up an easel on his property any time of year to paint the mountains whenever the mood strikes. And mood, he says, is a significant element in the creative process.

"I try to make the best possible statement with my paintings from the material that I have. I try to do that without repeating myself, and the best way is to work with the moods of nature.

Nature never repeats herself. So if you're feeding upon the great moments that God puts out there, what you do is to fly on a different area every time."

Schwiering alludes to the feeling that each canvas he starts "is bound to be the greatest painting I ever did, a masterpiece." But if during the course of filling in his "white board," he finds that his efforts are less than satisfactory, he destroys the canvas by burning it. Perhaps seventy-five percent of some 100 paintings he starts each year end up in the "ash can" because he doesn't want to leave "any bad footprints out for the public."

He exculpates with: "We, after all, are only human. We have to keep compromising with what we would really like to do and what we're able to do. So we settle for less than the great vision that we had. And in many cases, it's very frustrating because you never reach or achieve the thing that you thought you were going to do in the picture. When that happens, I burn it."

Despite the hardships and frustrations suffered by those in his profession, Schwiering feels that artists are "pretty lucky and special people because they have something they want to do more than anything else in the world, and they're able to work at it. It's not like I think other people feel about their jobs. With me it's like breathing. I want to work at it all the time and I do work at it all day, every day, seven days a week. Then I think at night before I go to bed about what I'm going to do the next day. And I'm excited," he says with a wide grin. "It's great therapy because your mind is involved in the problem solving process and that's what painting is—problem solving.

"You have to learn to concentrate if you want to be an artist. When you do that, it involves your whole mind. So no matter how bad you feel, how sick you are, or whether you're deeply in debt, that's all gone. Your mind only worries about the painting problem. So it is great therapy, and I feel a little selfish in that I have so much fun doing it."

Schwiering paints intuitively, not by filling in the lines with oils after he sketches a scene. He feels that staying within his original design is inhibiting. "A drawing or a design is just a base to throw your ideas on," he says, "and I've established a habit of painting the way I feel about a thing. If emotionally I feel it needs more expression in an area—or movement—I put it in. I don't worry too much about whether it's absolutely accurate to the landscape or foreground. But you can't change a horse's ears. They come out where they do, and you have to be fairly factual about them."

The artist rarely leaves his self-made paradise, but he exudes pleasure when he recalls a recent trip to central Mexico in early spring. "Wonderful people and wonderful, wonderful walls," he raves. "The light's like this light in Jackson – great light. And we paint out on the ocean near Monterrey where the light is good and clean and clear. The ocean is a great teacher, a strict disciplinarian. You have to concentrate to learn how to do it. So I enjoy it. It's a great opportunity to jump off the cliff into the cold water."

One of Schwiering's basic philosophies is that "an artist will never grow if he doesn't keep trying new things, experimenting with new ideas. To do it the same way you successfully did it before is the 'kiss of death,'" he says. "You must do something you haven't done before, some mood you haven't tried or some kind of landscape situation like the perking of the ocean. That certainly is entirely different every time you look at it and try to solve it."

Although he has no children of his own, Schwiering is often asked for advice from parents of fledgling artists. He usually replies: "If an individual is going to be an artist you cannot stop him or her because once that fire is kindled within that person, there is no way to put it out. If someone comes to me with a youngster they think has ability, I always ask the questions: 'Do you urge him to do this? Does he sneak off to his room to draw? Does he draw because God drives him to draw?' If that's the case, they have a chance of becoming artists. It takes that drive; there's no other way."

Casey Herschler, Wyoming's first lady

CASEY HERSCHLER

"I love this country-type state"

Wyoming's first lady is a rare blend of courage, earthiness and humor. Kathleen "Casey" Herschler is also a long-term victim of multiple sclerosis (MS), but she has managed to rear her two children, work as her husband's legal secretary and excel as his political partner during the intervening years. She runs the governor's mansion in Cheyenne with the expertise of a master chef despite a paralyzed left leg and memories of blindness and paralysis from the waist down. Casey considers her life a miracle.

Born on an 85,000-acre cattle ranch in the White Mountains of Arizona near Springerville, she was the middle child with two brothers in an active ranching family. She rode quarter horses as a ranch hand and was put on the payroll when she was fourteen because she didn't like housework.

"Before that I was the general chore girl," she says. "I rode fence, branded calves and did everything that was necessary. And I loved it. It's the only way for a kid to grow up." When she was fifteen, her parents enrolled her in a boarding school in El Paso, Texas, because the high school in Springerville was not accredited. "I cried myself to sleep every night for six weeks because I wanted to go home. I didn't like what they were trying to do to me—make a lady of me." She managed to survive the loneliness and confining girls' school atmosphere, however, and eagerly awaited vacations when she could transform herself into a ranch hand.

Following graduation she attended Christian College in Columbia, Missouri, and the University of Colorado where she majored in business administration. "My father felt it was a good idea for every girl to be able to support herself," she says. Her father, Burt Colter, arrived in Arizona at age eleven, where he worked hard and invested in then "bargained priced" land. Her mother, Elsie Wear, had been a schoolteacher and also wanted her daughter to get an education.

While studying at the University of Colorado, the dark-haired beauty met Ed Herschler, a tall, lanky young man with a sense of humor to match her own. She soon learned that he was also from a ranching family with a "spread" as large as her family's land holdings. But World War II was brewing at the time and Herschler, convinced that he wasn't going to get through law school before being drafted, enlisted in the Marine Corps. He was a machine gunner in a Raider unit and was wounded in the leg in the Solomon Islands and sent back to the States for recuperation and limited duty until shortly before the end of the war.

Casey, meanwhile, graduated from college and went to work for the State Department of Employment in Phoenix, Arizona. When her fiancé returned home from combat, they were married and moved to Kemmerer, forty-seven miles from the Herschler ranch in southwestern Wyoming. Her husband decided to return to school the following year at the University of Wyoming and graduated with a law degree in 1949. The young couple then moved to Kemmerer to set up his law practice with Casey as his legal secretary. It wasn't long before he decided to run for Lincoln County attorney and he won. He then ran for the state legislature where he served five terms in Cheyenne. During that period their daughter, Sue, was born and two years later their son, Jim.

Shortly after Jim's birth, Casey began experiencing areas of numbness in various parts of her body. She felt listless and "dragged down." Then she lost her eyesight for six weeks and could only distinguish between light and darkness. She also felt "wobbly" and was unable to walk. "But then I was fine for awhile," she recalls. The attacks began to occur every two to two and a half years and once she was paralyzed from the waist down, but she insists that "all those years when my kids were growing up I was fine. I've had a miracle worked in my life."

Ten years ago she "weakened" and lost the use of her left leg, but she manages quite well with a cane and, when necessary, a wheelchair. The governor bought her a golf cart so she can tour the nine acres surrounding the mansion. The cart stands ready outside her office during the summer months, but she spends most of her time at her desk answering the many phone calls with her ever faithful secretary and companion, Eve Souply. Casey arranges all the social events at the mansion and attends quite a few outside engagements with the governor. She entertains two or three times a week with teas, cocktail parties, dinners and buffets in the public half of the mansion, and she accompanies the governor to about three outside engagements each week. "We fill in as busy a schedule as we can," she says. "But, of course, there's some that we just have to 'regret' because we can't be in two places at once."

Since the Herschlers are rare birds in the political nest—Democrats among a flock of Republicans who fill all Wyoming's allotted seats in the U.S. Congress—Casey makes a point of entertaining both parties as equally as she can on a regular basis. "The mansion belongs to everyone who pays taxes," she explains, "and I'm just the temporary caretaker." She is also hostess to visiting dignitaries: "Well, we have some, but I don't consider them dignitaries," she says. "They're just nice people." She puts them in one of two guest rooms in the mansion, one decorated in cowboy decor, the other in Indian. The rooms are comfortably furnished with western artifacts such as branding irons, spurs and Indian prints befitting Wyoming's life-style of the past.

When asked about her daily schedule and the time she rises in the mornings, she answers: "That's a rotten question," and laughs. "Oh, between 7:30 and 8 o'clock. That's early enough. I get to work at my desk between 9 and 9:30 because it takes me awhile to drink my coffee and get my eyes open." She remains at her desk until 4:30 or 5:00 PM, usually, Monday through Friday. Weekends at the mansion are supposed to be days off for both Herschlers, but they rarely are. When state business is temporarily set aside they enjoy reading, but watch little television. Casey's favorites are mysteries and historical novels, while the governor enjoys history, especially Wyoming history.

Politics come naturally to Casey, although she denies any political aspirations of her own. She also denies that she influences the governor in any way, but admits, "I probably pop off sometimes when I shouldn't." Her father was an Arizona politician who ran for offices as diverse as sheriff and state legislator. His daughter fares as well with Wyoming voters. She campaigned for the governor in 1978 for his second term by "visiting" with people around the state. "I'm not the speaker of our house," she smiles, "but I really enjoy visiting with people." She travels one-half of the state with a companion, while the governor campaigns the other half. Then they switch locations. "I campaigned the last time," she says with a straight face, "because I wanted four more years of free rent."

Casey feels that the publicity her husband has earned with his humorous quips is "great. You know, at least he's getting people's attention. As long as you're in politics, even if they spell your name wrong, get in print often when you're running for office." When the press gives her husband a "bad time" she gets annoyed, but she says, "I've learned the more they stir things up—well, they get you into a contest, and it's just not worth it. And yes, I have gotten very upset, and I probably smoke too much as a result. I usually don't fight back although I have on occasion, like that time I wrote to the editor stating that maybe it wasn't the governor's fault, it might have been mine. He runs the state, and I run the mansion. Sometimes people criticize political groups being up here, but I've had as many Republicans as Democrats. Nobody gets elected by Democrats alone in this state, you know."

Despite the pressures of public life, Casey says she's had "such a marvelous life. I've liked every minute of it, especially being a mother and raising my children. Of course, now I'd like to raise my grandkids. I think I could do a better job [the second time around]." Her three grandsons live at the Herschler ranch with their mother, Sue Hunt, her Arizona ranch-reared husband, Jerry, and their uncle, Jim Herschler, all of whom comanage the ranch.

Along with her state duties, the spunky lady has done battle with a number of foes in her own quiet way. She serves as honorary crusade chairman of the American Cancer Society in Wyoming and other important causes besides her own private battle with MS. She has served as a "guinea pig" for many years, trying new "cures" such as acupuncture, which brought only temporary relief. She has also undergone various forms of physical therapy, which she says has helped a great deal. She "highly" recommends her local therapists in Cheyenne who have put her through a series of supervised exercises. She further explains that heat is very debilitating, so diathermy treatments cannot be used. Extreme cold is also intolerable to someone with multiple sclerosis, so she must guard against the frigid Cheyenne winters.

Casey worries about her beautiful adopted state, which experienced a forty-one percent increase in population between 1970–80. "I think progress is inevitable," she says sadly. "And I'm afraid that we're going to have such an impact of people that we're no longer going to be a country outpost. I love this country-type state. There's nowhere else in the nation where everybody knows the governor, and they're on a first name basis."

There's probably no other state—since "Happy" Rockefeller—where everyone calls the first lady by her nickname, but that's the way she likes it.

Chris LeDoux, Wyoming's singing cowboy

CHRIS LeDOUX

"I hope I have enough sense to never go back to it"

Chris LeDoux raises "kids, dogs, horses, Columbia sheep and hay" on his 500-acre ranch near Kaycee; but he's better known for his world championship bareback title and his songs about rodeo life. The easy-smiling, laid-back cowboy does things his own way because, next to his family, freedom is his most valued acquisition. That's why he quit the rodeo circuit in September of 1980 and continues to record under his own label, instead of being "owned by a big recording company."

"I don't know what makes a guy want to write songs and sing to people," he says, "but if you've got a message, you want to get it across. When I come up with an idea about the way I feel about something, I can really state it strongly in a song."

The shy "guitar picker" feels strongly about "family, freedom, the West and cowboy ways." He's just as adamant about his dislike of farm machinery and refuses to be photographed on his own tractor. His feelings have been transformed into nearly fifty songs which he has written, recorded and sold—more than

250,000 albums and tapes—since he and his father, a retired air force major, formed their own recording company in 1972 and began selling music from the back of the cowboy's pickup truck at rodeos where he performed as a bareback rider.

LeDoux (pronounced LeDo) began riding in junior rodeos while he was thirteen and living in Denison, Texas. The air force "brat" had previously lived in France, Mississippi, Pennsylvania, New York and Texas before moving to Cheyenne when he was a sophomore in high school, and the eldest of three children. While residing in the south, he acquired an accent and love of rodeo which led him to quit college during his third year to take to the "circuit" full time.

He majored in "art, P.E. and rodeo" at Casper and Sheridan colleges and received a rodeo scholarship to Eastern New Mexico University at Portales in 1969. After one semester at Portales, however, he performed at a rodeo at the Denver Stock Show. He didn't win any money, but he went on to Fort Worth where he won $400 in bareback riding. The win made him decide to "quit school and go to rodeoing."

While performing in high school and college rodeos, he rode bulls and saddle broncs and roped calves, but he found that he was best at riding bareback-bucking horses. So he began to specialize in that event. "I had to give everything I had to one event if I wanted to excel in it." And excel he did. He won the world championship bareback riding title in December of 1976 at the National Rodeo Finals in Oklahoma City, the "super bowl" of rodeo. That win, he says, made up for all his injuries and lean days on the road.

"I can remember sittin' in a cafe when I first started in rodeo, and waitin' until someone got done so I could finish what they left," he laughs. "You get to where you kind of like it, and it's a habit that's hard to break. I still find myself sittin' in a cafe, like a pizza parlor, and thinkin', 'Doggone, they sure left a lot of food.'"

When the prize money ran out, he was forced—like so many other cowboys on the circuit—to "rough it" between rodeos. "Sleepin' in the truck wasn't so bad. Shoot, I kind of liked that myself," he chuckles. "And takin' a bath in the creek. That's the stuff that really made it worthwhile. Anybody can stay in a motel."

The expenses are the worst part of "rodeoing," he says. "I remember when I first started out. I thought, 'Boy, if I just had enough to pay my entry fees and buy a hamburger once in awhile, I don't care whether I win any money. I just want to get on them buckin' horses and go.' But when you get a little older, you think, 'I'd like to make a little money and stick it away or buy a place — or win the world championship.' "

Entry fees are usually $150–$200 per event and cowboys look forward to sharing in the prize money which averages between $2,500 and $4,000. But the odds of winning are high. "In my event," he says, "at a rodeo like Houston, there might be ninety bareback riders that you're competin' with. You'll probably get three horses and you have to draw a good buckin' horse. That's mighty tough. The odds of drawing a good one is probably eighty percent against you. If you're lucky enough to draw a good horse, you still have to ride him, then the next ones. So it's probably eighty percent luck and twenty percent skill."

The six-foot, 170-pound cowboy averaged 80 rodeos a year. "I really didn't go that hard," he says, "although a couple of years I did. Some guys work 125 to 130 rodeos a year. They're just goin' all the time." Rodeo cowboys usually keep going until they are "crippled" (injured by animals), run out of money for entry fees and traveling expenses, quit or get killed in the arena. The comradery among them is unlike any other sport.

"We loan each other money to keep goin'," he explains. "And we yell for each other in the arena. It's not like football or basketball where the guys are competin' against each other. You're competin' against the animals and the elements. And you hope your buddies will win so you don't have to loan them any money."

LeDoux had second thoughts about his rodeo career during his second season. "I thought it was the worst mistake I ever made 'cause I only won $250 all summer," he recalls. "And then I got crippled. I had a horse step on me [while performing] and it messed me up for awhile."

The handsome bronc rider was fortunate that he never sustained any broken bones in the arena. His injuries were confined to separated joints: knees, collarbone and an elbow. The longest period of time he was off the circuit was from February until June of 1975, when he injured his knee. "It was a terrible injury," he says, "and it's still not right. I had to finally figure out a way to tape it so that it would hold together." Before his world championship win, he and his wife had to rig up a harness to hold his collarbone in place. "Shoot, everytime you get on an animal, you take your life in your own hands," he says with a shrug.

Some of LeDoux's predicaments were more humorous than life threatening. He recalls a horse that "mashed" his new western hat in the arena, and the time he performed in a race where he sat in a "scoop shovel" pulled by a rope that was "dallied up to the saddle horn" of a horse running a timed race around some barrels. "My partner and I won the race," he says, "and I threw my hat into the air and bent over to pick it up. Everybody started laughin' because I had split the back end of my pants out, and I didn't have any shorts on."

The cowboy married a girl from Kaycee in 1972. Peggy Rhoads had never been out of the state when she became Mrs. Chris LeDoux, but she soon found herself on the rodeo circuit, living like a gypsy. Her husband had intended to leave her home that winter and return whenever he could, but she attended a rodeo in Denver with some friends to see him perform and wound up traveling the circuit with him. He had $15 when they left Denver for Amarillo, Texas, but he won $800 there which got them as far as Fort Worth, Houston and San Antonio where he won a little more. That ran out in San Angelo so he borrowed enough to get them to San Diego.

"The tires were so bald on the truck that the air was showin' through, and I had to drive fifty miles an hour all the way out there," he says, "because it was vibratin' so bad." He won the bareback competition there, and they went on to Phoenix where they bought two tires, paid his entry fees and the motel bill. Then they were broke again.

Peggy left the circuit to give birth to three sons and a daughter, and her husband went home during his off-time, whether due to injury or fatigue. While he was home, LeDoux began building a log house in "downtown Kaycee" which took him over five years to complete. He also began thinking about becoming a recording artist in his spare time. He had been composing his own songs with guitar since high school as well as dabbling in other artistic endeavors such as painting and sculpture. In 1972, he and two

LeDoux in Championship Rodeo finals, 1976 — *courtesy National Rodeo Association*

friends recorded some of his songs on a four-track tape recorder in the basement of a country music lover's home in Sheridan. LeDoux then sent the reel-to-reel tape to his father who had retired from the military and was living in Mt. Juliet, Tennessee, near Nashville.

"There was a big lack of songs about rodeos," he says. "There were songs about truck drivers, love, barrooms and every other doggone thing, so I figured that with all the rodeo fans and cowboys out there, I'd give them some rodeo songs. And it worked."

LeDoux's father at first recorded the tapes, one at a time, on a small device in his home, and they were distributed by his son from the back of his pickup at rodeos. Later, they rented a recording studio in Nashville and hired musicians to play backup music. "They're so good that you just have to sing the song to them once and they've got it," he smiles. "It's amazing. Sometimes it doesn't come out the way you wanted, but it's good." His albums take three or four sessions of three hours each to record without rehearsal time.

Country music fans have purchased over a quarter of a million copies of his recordings since he began. His renditions of songs like "A Cowboy Like Me," "Too Tough to Die," and "What More Could a Cowboy Need" have been selling increasingly well each year in stores and music outlets; they are broadcast on country music stations across the nation. Radio station KSOP in Salt Lake City has promoted the young "Roy Rogers" since his early days of recording, and he stages a concert in the area regularly. He has also appeared twice in Germany on television in Munich and has a fan club in Iowa.

His father, Al LeDoux, who serves as his business manager, has negotiated with several large recording companies and found that his son's valued freedom would be severely impaired if he signed with any of them. "Shoot," the cowboy says, "they would own me. They'd tell me which songs to sing and where to appear. That would be terrible."

Although he continues to write songs about his rodeo days, LeDoux says, "I hope that I've got enough sense to never go back to it. I might consider it if rodeoing starts paying anywhere near as much as other sports, though." He decided to give it up in 1980, while he was "down behind the chutes with this big snatchin' horse—that's one that really jerks on you like a hobo grabs a freight train as it goes by," he says in mock seriousness. "I was sittin' there with both knees taped and my elbow and collarbone. And I thought, 'Doggone, what am I doin' here?' I just wanted to get in the truck and go home. . . . When I finally got there, I threw my glove away and tossed my rigging bag in the cellar. I haven't been back since."

Beth McElfresh, circa 1908—*McElfresh Collection*

BETH McELFRESH

"Boy, I sure like the looks of that cowboy"

P earl Elisabeth Mary Cockelreas Ash McElfresh could break horses, brand and trail cattle and chuck wagon cook with the best of 'em. The five-foot-tall, ninety-five pound beauty worked for former Wyoming Governor Bob Carey as her husband's "right hand man" and was called "Mrs. Scout" by cowboys and "Jack" by her husband. Well into her nineties, she has written numerous autobiographical short stories and a chuck wagon cookbook.

Beth was born in Chehalis, Washington, December 10, 1888, the only child of John Cockelreas, a race horse breeder who died of pneumonia before she was five. Her mother, a rural teacher, remarried when Beth was nine; she grew up on a ranch in northern Montana and was adopted by her stepfather, Frank Ash, who was a sheep foreman and rancher. The Ash family moved to North Dakota in 1902, forty miles from Ekalaka, Montana, where Ash trailed 6,000 head of sheep to his 160-acre homestead.

Beth had been taught by her mother until the fourth grade and had to be boarded in Wibaux and Big Timber, Montana, from the seventh grade following the move to North Dakota. Leaving the ranch to further her education was always an emotional crisis because she felt that "school was for the birds." She much preferred ranch chores; "tending" her two younger sisters, Joy and Jesse; and cooking for the cowboys. "I used to break every one of Dad's colts from the time they were babies," she says.

The petite tomboy was returning from a neighbor's home one afternoon on her horse, Midget, when she met her future husband, Waitman Wiley McElfresh, who was wagon boss for the CY Cattle Company across the state line in South Dakota. Not quite fourteen, she thought to herself, "Boy, I sure like the looks of that cowboy." The wrangler was quite a bit older and had come from Texas as a scout on the Chisholm Trail, but would never admit that, or his age, for many years after they were married. The West Virginian had attended private schools as the son of an eastern horse breeder before leaving home at eighteen, for Texas. After the Chisholm Trail drive, he was known as "Scout" the rest of his life.

Beth didn't see her cowboy again until the following winter when she was boarded with a couple in Wibaux and attending high school. Scout was living nearby. "I said, 'sure,' I'd like to go [steady] with him, but mother didn't much approve. She thought I was too young." The ninth grader attended dances with Scout although her maternal grandfather and four uncles were all Methodist ministers who disapproved of dancing. But her mother made her "beautiful silk riding suits" to wear to dances held on nearby ranches and in Wibaux. Beth had other boyfriends, but she decided to marry Scout McElfresh over her mother's objections.

The cowboy arranged for the "sky pilot," as the wranglers called ministers, to travel forty miles to the ranch from Ekalaka, Montana, to perform the ceremony. Several days before the planned nuptials, however, a letter arrived from the minister saying: "I am sorry to inform you that I will not be able to perform your wedding ceremony as I promised. I am holding a protracted meeting. I am busy saving souls." Scout was upset and was advised by Beth's father that they should leave the following morning to be married by the nearest justice of the peace in Sentinel Butte. The young couple left the ranch early and returned in time for

50

the planned ceremony and reception that was attended by a crowd of CY cowboys and neighbors. The bride was almost seventeen on her wedding day, October 21, 1905. The groom was thirty-four.

Scout had planned to leave the CY Company which was owned by R. W. "Bob" Carey, who later became governor of Wyoming, but Carey convinced him to stay on and run some of his own cattle across the state line in North Dakota. Carey also presented the newlyweds with a horse that was the pick of the remuda. The cowboy stayed on with the CY outfit and Beth (or "Jack" as her husband always called her) worked with him — helping with branding, chuck wagon cooking and cattle trailing. "But he wouldn't let me rope or pitch hay or do any heavy things because he was afraid I'd get rope burns or get hurt," she says.

The spunky little ranch hand did get hurt on a number of occasions and had seven major surgeries during her lifetime due to serious illnesses. She recalls the time she was "cutting out cattle" from the herd on Elk Mountain, Wyoming, when a balky mare threw her over its head and Beth landed on her back. Scout rode over and laughingly said, "Jack, that's an awful poor place to take up homesteading, the land is dry." Beth suffered a dislocated hip but got back on her horse. Years later, the injury was diagnosed while she was undergoing surgery for another problem.

She also broke her anklebone by falling off a sheep wagon because her husband hadn't gotten around to building some steps. Beth refused to be hauled off the mountain in a litter and insisted that Scout get instructions from the nearest doctor and apply the splint himself. "I was out of the saddle for two weeks and then one day we were riding in the timber when one of the trees that was very supple flew back and hit me across my broken shinbone. Scout looked back and saw me out of the saddle passed out." The cowboy removed her stocking and bandage "and he said that he'd have to put some alum on my leg. I began to cry. He said, 'Why are you crying, Jack? Don't you help me put it on horses and cattle all the time?' And I said, 'Yes, but they can't tell you if it hurts.' And I looked down from my camp chair and saw tears streaming down his cheeks. He felt terrible that he hadn't made those steps."

When they had been married four years, they moved across the Montana state line to Box Elder. They were expecting their first child, which didn't survive, and Beth was never able to conceive again. Tragedy struck again several years later when a blizzard killed their entire herd of 500 head of cattle. "We went broke and had to leave our new cabin, the first one of our own." So they leased out their ranch and became partners in a large furniture store in Spokane, Washington, for a year before returning to Montana, where they went into partnership with Beth's father in 1916, on the Yellowstone River near Miles City. There they prospered, built a cabin with a beamed ceiling and weather board exterior and were able to buy a year's worth of groceries to line the walls of their storehouse. "Boy, we lived good," she says. "And then the Carry Law came in that allowed you 160 more acres of homestead land. They advised my husband to relinquish all his desert land and keep only 40 acres right around the ranch buildings for thirty days until he could refile. But people in those days were awfully jealous of someone who was prosperous, and they got some fellow to come in there and file on the land we relinquished and he had us surrounded. There we were with our stock and all those expensive buildings." Disgusted, they sold the ranch buildings to her father, with whom they had previously dissolved their partnership, instead of selling their cattle and waiting for the new landowner to go broke. "He didn't even have any water," she says. "He had to use our well."

After a number of years commuting between Spokane, Washington, and Montana as a cattle broker and later an auctioneer, Scout was persuaded by Bob Carey, then president of the Stock Grower's Association, to go to work as the Wyoming-Nebraska brand inspector. They moved to Denver. Bored with city living, Beth attended a beautician's school, helped her husband at the stockyards and frightened Denver ladies who rode streetcars by riding her horse alongside, knowing that he would rear "up on his heels and squeal." She also had serious bouts of illnesses and spent considerable time in hospitals with complications from strep throat, tonsillitis, ruptured appendix, gall bladder, etc.

A year after Bob Carey had won his bid for the Wyoming governor's office in 1919, the new president of the Stock Grower's Association tried to transfer Scout to St. Joseph, Missouri, so that the President's nephew could assume the brand inspector's job, Beth says. Scout resigned his job and became cattle foreman

McElfresh, nonegenarian writer and former "cowboy of Sheridan."
(She died in July of 1982.)

of the Faddis-Kennedy ranching operation at Elk Mountain, Wyoming, where Beth broke her ankle. She worked alongside her husband and cooked from the back of a chuck wagon for eight years, not only on the mountain, but in the Crazy Woman and Power River areas.

Scout then worked as cattle foreman on the Crow Indian Reservation where he had introduced his wife in 1914 to Two Moons, the Indian chief who led the Sioux attack on George Custer's troops at the Little Big Horn. With him was Curley, Custer's Indian scout who survived the battle. Both Indians were present in 1926 for the fiftieth anniversary of the battle along with the Seventh Cavalry and General Godfrey who had missed the battle because his company lost its pack horses, mules, ammunition and pack saddles in quicksand while trying to cross a swamp in an attempt to reach the battle site. The aging general asked the Crow Indian agent for someone to lead him to the swamp, "and Scout took him cross-country to see it," she says.

Beth began photographing Indian burial trees on the reservation and writing about her experiences. She knew Plenty Coups, famous Crow chief born in 1848, who attempted to school his tribe in the ways of the white man. Beth and Scout "met Plenty Coups in 1925, and we liked him very much," she says. "He had been married three times when the old chief passed away in 1932; he was buried on his beloved ranch which he left to the Kiwanis Club in Billings because he had been a member for many years."

The McElfreshes quit their cattle company jobs on the reservation because their salaries had been cut three times during the early days of the "Great Depression." They then bought a herd of cattle for $150 a head, "had a terrible drought" and had to sell them to the government for $22 a head. "So we were broke again."

Scout was hired as a special guard at the Montana State Prison in 1938, where he worked until just before his death ten years later. Beth's mother, then in her 80s, prevailed on her to live with her and Beth's sister, Joy, in Sheridan, Wyoming, where she's been ever since. Although legally blind, she's written short stories about her life and the *Chuck Wagon Cookbook* which has recipes for "Leather Aprons" (steak and beans) and "son-of-a-gun" pudding in a sack. She also lists old timer's remedies for boils and gallbladder colic. Beth has pen pals and receives fan mail from as far away as England and Canada, from retired cowboys and from city slickers alike who still call her "Mrs. Scout."

(Note: Beth joined her beloved "Scout" during July of 1982. More than 300 of his letters to her—written during their court-ship and tied with a red ribbon—were buried with her as per her request.)

Dick Cheney, U.S. congressman—*courtesy Dick Cheney*

DICK CHENEY

"One-four hundred and thirty-fifth view of the world"

Dick Cheney has been called "Washington's best-kept secret," a White House "hired gun" and "an iron hand in a velvet glove" by political observers who watched his meteoric rise from congressional intern in 1968 to White House chief of staff, the top post in President Ford's administration, seven years later. The thirty-four-year-old presidential assistant reached the staff summit when his predecessor, Donald Rumsfeld, was reshuffled into the defense secretary's post following the dismissal of James Schlesinger. The overall improvement of the Ford administration under Cheney's management was obvious, but his White House career was short-lived because the president lost his election bid the following year, and Cheney returned to Casper.

Wyoming's only congressman is a native Nebraskan who was born in Lincoln in 1941, the eldest of three children of Richard and Marge Cheney. His father was a civil servant and worked for the U.S. Department of Agriculture for forty years in Nebraska and Wyoming. Now retired, he lives in Casper. His son, Richard Bruce "Dick" Cheney, spent his adolescence in Nebraskan schools before he was transferred to Casper. Dean Morgan Junior High came next, and he was a football "jock" at Natrona High School where he began his political career by getting himself elected senior class president. During his youth, he was a cub and boy scout and played a number of sports including baseball. Before graduation from Natrona High, he worked in a candy store and a "five and dime."

Cheney majored in political science at the University of Wyoming where he earned his B.A. and M.A. before transferring to the University of Wisconsin to become a Ph.D. candidate in 1968. He married Lynne Vincent, an attractive petite blonde he had dated in high school, during the summer of 1964 while Lynne was teaching literature at the University of Wyoming, having earned her Ph.D. in English. Cheney had taken time off from school during his second year at the university to work for a construction crew, installing electrical power lines throughout the northern Rocky Mountain states. He later returned to UW to complete his undergraduate work in political science and earned his master's degree.

The compact model congressman began his public service career in 1965 as an intern in the Wyoming legislature and won a fellowship from the National Center for Education in Politics to intern on the staff of Governor Warren Knowles of Wisconsin the following year. In 1968, he received yet another fellowship to serve under the late Congressman William Steiger, R-Wisconsin. Cheney had planned to write his dissertation for his doctorate degree following his year in Washington, but he never went back to the University of Wisconsin because Congressman Steiger loaned him to Donald Rumsfeld for ten days when Rumsfeld left Congress to head the Office of Economic Opportunity (OEO) in Washington. Cheney stayed on with Rumsfeld at OEO and the two men formed a working relationship which complemented each man's image and production. Rumsfeld was known for his "bluntness and hard-driving competence" and his young assistant for his diplomacy and capability. Cheney moved with his boss to the Cost of Living Council in 1971 where the relationship continued until 1973 when Rumsfeld was appointed by President

Nixon as U.S. ambassador to the North Atlantic Treaty Organization (NATO). The Cheneys decided to remain in Washington where Lynne was teaching part-time at George Washington University, and their two daughters, Elizabeth and Mary, attended elementary school. Cheney then became a partner in a small brokerage firm with offices in Washington and New York.

The following year, he received a call from his former boss from NATO headquarters in Brussels telling him that Rumsfeld was returning stateside to head up Gerald Ford's team of advisors. The call was made the night before Nixon made his formal announcement of resignation. Two months later, Cheney became Rumsfeld's deputy chief of staff. As "Staff Coordinator," Rumsfeld's job was to reestablish confidence in the nation's highest office, and he began by setting very frugal standards of White House staff expenditures in sharp contrast to Nixon's "lavish spending." Cheney followed suit and told a *Washington Post* reporter: "I've got this ten-year-old Volkswagen, and I'm going to drive it until it dies." The young deputy earned a reputation not only as a conservative who shared President Ford's view on limited government intervention, but as a conciliatory who could pour oil on the troubled waters of Ford's staff relationships. He also became the president's confidant and advisor on an equal footing with Rumsfeld.

When Ford created his big staff "shakeup" in 1975, Rumsfeld was "talked into" taking over as defense secretary when James Schlesinger was fired, and Cheney was promoted to chief of staff. Only thirty-four, he was the youngest member of the White House staff and held the ultimate post on the president's administrative team. A self-effacing man, the new chief of staff worked to maintain a low profile. "I really do believe a staff man should be anonymous," he says. A few weeks after Cheney assumed his new post, most observers noticed a dramatic change in the White House atmosphere—in both mood and a lessening of former tensions.

Cheney is credited by Michael Medved in his book, *The Shadow Presidents*, with playing a key role in winning Ford's nomination for the Republican candidacy in 1976 against Ronald Reagan: At the convention, the Chief of Staff's painstaking efforts paid off handsomely when Mississippi gave Ford the key votes he needed to nail down the nomination. Had Cheney failed to act in backing up (Ford's southern coordinator Harry) Dent's audacious and timely maneuver, it is entirely possible that the Republican Party would have rejected Gerald Ford in 1976.

When Ford lost the election to Jimmy Carter in 1976, Cheney prepared the president's concession speech and read it over the phone to Carter because Ford's voice was so hoarse that he could only croak "congratulations" to the new president-elect. Following Carter's inaugural address and goodbyes to the Fords and his former staff members, Cheney took his family to McDonalds for lunch in the family station wagon and slid into further anonymity.

The Cheneys returned to Wyoming where he secured a job as an investment broker in a Casper firm. A year later, Teno Roncalio declared his intention to retire as the state's lone congressman, which prompted the former chief of staff to throw his political cap into the ring. Cheney loaded up his family into a camper to hit the campaign trail in December of 1977 and worked so hard greeting voters that he suffered a heart attack the following spring. While convalescing, he decided to send a letter to every registered Republican voter in the state to tell them that he was going to follow doctor's orders by giving up his three packs of cigarettes a day and by getting regular exercise. He also wanted them to know that one little heart attack wasn't going to stop a man, not yet forty, from representing them in Washington.

The publicity generated by his coronary probably gained him more recognition, if not more votes, than he would have had without it, and he won easily in the November 1978 election; thus, he went from the most powerful White House staff post to the least influential position as a freshman congressman. To which Cheney replies: "My vote counts for one-four hundred and thirty-fifth view of the world, and that's very satisfying."

Cheney ran for reelection in 1980 and was elected to serve as chairman of the House Republican Policy Committee during the Ninety-seventh Congress, thus making him the fourth-ranking leader among his party in the House of Representatives, and the only westerner among the Republican leadership. He ran for his second term on his record of attempting to hold down federal spending and opposing federal intervention in state affairs, such as coal legislation and the proposed federal Energy Mobilization Board which would have had the authority to override certain state laws. His Democratic opponent was Jim Rogers, a former oil field worker and bar owner who spent $9,000 to Cheney's $50,000.

While in Washington, Lynne Cheney wrote a political novel, *Executive Privilege,* and an historical novel dealing with nineteenth century Wyoming women, due out in 1982. She says: "Dick thinks [being in Washington] is important. It's the place where he can do something about the problems he cares about."

The congressman's concerns include "preventing energy activity in congressionally designated wilderness areas of Wyoming and the West. I have generally been strongly supportive of the development of energy and minerals on federal lands in Wyoming, knowing that this development is the backbone of the state's economy and a vital element in the national effort to achieve energy independence and economic recovery. Nevertheless, there are two categories of land in Wyoming that should not be allowed [to be developed] at this time; these are our national parks and our designated wilderness areas. Because development applications have been filed in many of these areas, including the Washakie Wilderness in Wyoming, Congress had to act to prevent development in wilderness areas.

"I've also found it challenging to be involved in congressional decision making on President Reagan's Budget Policy Committee. I have been privileged to be part of the White House discussions on these issues and the strategy in Congress to enact the President's programs," he says. "A representative's job is to represent his or her constituents' views and philosophy in Washington. I take very seriously my responsibility to cast Wyoming's sole vote in the House of Representatives on important issues and to try to influence the legislative process in favor of my state's best interests. It is both challenging and frustrating to participate in the political process. It can also be very rewarding.

"The best parts about the job are the ability to influence in a small way the policies of our national government, and working with Wyoming people. It is fascinating work which I enjoy very much. The worst part of the job is the loss of time to be with Lynne and the girls—and the loss of privacy."

Gene Gressley, archivist, University of Wyoming—*courtesy University of Wyoming*

GENE GRESSLEY

"As an archivist, you're compared to a mortician"

Acquiring "literary archaeology" is Gene Gressley's flaming passion; he's done so well that the University of Wyoming's archives rank among the best in the nation. Dr. Gressley has amassed some 8,000 separate collections of not only Wyoming history, but of the performing arts, aviation, theatre, cinema, radio, music, mountaineering, water resources, petroleum, mining, livestock, western literature and others.

Among the many treasures housed in the American Heritage Center (and five warehouses) is memorabilia from Barbara Stanwyck, Harry James, Dean Martin, Owen Wister, daredevil pilot Roscoe Turner, Larry Hart (of Rogers and Hart), many wealthy industrialists, oil and cattle men as well as movie cowboy Tim McCoy's western saddle and J. P. Morgan's Curtis Indian book set valued at $135,000—to name a few. Gressley has been collecting memorabilia since he was hired as a twenty-five-year-old archivist in 1956, with one assistant and 284 collections in three rooms in the old library. His annual expense budget was $400, and he spent considerable time hitchhiking around the country to acquire material for the archives. Gressley and members of the faculty still talk about his adventures.

"My first major trip," he says, "was to Texas and Oklahoma to collect oil history." The fast-talking, enthusiastic young man had two suitcases, a brief case and a forty-pound tape recorder with him when he was given a ride by a traveling salesman between Dallas and Houston during the fall of 1957. "He picked me up because of all the baggage, and he couldn't believe that anyone from the University of Wyoming would be hitchhiking. When he left me off at a second-rate hotel, he said 'Gene, if you ever need a job, I'm sure that Lone Star Steel Company can do a lot better for you. . . .' "

Circumstances and Gressley's budget have improved considerably since that time. The university now pays for packing and shipping of all donated materials as well as processing and indexing. He doesn't have to hitchhike anymore and his original 800 square feet of archival storage space has increased to 65,000 square feet. His staff now numbers eighteen; his dream now includes a new $10 million archives building which has left the drawing board, is awaiting funding, and will house the "Western Writers Hall of Fame."

"I didn't have a primary goal when I first started out," he says. "After flunking out at Johns Hopkins University [at age sixteen] I was like 'What Makes Sammy Run?' I was insecure in a sense and I always wanted to build and develop. I had no idea of getting where we are today. I just wanted to build a decent archive for the state of Wyoming."

Gressley's outgoing personality was his greatest asset when it came to acquiring "treasures" for his archives. He developed it early as the son of a Congregational minister in Huntington, Indiana. "We were always on display," he remembers. His family of four frequently moved about the Midwest, and young Gene decided early on that he would never get himself into a job situation like his father where he would have to ask people for money. That determination has carried forward into his present job although "archives always need money." He quickly learned that people who donate their "papers" to the university are also inclined to fund the institution, often as a bequest.

A better than average student, Gressley graduated from high school at the age of sixteen, "went to Johns Hopkins University in 1948, flunked out in 1949 and came home. I thought I was pretty bright," he says, "but I came home thinking I was pretty dumb. Then I went off to Manchester." He graduated from Manchester College in Indiana in 1952 with a B.S. in history; married Joyce Eleanor Bourrous, a foreign language student; and moved to Denver where she earned her M.A. in languages. He found a job at the Colorado State Historical Society as a guide in the state museum under Agnes Wright Spring. "It was a peon's job, frankly, but it had great value to it because I got to know one of the great ladies of western history by pure accident. . . . We used to eat our brown bag lunches together, and she would tell me stories of Wyoming and how she grew up in the state and the characters she had known." Although Gressley had been primarily interested in African diplomatic and economic history, Mrs. Spring sparked his interest in Wyoming and western history.

The Gressleys returned to Indiana where he earned his M.A. in western history in 1956, but he "missed the west." Their daughter, Debbie, was born with the "Gressley curse," too-small bronchial tubes which made her dangerously ill. So her father called Agnes Wright Spring and asked if she could help him find a job in a drier climate in the Rocky Mountain states. "And she bent every arm to help me," he says. The result was a call from the University of Wyoming's library director, who offered Gressley the archivist's job.

Gressley's domain has increased dramatically over the ensuing years, due mainly to his own efforts. "I'm a workaholic," he admits, "and I'm very persistent." He writes thirty to forty letters each day requesting records, manuscripts and memorabilia from sources all over the nation and several foreign countries. His efforts have been rewarded handsomely in donations of valuable paintings to the archives such as the Henry Farney and Remington collections; rooms full of memorabilia from personalities such as actor Edward Everett Horton; and literally tons of records from the American National Cattlemen's files and the American Wool Growers. The Farney paintings took twenty years to obtain, and the cattlemen's records nearly caused a riot.

The archivist's friend, Joe Watt, a former Sheridan rancher, was asked to obtain the cattlemen's records by lobbying at the American National Livestock convention during the mid-sixties where a floor fight ensued and one of the delegates called Watt's Wyoming group a "bunch of horse thieves." Gressley says: "We won because there was a natural reaction against that [allegation]. You don't call anyone a thief, especially a cattleman," he laughs. A number of other archives were after the cattlemen's records, including "the Cowboy Hall of Fame." To further utilize the records, Gressley would like to "follow the cow historically from the range to Safeway" by obtaining packinghouse records as well as those from a number of small ranches.

Competition is fierce among archivists, and Gressley would feel badly if another facility bagged a valuable collection from his own territory. He delights, however, in telling of his archival "coup" that occurred when Emerson Hough's papers were donated to UW, from the attic of a house located two blocks from the University of Kansas library, by a university staff member.

One of the more humorous incidents that occurred while Gressley was still relatively new at his job happened during an acquisition trip to the home of a Wyoming politician's widow who met him at the door in her negligee. Gressley ran for his car but fell in a puddle of water in her yard. "I don't know who laughed harder, she or me," he says. "But I never got that collection, needless to say."

Gressley's letters to prospective donors (20,000 a year) net him an eighteen percent return, up from seven percent when he first began his mail campaign. He credits the increase to public relations. "I now get replies from Hollywood to New York. The University of Wyoming is much better known now than when I first came here," he says. "And wealth begets wealth. When you have fifty composers [already in the archives], it's much easier to get fifty more."

UW's archives have the largest radio script and music score collection in the country as a result of his Hollywood and New York connections. The most copied music score, requested and received by forty universities, is the "Sound of Music." Gressley has the original score but lost the Max Steiner collection to Brigham Young University (BYU).

University of Wyoming Archives

"They put on a Max Steiner program in the music department and invited Mrs. Steiner up there," he says. "She became intrigued with it and gave them her husband's papers." Gressley had tried to acquire the collection for years and admits that BYU "outdid" him.

Writing to widows can be a problem. "Some widows throw everything out within two weeks," he says, "while some will hold on to it for six years. I don't know when the right time is to ask for their husbands' papers, but I usually write within a month or two. A lot of wives are possessive about their husbands' careers and don't want to share them."

When asking someone for his or her papers while they're still alive, it's "psychologically bad," he says. "He thinks, 'Am I dead yet?' or 'Am I about to go?' As an archivist, you're compared to a mortician." Gressley has written to hundreds of western writers and received myriad manuscripts for his literature collection.

When he wrote to David Niven requesting his personal papers, the British-born actor agreed but insists that his papers will be bequeathed to UW. Niven was asked several years ago at a news conference at London's Heathrow airport why his memorabilia is going to Wyoming. "For the simplest of all reasons," the actor replied. "They asked me."

Gressley has shared many of his archival "secrets" with others at conventions and universities but few take advantage of his knowledge, he says. "They're more interested in processing and preserving the papers than acquiring them." But to him, the "thrill" is in the challenge of acquisition. He has been accused by faculty members of collecting a lot of "junk," but the archivist counters with, "Nobody gave me anything to throw away. Let some other archivist with perception a hundred years from now go through all this material and decide what's important and what's not. I'm collecting for scholars of the twenty-first century as well as today."

Recent appraisals of the American Heritage Center collections from distinguished authorities include: "UW's popular cultural materials are unmatched anywhere." (Prof. Russell Nye, Michigan State) "The aeronautical collection is the most comprehensive in its field." (Prof. John Rae, Harvey Mudd College) "The petroleum history is unmatched as a center for research." (Prof. Gerald White,

University of California, Irvine) "The manuscripts on ranching comprise the most valuable and unique collection to be found anywhere." (Wayne Rasmussen, chief, U.S. Department of Agriculture) "The American Heritage Center is today one of the major manuscript libraries in the nation, and the world of scholarship and research owe a debt of gratitude to the University of Wyoming and Dr. Gressley for what has been achieved." (Sidney Fine, Andrew Dickson professor of history)

Thyra Thomson, Wyoming Secretary of State—*courtesy Thyra
Thomson*

THYRA THOMSON

"I like them—chauvinists and all"

Wyoming's glamorous Secretary of State Thyra Thomson has not only achieved state, national and international recognition as a capable public servant, she is also an outspoken advocate of women's rights. As ex officio lieutenant governor, the Republican stateswoman has served as chief executive on numerous occasions during the absence of three governors; ranking the highest woman state official for five years before the election of Alabama Governor Luraleen Wallace.

Thyra's entrance into politics occurred two years after her husband, Keith, died of a heart attack at forty-one, just after his election to the U.S. Senate. The Thomsons had lived in Washington for six years while he served in Congress before winning his senate seat in 1960. When he died a month before taking office, "I was in Washington with my three small boys," she says, "and I stayed there through the school year before moving my family back to Wyoming." She decided to run for the post of secretary of state two years later because of a set of circumstances set in motion by her husband's death.

71

Governor J. J. Hickey resigned as governor and appointed himself to fill Thomson's vacant U.S. Senate seat, thus making Secretary of State Jack Gage acting governor. The vacant secretary of state's post was filled by a deputy for two years, and Thyra decided to run against him in the next election. "I knew a lot about government," she says. "We had invested seven years of our lives in statewide elections, so I had been all over the state to campaign."

Thyra thrives in a male dominated atmosphere, perhaps because of her background. She was born the youngest of seven children and admits to being spoiled by six doting brothers and her father, John Godfrey. Her mother, Rosalie Altmas, a native of Bavaria, Germany, married Godfrey, a Welchman who was a widower with five young sons. Thyra was born when her eldest brother was eighteen, and she lost her father in a mining accident when she was three. Godfrey had been superintendent of the Colorado Fuel and Iron Company in Florence. Following his death, his wife was forced to find work to support her large brood.

"We moved around, and I attended a lot of different schools," Thyra says. A somewhat precocious child, she played cribbage when she was five; spent considerable time reading; "daydreaming"; and playing caddy with her brothers, a game played with sawed-off broomsticks out on the prairie. "We played a lot of cards, baseball and danced to fiddle music," she says. "There wasn't much else to do in those days."

Her mother was hospitalized in Denver for two years and Thyra worked as a "family helper" while attending high school. Following her release, Mrs. Godfrey found a job in Cheyenne managing housekeepers for the local hospital, and Thyra graduated from Central High School. She attended the University of Wyoming where she majored in psychology and minored in business and sociology while holding down jobs such as telephone operator and secretarial positions in the economics and agriculture departments. A member of Phi Beta Phi social sorority, she was also in the Scholastic Honorary Society and "Spurs," an honorary pep squad; she graduated cum laude. Thyra later completed graduate studies at American University in Washington, D.C. While studying at UW, she met Keith Thomson at a skating party in Laramie.

Following their marriage, she worked at the university until he earned his law degree.

Since taking office as secretary of state in 1963, Thyra has been reelected four times with a predicted approval from voters in 1982. She's currently in the process of completing a computerized records system which she calls "the sweetest system in the U.S." After visiting other states to check out their computer records systems such as Lansing, Michigan, and Reno, Nevada, she decided to design her own software. A state data programmer has been completing the records system to include the registry of voters, payrolls, licensing, continuing corporations and partnerships and security brokers. The broker-dealers will be listed on a nationwide registration system in Washington, D.C. "I've been working on it for two years and it should be on the line by January of 1983," she says. "There will be access from state libraries and the university."

In addition to her secretary of state post, Thyra lectures on economics, business and women's rights issues to various groups around the state. "I like to talk about new directions, plans for quality growth and the environment," she says. "I try to keep up-to-date on new thinking. Any age group can talk to me on most subjects, and I'm not divorced from academics or foreign affairs."

A women's rights activist, she has worked to promote the equal rights amendment (ERA). "I don't think ERA will be ratified by the deadline," she said in early 1982. "It's a great tragedy, but ultimately, it will be passed if it takes a thousand years. The saddest commentaries are from opponents who traffic in fear, and it's irrational. . . . The myth is that it's a man's world and a woman's place, so we're forced to live that way. I find men are, in most cases, more receptive to women's rights than one might suspect. Once they understand the problem and see the bias, they are pretty good about it."

A delegate to the 1977 National Women's Conference in Houston, she feels that men no longer feel threatened by ERA, although there is still a generation or two of hangers-on who will not accept it. "I look at my own sons—the eldest, Bill, and I don't see eye-to-eye on the subject half as much as my youngest son,

K. C. and I do," she laughs. "Bill was working for Senator Cliff Hansen when ERA saw its first blush of publicity." The senator was opposed to the Equal Rights Amendment at that time, and Bill Thomson, who worked in his office, took the same position.

"I'm sure that Senator Hansen has changed his mind on the subject, but at that time he was getting letters from women who wanted protection legislation. The anti forces were filling in the walls of those fears—fears that I won't repeat because I feel that it's foolish for anyone to make a decision based on fear. Senator Hansen is a very chivalrous man who was filled with the old ideas of protecting women. But I look at it this way: in Wyoming more than half of all women, married or not, are employed up to half a century of their lives. We live until we're seventy-five years old, which is average, and a woman has her last baby when she's twenty-six. So what are they going to do for fifty years of their lives? Most women are going back to work."

Thyra feels that "it is absolutely intolerable not to be included in the constitution. If women had been included, it would not have taken a separate amendment to give us the vote in the Nineteenth Amendment. The Equal Rights Amendment had almost impossible odds to overcome from the beginning. Senator Sam Irvin, that wonderful old southern gentleman, was responsible. It was the old idea of protecting women and that sort of thing. Never mind that most of them were out working in the fields. In order to get ERA on the ballot, lawmakers had to make concessions to old Mr. Sam, so they foreshortened the time period for ratification."

As a demonstration of the need for public enlightenment, she cites governmental pay scales: "Fifty-two percent of the jobs in this state's government are held by women, yet nine out of ten highly paid jobs are held by men. The lowest paid job for a man is a janitor, and he's paid [considerably more] than the lowest paid women's job which is a records and communication technician. Even grounds workers are paid more than clerks and stenographers. And security guards who stand in the capitol are paid more than an executive secretary who holds such a high-ranking job that there are only seven of them in all of state government. Yet, the guard starts out higher than the executive secre-

Thomson on a horseback hunting trip—*courtesy of Thyra Thomson*

tary who has to pass a written test and have six years of experience."

Thyra's work has consumed most of her life since her husband's death. She reared her sons in Cheyenne, putting them all through school, including "five degrees." Her eldest son, Bill, is a Cheyenne attorney; Bruce is an actor and director in New York; K. C. is manager of a savings and loan company in Sheridan and married to a lawyer, Karen Thomson, who won her first Supreme Court case in 1981. Thyra's four grandchildren live in Cheyenne.

The attractive secretary of state has not remarried but has been seen in the company of eligible Wyoming bachelors, including a judge. "I'm a type A person, and I'm always attracted to type B men; that is, men who are quiet by nature and calm and thoughtful. I find them hard to resist. I always try to approach people from the viewpoint of how they're looking at things," she says. "There is a saying that young people have used that's very true: 'You have to find out where people are coming from to understand them.' And while I don't always agree with men, I like them—chauvinists and all."

Thyra moved several years ago from her "big old house" near the capitol to a smaller house two miles away. "I fixed it up just for me," she says. "This is a feminine house. I have bookcases on all my walls, music piped into every room and lighting on every painting. There's also white carpeting and a little French kitchen. I'm gloriously happy in it."

During her nearly twenty years as secretary of state, Thyra Thomson has accumulated a number of honors. In 1974, she became the first woman to serve as president of the North American Securities Administrators which encompasses fifty states, ten Canadian provinces and Mexico; she was named an "International Woman of Distinction" by women educators, a Distinguished Alumna of the University of Wyoming, and a "Woman of Achievement" by Press Women. She has also been cited by professional and academic honor societies in economics, commerce and education as well as serving on the UNESCO's Youth Committee and HEW's Allied Health Professions Council.

Internationally, she participated in Wilton Park Conferences in England, sat on the United Kingdom's Marshall Scholarships

Committee, and was a guest of the Federal Republic of Germany for "International Women's Year," one of only six women from the United States. Thyra also writes. Her opinions have been expressed in various textbooks, newspapers and magazines, including *Reader's Digest*. Although she has a proven track record of efficiency and progress, she would most like to be remembered as "a compassionate person."

T. A. "Al" Larson, historian and author

T. A. "AL" LARSON

"A big frog in a small pond"

Wyoming's colorful past is eons from English medieval history, Taft Alfred Larson's original specialty, but he has few regrets in giving it up. During his course of becoming the foremost authority on Wyoming history, Larson has authored four books on the state's ancestry. He also enlightened the lives of more than 16,000 students in his thirty-nine years at the University of Wyoming prior to his retirement in 1975.

His first love, however, was medieval history. He spent seven years studying it at three universities, and a year in England researching fourteenth century relations of church and state, the subject of his doctoral dissertation. But economic circumstances during the depression of the 1930s changed his own course of history; for the only job available to the young man with a hard-earned Ph.D. was a substitute teaching job at UW.

Larson taught European, English and Western civilization courses during the 1936-37 school year, while the tenured professor was on sabbatical leave. Then, jobless, he borrowed $400 from his brother to help finance a trip to England where he ferreted through 600-year-old parchment rolls in the Public Records Office to complete his research. His efforts culminated in two articles which appeared in the *English Historical Review*, the top history journal in England. Larson also took some night courses at the University of London, without credit, from the head of the Public Records Office.

The trek to England cost him $1,100, including round trip fare and a year's living expenses. "The next year, I still couldn't find a job—a tenure track job as they call it—so they brought me back to the University of Wyoming to substitute for the other history teacher, Laura White, who taught American history." During the year, he began to develop a course in Wyoming history and was offered a permanent teaching position with the university.

"They kept me on," he recalls, "but if there had been more jobs available, I probably would not have stayed here because of all my extensive training in medieval English history from the universities at Boulder, Chicago and London. But I gradually shifted to teaching American history and concentrated my own research in the field of western history. By doing so, I disqualified myself, really. Nobody in New York, Chicago or California would hire an expert on Wyoming history." The teaching assignment at UW gave him the chance to become "a big frog in a small pond, you might say, and the students appreciated it as did some of the citizens." It also gave him the opportunity to teach more students than any other instructor in the history of the university.

Larson was named head of the history department, a job he held for twenty-one years. And except for a three-year stint in the navy during World War II, when he taught air navigation and wrote the history of the Great Lakes Naval Training Center, he taught western history continually during his career as well as heading up the American Studies Program.

When he returned to Wyoming after the war, he was encouraged to write about Wyoming's participation in it. The result was a 400-page book titled *Wyoming's War Years, 1941–1945*, published in 1954. A chapter on Heart Mountain describes the relocation center, located between Powell and Cody, which housed a number of Japanese Americans from the West Coast. Another site, a German-Italian prisoner of war camp, was located at Douglas.

The book took seven years to research and write and preceded his "big Wyoming history book" which was published in 1965.

"I thought it was high time that we had a one-volume history on Wyoming for adults," he says. "And by that time, I had been teaching Wyoming history for many years when this chap came around and wanted me to write the history part of what they called 'mug books.' They used to put out a three-volume set on Wyoming history. There were two, one by Bartlett and one by Beard. People got their pictures and biographies in the book by paying $50 or $100 a page for the privilege. So that's what we had in Wyoming history up to that time. Although Mrs. Beard and Mr. Bartlett were pretty good historians and those histories are somewhat useful, I don't think the biographies of the people who paid are necessarily the ones who should have been in there. Some people refused to pay, so they were left out. And there were a few—like a U.S. senator or the governor—if they wanted in there, they probably got in free."

Larson's comprehensive, 619-page *History of Wyoming* took nearly ten years to research and write, sold out in four editions and won the prestigious American Association of State and Local History Award. He followed it in 1977 with *Wyoming, A History*, for the bicentennial; and a 663-page revised edition of *History of Wyoming* in 1978. Sandwiched in between was an anthology he titled *Bill Nye's Western Humor*, published in 1968.

He also authored a number of articles on the women's rights movement. He plans to incorporate his extensive research material into another book which he says he planned to start after completion of his third and "last" term as a Democratic member of the state House of Representatives. Dr. Larson labels himself "a great believer in women's rights" and was a charter member of the first ERA chapter organized in Cheyenne. He gave the women present a "pep talk" and signed the charter along with another male teacher, Sid Speigel, to make sure that the organizers had enough signatures to qualify as a chapter.

"In the first place," he says, "you have to have men who believe in the thing or you'd never get through any legislation. Even at the meeting in Seneca Falls, New York, in 1848, when they adopted the big resolution and got the thing rolling, one-third of the people who signed the resolution were men. I must admit, though, that men who are active in the women's rights movement usually have wives who are interested in it, but not necessarily active. Certainly, my wife, Mary (a former UW librarian), is enthusiastic about equal rights. And I have two daughters (one from each marriage). I've observed that men who have daughters are more inclined in that direction.

"ERA just makes sense to me, and I'm completely sold on it," he says. "The more I read about what all those women said and did, I couldn't help recognizing that they had a lot of ability, and they were getting short shrift in a lot of things such as employment. All the arguments they were using are persuasive if you read and listen to them."

Larson, his three brothers and sister, may have been short shrift as children after their mother died, a victim of the 1918 flu epidemic, but all grew up to be successful adults. The next-to-the-eldest Larson child, Alfred—as he called himself—was eight when his Swedish mother died in Wakefield, Nebraska. His father, also an immigrant of Sweden, had retired three years earlier from his corn-hog farming operation at the age of forty-three, and the family had moved into the town of Wakefield, population 1,100.

"My father was left with five stair-step children," he says. "And we hired a housekeeper for awhile. Later, my father's widowed sister lived with us and took care of us after a fashion. We certainly didn't have what we should have had, but my father was a pretty hard-driving man who instilled the spirit of going ahead and working hard—the work ethic; he was steeped in the work ethic."

The Larson children all excelled in school and became avid readers. Shy, introverted Alfred won an interstate spelling contest for the South Dakota-Minnesota-Nebraska-Iowa region for sixth, seventh and eighth graders while he was in the sixth grade. "We went to Sioux City and spelled them down," he says. He still has the gold medal. The tall, slender youth later held the highest grade point level of any student to graduate from his high school, a record broken by one of his younger brothers. By the time the oldest Larson children were ready for college, "the Great Depression came along." Their father had "overbought in World War I" and the family was "land poor." So they had to work their way through colleges and universities. "Al" Larson received some financial assistance during his freshman year but had to work his way through the next seven years with odd jobs, assistantships and fellowships. He was listed number two in grade point average among a thousand students in his freshman class.

The young man completed his undergraduate work at the University of Colorado at Boulder where he lived in the basement of the fraternity house with three other male students who fed coal to the furnace and food to the Phi Beta Phi sorority sisters by working in the kitchen to earn some much needed funds. He then spent a year at the University of Chicago to complete some undergraduate work where he lived on $300 for an entire school year by eating very miserly and unnutritionally. Four of his summer vacations were spent working at Yellowstone Park as a yardman, night watchman and cabin scrubber.

He had been editor of his high school newspaper, but there were no freshman journalism classes at Boulder, so he allowed himself to be recruited by a history professor who told him that the journalism department would " 'just make a proofreader' " out of him. " 'Learn something before you go out and write,' " he was told. "And being an impressionable youngster, I followed that path," he laughs. "Otherwise, I'd probably be editing some small town newspaper."

Since his first teaching job at UW, Dr. Larson has received national recognition, a number of prestigious awards and has generously donated his time and experience to various organizations. His biography has been carried in *Who's Who in America* for over a quarter of a century, and he has held elective office in national, regional and state historical societies. He also served on the board of three scholarly journals; is a member of the Wyoming Judicial Planning Committee; and received in 1966 the G. D. Humphrey medal as the university's most outstanding faculty member. In 1975, a chair was endowed in his honor by a former student from Casper. In appreciation, Larson donated 450 books from his personal library to Casper College.

Bunny Connell, sculptor – *courtesy Bunny Connell*

BUNNY CONNELL

"Art is ten percent talent and ninety percent hard work"

"**I**'m really glad that I didn't find sculpture until my children were grown or I would have been a terrible parent," she laughs. "I would have neglected them totally." Wyoming sculptor Bunny Connell jokes about her artistic ability but is voraciously committed to it. She didn't begin to take her talent seriously until after her children were born, and a friend suggested that they take a class in oil painting that was being taught above a drugstore in Sheridan during the 1950s.

"It was the first thing I'd done with art since high school," she remembers, "and I was sort of intrigued with oils, so I just kept painting." Her work was featured in one-woman exhibits as well as traveling and congressional shows—until her family took a six-week vacation in Africa in 1972. Then her painting stopped abruptly and her sculpture began.

Bunny had not had time to unpack from the African trip when an artist friend told her of an "approach to sculpture class" that was commencing that evening. "It was the first time I had been

85

instructed in sculpture, much less in bronze, and I realized that I had found the media that I had been looking for," she says. Her intention to paint "all those marvelous animals" she had photographed in Africa was almost forgotten. "I wanted to build things—sort of construct—so I took a course in welding at Sheridan College, and I did welded sculpture for three years before I tried bronze."

Her children were "completely in awe of their mother," she laughs. "They were afraid that I was going to blow up the house when I was welding in the basement, and they were terribly relieved when I got into bronzes and simply working with wax— something as innocuous as that. Orin, my youngest son, took this rather extended course in welding at the college and when I finally got to bronzes, he said, 'Mother, we're not going to pour them in the garage, are we?' And I said, 'No, I know it would go right in my shoe.'"

As a child, Irene "Bunny" Smith drew pictures, was a good student and took part in "lots of athletics such as horseback riding and swimming. I was a tomboy," she says, "and my older sister, Jane, and I had a marvelous set of electric trains instead of dolls. They ran all over the third floor of my grandmother's house." The Smith sisters grew up in St. Louis, Missouri, and spent their family summer vacations in Wyoming while Bunny and Jane were in elementary school. "It took my parents three years to find a ranch [near Sheridan] and we moved here." She and her sister attended a boarding school in Santa Fe, New Mexico, which doubled as a dude ranch during the summer months. "Bishop's Lodge is where I learned to ski," she recalls, "but it didn't have the tows like we have now." She spent summer vacations at home on the family ranch where her parents raised Thoroughbreds and had a herd of 900, the largest in the Rocky Mountain West.

She attended the University of Colorado at Boulder where she majored in geology because it was interesting but never sat down to think, "What am I gong to do with my life? Actually, I was going to teach skiing at the Teepee Lodge [in the Big Horn Mountains] when I got out of college, but that fell flat because it never reopened after the war."

Bunny married Bob Connell, a friend and neighbor she had known since they were both eight years old. "Bob encouraged me to go to the Disney Studios in California to study art instead of going to college, but I didn't think that I had much in the way of talent. I didn't take an art class in college, but I really think it's an advantage not to have gone the academic route because I feel it inhibits you in a way." One of her first pieces of sculpture was a lioness leaping from a pedestal with only one foot on the base. "A real sculptor came to the house when I had just gotten my first casting and he said, 'You can't do that because bronze won't support that much weight on one foot.' " Her response was: "I'm glad you didn't tell me that before I did the piece, because if I had known ahead of time that you can't do it, I never would have tried."

The artist's bronzes consist of graceful, limited edition sculptures: African animals, equine figures engaged in the sport of polo, American hunting dogs and North American big game animals. Original pieces take a minimum of three months "if everything goes well." The original design is made from wax although clay, paper maché and other materials can be used; the mold is made at a foundry. "I'm sure that most people think that once you have a mold you can crank out bronzes, but that's not how it works, because the original is dismembered when the mold is made. There are imperfections when a wax is poured; the mold lines are taken off, and the arms, legs and horns have to be put back on."

The hollow wax form is taken to the foundry where it is attached to a screw bar with numerous screws and risers which allow the gas to escape, the wax to run out and the bronze to flow into the mold. Then it is encased in a ceramic shell formed by a process of dipping the mold in a very "goopy" mixture, alternating it with a dusting of fine silicone which builds up a coating about a quarter of an inch thick. The mold is fired at 2,000 degrees, covering the piece with a ceramic platelike finish. The wax burns off and runs out leaving a hollow, and molten metal is poured in. When the metal cools, the ceramic shell is broken off and all the screws and risers are cut off. A section is taken out of the side of the art piece so that a shell can build up inside to fill with wax so that it will be hollow. "Otherwise, it would be a solid piece, and you wouldn't be able to pick it up," she explains.

Bunny's sculptures sell anywhere from $450 for a number of

her hunting dogs up to $7,000 for one of her equine polo pieces. Most of her thirty-five designs are action pieces and exquisitely lifelike. She watches home movies taken in Kenya, Africa, to get the rippling muscled effect of her large jungle cats and video tapes of polo games to put realism into her equines. She also clips still photographs from magazines for future references. Giraffes, "those marvelous, gentle giants," are her favorites; she makes sure that every one of the animals' neck vertebra can be counted. "The advantage of sculpture over two-dimensional work, as in a painting, is that you can turn the piece around if you have a problem and solve it in five minutes. It's like turning the painting upside down to get a little bit of perspective."

Bunny's biggest problem is being interrupted while she's working. "I told my husband that I married him for love, not lunch," she laughs. A veterinarian and fulltime rancher, Bob Connell is usually home for his midday meal, "and he's starting to get a complex because I say, 'Oh, not you again.' I love him coming home but things just start to happen in my studio by 11 o'clock in the morning." Her small studio is just off the kitchen of their spacious ranchhouse and was converted from two maids' rooms. "Who has maids anymore?" she says with a grin. "Even a cleaning lady is hard to find."

The Connell Ranch, located in the Big Goose area southwest of Sheridan, is a "moderately sized operation" that includes land across the border in Montana. Bunny and her husband Bob have a herd of Angus cattle, some Thoroughbred horses and six dogs (five Labs and a Doberman). Their daughter and two sons have homes of their own, and ranchwork during the summer months precludes any time for artwork. Her oldest son is ranch foreman and her daughter supervises the Thoroughbred operation, but there is "too much going on ranchwise during the summer, and guests arrive so I wait until the first of September to get back to work," she says.

Her sculpture has been shown in a number of prestigious art exhibits in Philadelphia, St. Louis, Sun Valley and elsewhere but taking time off from the ranch and her work happens only several times a year. Two galleries in New York have been selling her work for a number of years, and she has a group of patrons who collect her sculpture. She was "juried" into a prestigious equine artists show with sculpture from various parts of the world in October of 1980 and "juried out" the following spring. "You sort of have to pick where you want to be shown, and like a writer's manuscripts, you get a lot of rejections," she explains. Sculptors usually submit slides of their work to large art exhibits, displaying three angles of the same piece. "You're allowed to submit one or two or possibly three pieces."

Bunny rarely gives advice to budding artists. "I think that art is a very personal thing. You have to have something to say first, and you have to be able to put it out there, ready to take criticism. I don't think that art is a matter of great talent. It's a matter of grim determination. I'd say that art is ten percent talent and ninety percent hard work. And I know that I would get a lot more produced if I were better disciplined. Sometimes I get to my studio at seven in the morning and work until four in the afternoon. But you can't create every day either. There are days when I'm easily distracted."

Young artists need encouragement, she says. "I think anyone interested in getting into art must realize that there are few artists who can support themselves. I don't know what the percentage would be, but it's not even ten percent. So they must be realistic. Art is something you always have, and it's a marvelous avocation as well as a vocation. So it will enrich their lives and they may end up really doing a lot with it, but it shouldn't diminish their own sense of accomplishment by the fact that they may have to work at another job as well. I think they should expect that. The thing of a starving artist is not so farfetched."

'Ed Herschler, Wyoming Governor—*courtesy State of Wyoming*

ED HERSCHLER

"People know me for what I am"

Ed Herschler is an impressive figure seated behind his desk
at the capitol building in Cheyenne, dressed neatly in Saturday attire, his deep voice pleasantly modulated. The Democratic
governor's infamous wit and toothy grin fail to surface during
the first few minutes of conversation, and he lights one cigarette
after another as he talks about his life.

Although he had not yet officially announced his intention
to run for an unprecedented third term as governor of Wyoming,
he gave every indication that he would accept the challenge.
Speculation that he would run against Malcolm Wallop for the
senior U.S. senator's seat was only that—speculation—for neither
the governor nor his wife, Casey, want to leave Wyoming.

Herschler's roots run deep in Wyoming's soil. Five generations
of his family have lived in the southwestern section of the state
near the Fontennelle Reservoir where his grandfather homesteaded the land during the 1880s. The cattle ranch prospered
and he bought out other homesteaders when they decided to leave

Lincoln County. Only three or four ranches remain where fifteen or twenty once existed while young Ed grew up during the 1920s. He was an only child and calls himself "a spoiled brat" although he punched cows, irrigated, built fences, cleaned ditches and helped in the hay fields. He attended a rural elementary school with three other students whose number later added up to five. After eighth grade, he was boarded at a private home in Kemmerer so he could attend high school and work the ranch on weekends. He remembers his father as a very even tempered, kind man. His mother, a coal miner's daughter, was very strict and he had to "toe the mark" around her.

Herschler studied prelaw at the University of Colorado but switched to business administration when it was apparent to him that World War II would prevent him from graduating from law school. He had attempted to join the air force to utilize his pilot's training, but color blindness kept him out, so he enlisted in the Marine Corps as a private early in 1942. His Raider unit "saw action at the tag end of Guadalcanal" and the machine-gunning corporal was hit in the left leg on Bougainville in November of 1943. He subsequently spent the rest of the war in military hospitals and on limited duty at Great Lakes, Illinois. Before the end of the war he married Kathleen "Casey" Herschler, an Arizona ranch girl he met at the University of Colorado at Boulder.

After the honeymoon, they moved to Kemmerer for a year before he returned to college courses and the University of Wyoming's law school. He graduated from UW in 1949 and set up his law practice in Kemmerer with Casey as his secretary. Herschler also worked the ranch part-time during his father's long illness. After Edgar Herschler died, his son practiced law three or four days a week and worked the ranch almost equal time until his own son, Jim, finished school.

The governor is disappointed that his son didn't follow in his legal footsteps. He took Jim to court and his son seemed interested but only had eyes for the ranch. So now he pins his hopes on his three young grandsons, his daughter Sue's children. The eldest, Will (born in 1971) has the inbred ability, Casey says.

Herschler first rode into the political arena shortly after he passed the bar exam when he ran for Lincoln County attorney and won. He then served five terms in the Wyoming house and only lost one election in his entire political career. That was to Teno Roncalio in a race for the U.S. Congress in 1970, but undaunted, he ran for governor in 1974 and was reelected in 1978. His 1982 bid is the first time a Wyoming politician ever attempted a third term as governor in the state's history.

Although in his early 60s, the governor is relatively young compared to the nation's chief executive, and retirement is something he's not overly enthused about. If he had decided to retire from politics, he could have returned to the family ranch where he enjoys "the fresh air, good clean work and the exercise." Or he could have resumed his law practice with a brush-up course on legalistics following an eight-year absence from the courtroom.

"I miss the trial work," he says, "but I certainly don't miss examining abstracts or defending drunken drivers. I tried to specialize in personal injury cases and I liked criminal work, but you can't make any money at it because if a guy had any money, he probably wouldn't be stealing things. But it didn't matter whether I was on the defense or for the plaintiff. It was the challenge that mattered and getting psyched up for the trial. I never tried a case that I didn't throw up my breakfast the first morning before I went to court.

"I had to do a lot of things I didn't like because I was in a small town and represented a lot of business people. I hated divorce cases. There's nothing nastier than a contested divorce, but when you're on a retainer the first thing you know, a businessman's daughter is getting a divorce and you've got to handle it. Or his son gets picked up for drunken driving and you have to defend him." But Herschler thoroughly enjoyed the diversity of his work. "One day you're collecting a delinquent garbage account and the next day you're appearing before the Federal Power Commission. I never knew what was going to come in when I went to work; what strange and wonderful thing was going to happen that day."

The governor's favorite fellow attorney, whom he battled and befriended during his legal heyday, is Gerry Spence. The controversial, flamboyant Jackson lawyer tried many cases against Herschler, and the governor says he always had to work "his fanny off getting prepared because Spence is tough and you'd better be prepared or you're done. When Gerry's grandstanding, he knows exactly what he's doing. He'll say nasty things to you and try to get you mad, but I'd always kill him with kindness. He couldn't understand that," Herschler says with a wide grin. "The first time I tried a case against him I argued a motion for a new trial, and he made me so mad that it's a wonder that I didn't poke him one. But I went home and had a little talk with myself and said, 'How stupid can you get?' From that day on I used to boil inside but he never knew it. . . . I really enjoyed matching wits with the other lawyers and figuring out what kind of jury I wanted," he says. "It's all part of the drama."

Herschler enjoys his job as governor even more. Although he misses the company of other lawyers, he makes up for it, somewhat, when he attends governor's conferences. "We get together to exchange ideas and get all kinds of information. Sometimes you'll have a problem and if you know these guys, you can call them and get their ideas. It's very helpful. Most of the governors are very likable guys and pretty down to earth. If we find something going on at the national level that we don't like, we really let them know about it," he says. Herschler has served on the Crime and Prevention Committee as subcommittee chairman of the National Governor's Association, and as a member of the Agriculture and Public Lands committees.

As compatible and agreeable as the governors seem to be, they are not above hiring away staff members from their colleagues. It's tough to find good people, Herschler says, and you worry about other politicians pirating them away from you. The governor got his "water man" from Governor Exon when the Nebraskan ran for the U.S. Senate. And he hired another cognoscente away from the Old West Regional Commission. He, in turn, lost one of his best staffers to his friend, Cecil Andrus, when the former Idaho governor served as secretary of the interior under Jimmy Carter. Herschler's staff is small: two secretaries, a receptionist, administrative assistant and planning coordinator with a four-man office team. The governor's secretary, Bonnie Grivet, has been with him since 1970, making the move from his law office in Kemmerer.

Governor Herschler gained national attention several times with his humorous quips and outspoken appraisals of pending legislation. "People know me for what I am," he says, "and I'm not going to change my philosophy of how I live simply because I'm governor. I say what comes to mind and sometimes put my foot in my mouth, but if you say something very seriously and express your beliefs, you're going to get into trouble anyway because there's always someone who will disagree with you.

"You get awfully discouraged sometimes when you feel that you've done something well and would like the public to say 'Governor, you did a fine job.' They're not going to say that, but you do get some inner satisfaction. There's a lot of things that you can take some pride in, particularly helping individuals with problems. Sometimes you can find an agency head or some department of state that's able to help them and that makes you feel good. That's the best part of being governor. The worst part is sometimes you have to do things that you know will upset people, but you have to do them because you feel that you've made the right decision."

Herschler considers himself a frugal head of state and his eight years in office lend evidence to support that belief. He's proud of his conservative fiscal record as well as his water development program. His unswerving environmental course may have ruffled more liberal feathers along the way, but his dogged determination to preserve and protect Wyoming's natural resources—including water—have made him popular among conservationists. He's also proud of his "no-strings" label. No one owns Ed Herschler.

The conservative Democrat has been referred to as a "democratic Republican" and hails from a staunch Republican family. "My dad and mother were strong Republicans," he says, "but I've been a Democrat ever since I was old enough to vote. I guess my feeling is that people come ahead of property, and there are more important things than a profit and loss statement."

Lucile Wright, queen of the air lanes—*Wright Collection*

LUCILE WRIGHT

"I always flew for the joy of flying"

The grande dame of aviation in this country and the world is Lucile Wright of Cody, Wyoming. With more than five million air miles under her seat belt, Lucile is undisputed queen of the air lanes. Although she isn't as well known outside the industry as her late friend, Amelia Earhart, the feisty redhead has worked long and hard to preserve Amelia's memory and to improve the aviation industry in general.

Her first plane ride was with the infamous General Billy Mitchell in 1922, when the aviator took her for a spin in his X-5 Jenny, a canvas-skinned, open cockpit, single engine plane with an OX5 engine. They flew over Long Island and Staten Island, New York, for half an hour, and Mitchell allowed Lucile, who was seated behind him, to "hold the control stick" while they were in flight. "It was the greatest thrill of my life," she says. "As I was crawling out of the cockpit, he patted my shoulder and said, 'Lucile, I think you'll be a very good pilot.' " She had a difficult time keeping her feet on ground from that time on.

Lucile's father was aghast. He had persuaded his friend, Mitchell, to take his daughter for a ride to "scare the crazy notion of flying" out of her. "But from then on, I couldn't do anything else but think of flying," she says. It was a number of years before she was able to earn her pilot's license, however, and she had to buy her own plane to accomplish the feat.

Lucile Miller was born in Beatrice, Nebraska, in August 1900, a small town forty miles south of Lincoln. Because her parents had no name picked out for a girl, the doctor, a Scotsman, named the baby Lucile ("with one L") after Lady Gordon of Scotland. The fiery-haired youngster was seven when her brother, Harley, was born. Then the entire Miller family moved to Billings, Montana, in 1910, where they tried ranching. "They collected the whole clan and came west," she says. "They were an adventurous group and they all became ranchers and homesteaders. But they were city folks and I guess the ranches were too big for them and took too much time to take care of, so I grew up in Billings and didn't spend much time on the homestead or the ranch."

Bored with ranching, her father got into the Salt Creek oil field in Wyoming with seven partners while Lucile was in elementary school. "I'd spend a couple of days of my vacation down there with him," she remembers. "I just loved the excitement of the oil fields." Miller and his partners were early drilling pioneers at Salt Creek and in Lusk, owning valuable pieces of oil property which Standard Oil attempted to buy from them, and later tried to lease. "They were drilling wells so close together that you could hardly walk between them and all the while Standard Oil was quietly buying up the land around them until they were completely surrounded. So there the boys sat—fat, dumb and happy— until one morning they woke up to find that their oil had been prorated and they were bankrupt."

Lucile's parents then divorced; her mother stayed on in Billings, while Miller wandered around until he settled in St. Paul, Minnesota. Their daughter graduated from high school in Billings in 1919 and enrolled at the University of Minnesota to be near her father. "I wanted to go to medical school," she says, "but my father wanted me to go to law school because I had an aptitude for languages." While attending classes, she also worked as a news reporter for the *Minnesota Daily*. Miller then transferred her to Washington University in St. Louis in her junior year "because he wanted me in the center of the country." There she earned her B.A. degree in languages and B.S. in science.

She then transferred to George Washington University in the District of Columbia to attend law school. "I had been auditing medical classes without my father's knowledge, because he would have raised cain if he knew," she says. "I really wanted to be a doctor." She married a medical student, instead, after she completed one year of law school. Her husband, Edward Winkler, wanted to specialize in obstetrics and gynecology so they moved to New York City where he served his internship and residency. Lucile went to work in a medical laboratory in a New York City hospital where "we did a lot of work for five of the other hospitals there, everything from autopsies to bacteriological sciences." She was able to capitalize on her background in science and sat in on autopsies, photographed gross specimens and was promoted to supervisor of twenty-five lab employees. "Several of the doctors were sorority sisters of mine, and they put in a good word for me. I held the job for six years."

Winkler finished his residency in 1926, and they moved to his hometown, Buffalo, New York, where he set up his medical practice. Lucile worked in the office as his receptionist, nurse and occasional scrub nurse when he delivered a baby. "That was when obstetricians made house calls and sometimes even delivered at the home," she explains. "I was 'Johnny on the spot' and whenever he needed something, I handed it to him. That went on for several years, and he eventually became the outstanding OB and GYN man in Westridge, New York. My husband was so prominent that it went to his head." They were divorced in 1940.

Lucile continued to work as the official laboratory photographer and branched out into nurse's wedding pictures. "I took so many pictures that I began putting them in albums," she says, "and the other photographers followed suit." In 1942, she became the official photographer for Spencer Lens, a large Buffalo optical company. She had also earned her pilot's license.

"There was a civilian pilot training program at the Buffalo airport before we got into World War II, and all the young boys were out there learning to fly, so I figured that I could get some instructions, too. But I had an awful hard time learning to fly because women were not popular around airports. They just didn't want us." Lucile met another woman pilot at the airport who worked in the office to earn her flying time. "She already had her private license—her whole family, all the boys were pilots and most of them in the service, but her father wouldn't let her take flying lessons, like my father."

Lucile passed her written test "with flying colors" but it was a year before she was able to earn her license because "I spent so much time on the phone trying to get some flying time. It was 'maybe we can give you an hour this week' or 'it might be another half an hour in ten days.' You can't learn to fly that way." The airport manager had Lucile in a holding pattern, not allowing her to solo, but taking her money for an extended period for flying lessons. "So I got fed up with that. It took me awhile to realize that I was being skunked, but I decided to buy my own plane." She then asked Betty Shay, the airport secretary, if she would fly with her until she could solo, then Betty could fly Lucile's plane to log enough hours to get her commercial license. The bargain was struck.

Lucile "scouted around" and found a Rearwin single engine plane with side-by-side seating. Betty flew her to another field where Lucile knew an airport manager who would solo her and give her a beginner's pilot's license. When they returned to the sod field at Buffalo, Lucile said nothing about her license but locked her plane in the hangar and reminded "all the boys that nobody could fly it except Betty or me." The women subsequently flew all over New York State and Pennsylvania with Lucile building up time for her private license and Betty working on her commercial license on alternate flights. The redhead earned her private license before the war began and served as the first woman courier for the Civil Air Patrol (CAP). CAP officials tried to borrow her plane without her services, but Lucile insisted that she and the plane were inseparable. It wasn't long before she was flying messages and supplies all over the country.

The flyer also went back to school, this time to study medicine. She didn't finish, however, because there were too many other things she wanted to do. Her graduate and "extra curricular" studies amounted to two years of medicine and a year each of law, journalism, business, art and geology. "I'm a jack of all trades," she laughs, "but I'm not a master of any."

Lucile joined the "99s," the international association of women pilots founded by Amelia Earhart in 1929. The redhead wasn't eligible for membership until she earned her pilot's license in 1935 but is now a life member. Amelia Earhart was her idol, and they met shortly after Amelia's first flight across the Atlantic as a passenger in 1928. They became friends. "She was warm and friendly, perfectly charming. One of the most charming girls you'd ever want to meet and dedicated to aviation." Lucile didn't think much of Amelia's husband, George Putnam. "She didn't want to marry him, but he promised her the world. She was in love with a handsome aviator, but he didn't have any money and she wanted to fly. Putnam married her for one reason only and that was to promote her, and she knew it. On her last flight, the fatal one across the Pacific, Putnam had everything subsidized, some of it experimental. He was dead broke, but he was a promoter and if the flight had been successful, they would have been set for life. Unfortunately, he made some wrong calculations."

Lucile has drawn her own conclusions about her friend's disappearance which don't include the theory that she was captured by the Japanese in 1937. She refuses to divulge the name of an aging aviator who has spent the better part of his life researching the disappearance in the area where the plane allegedly went down. "He's in California, and he's positive that he's charted it, and he has taken soundings," she says. "He's spent a lot of money and time researching it and has flown that route many times. The day will come when he can raise enough money to find the plane. He expects to find the skeletons of Amelia and Fred Noonan in the plane. And I think he's right. I've flown across the Pacific many times on commercial flights and it's a long, long haul. And it's awfully deep."

Lucile keeps in touch with Amelia's older sister, Muriel Morrison, who is Lucile's age and three years older than Amelia. "Everytime I go to Boston, I call her and we have lunch, but I'm usually so short on time that she hops on a bus and comes to see me." Lucile was instrumental in arranging financing for the monument erected to Amelia's memory in Meeteetse, Wyoming, although her name isn't on the plaque because she was not yet a Wyoming resident. She also donated a large, impressive wooden plaque with medallion in her honor to the Atchison, Kansas, library (Amelia's hometown) in conjunction with the Amelia Earhart commemorative stamp celebration by the "99s" during the late 1940s.

She's been awarding the Amelia Earhart medallion to outstanding women pilots every year since that time, including Hideko Yokoyama, first woman-licensed pilot in Japan in 1959, and Emily Warner, first woman pilot hired by United Airlines during the late 1970s. In 1956, she presented the award to Madame Paul, the wife of the president of France, and has given scholarships and Earhart memorabilia to various museums.

Lucile met John Wright at a chamber of commerce "fly-in" breakfast in Syracuse, New York, in 1947, and it was "a head-on collision," she says. "I never met anyone who was as enthusiastic about aviation as he was." She became his private pilot and his wife three months later, moving into his home in Jamestown, New York. Wright owned his own plane, although he wasn't a pilot, so Lucile now had a larger craft. Her husband owned five independent telephone companies and was also a banker. Wright authored the Kingsbury Commitment and "pushed it through Congress" to prevent the Bell System from becoming a monopoly during the early 1930s. "Now Ma Bell is buying up everything like crazy," she says. Lucile served as treasurer of the consortium for thirty-five years.

The aviatrix singlehandedly founded the Jamestown, New York, airport by convincing local farmers to donate portions of their land and by securing funding after World War II. "We had just a little landing strip, and I wanted airline service to the community," she says. "The airport was nowhere near adequate for a DC-3, which was the only airplane that was really in operation then. But the town was too tight-fisted and I couldn't convince them that it was the mode of transportation for the future." Lucile persevered and the airport became a reality. She served on the airport commission for eight years and was the first and only female member of the American Association of Airport Executives for forty years until another woman joined the ranks in 1975. "I'm now the grandmother of the whole crowd," she laughs. "They're all my boys."

Lucile flew in a number of Powder Puff Derbies, the last one in 1954 when she was fifty-four years old and the fifty-fourth to take off in the race. "Mine was the last one to take off because I wasn't sure that I would be able to fly in that one; I had a lot of business commitments so I was a late entry." She was the first pilot to finish the race, however, "and the press was there in Long Beach and thought that I was the winner, but I just happened to be the first one in. It's all computed on horsepower and time and all that stuff. I finished way down the line because I wouldn't push my airplane that much. I always flew for the joy of flying, not to win. The girls who fly to win firewall their engines at top speed. I have too much respect for moving parts and mechanical things to do that."

She entered her "little putt-putt Rearwin" in her first race, and later acquired, with her second marriage, a Stinson Reliant with a 450 Pratt and Whitney engine. John Wright donated the Stinson Reliant "station wagon" to the government to be used for training purposes, and they bought a Beechcraft Bonanza, the "Cadillac of the single engine fleet." Lucile kept the Beechcraft for five years after her husband died and sold it when she was sixty-five, "because the insurance was prohibitive and I couldn't afford it. It almost broke my heart and I haven't flown since." She later resigned her post from the telephone company and moved to Cody, Wyoming, where she had a house built in 1975.

Lucile continues to circle the globe on commercial planes, however, and is a member of seven VIP air travelers exclusive clubs including Lady Sabena. The seasoned air traveler is recognized worldwide as a public relations and airport facilities consultant; she speaks to civic clubs, airport organizations, women's groups and others to publicize the importance of aviation in a community. "In the early days, women were afraid to fly and didn't even want their husbands to fly. But that's all gone by the board now. There is a lot of hesitancy, though, probably because the fares have gone so high," she says. Among her many aviation organizational ties is the British Columbia Aviation Council and the Alberta Aviation Council of which she's the only member from the United States. She's also a longtime member of the Jamestown Zonta

Lucile Wright presents the Amelia Earhart medal to Hideko
Yokoyama, first licensed woman pilot in Japan, 1959—*Wright
Collection*

Club and an international member of Beta Sigma Phi. Through her interests in the Northwest Aviation Council, she established the NAC Achievement Award in the names of both Amelia Earhart and Billy Mitchell.

Although Lucile never had children of her own, she established a citizenship award for the Girls Clubs of America in 1957. She personally awards the scholarship and trip to Washington, D.C., to the winner each year. A member of the board of the Girls Club since 1947, she tried for several years to convince the directors to let her give the award. "In 1955, I was called a square," she recalls. "Who wanted a citizenship award that was founded on homemaking, good grooming, child care and civic involvement?" But Lucile persisted, feeling that the girls, most of whom come from disadvantaged homes, should have the opportunity to visit the District of Columbia "to see what makes this country tick" and to receive a scholarship to continue their educations.

The aviatrix was unable to personally award the scholarship in May of 1981, the first time in twenty-four years. She also missed several important aviation conventions she always attends because she was involved in a accident. Lucile was driving home from the Billings airport in her late model car when the steering mechanism locked, and the car rolled over into a ditch, breaking her left arm and shoulder. The eighty-year-old driver was rushed to the Cody Hospital in March where she remained until July, chomping at the bit to go home. After a series of therapy treatments, she was able to return to her own home and is once again driving and flying commercially around the country.

The delightful octogenarian continues to speak to various organizations. "When I'm speaking to a crowd that needs a bit of levity, I begin by saying that I'm hale and hearty, have 20/20 vision and all my own teeth," she laughs, "and my hair is my own [still vibrant red], and at least nine-tenths of my brain. That breaks the silence.

"You know, life's been good to me."

105

Bill Cody, Buffalo Bill's grandson, at home at his "guest ranch" near Cody

BILL CODY

"My own kind of pony express"

B ill Cody has not only followed in his famous grandfather's bootprints as showman, dude rancher, soldier and entrepreneur: he's made some history of his own. The unpretentious Harvard Law School graduate has lectured to more students about "American heritage," surrendered more American troops in Europe during World War II, married more times than the average Wyomingite, dropped his last name and learned to downhill ski at the age of sixty-five.

William Cody Garlow was "conceived in Wyoming and born at the Scout's Rest Ranch in North Platte, Nebraska," January 4, 1913. He and his mother, Irma (Buffalo Bill's youngest child), "returned to Cody country" when he was two weeks old. He and his older sister and brother, Jane and Fred, were orphaned in 1918 when their parents died two days apart during the influenza epidemic. Their grandfather, William F. Cody, had died the year before and his wife, Louisa, adopted her grandchildren and raised them until her death in 1921.

Bill and Fred were taken to a military school in southern California by their grandmother when they were in first and third grades, respectively, and Bill continued his education at the Riverside Military Academy in Georgia. Fred, however, never progressed past the ninth grade; the mountains and streams surrounding the small town of Cody held a special fascination for him and he spent the rest of his life exploring them extensively.

Bill Cody doesn't recall much about his illustrious "granddad. I remember him distinctly only three times," he says, "on his death bed, once at the TE Ranch [on the Southfork west of Cody] and his funeral in Denver up on Lookout Mountain." He was four when "Buffalo Bill" died. Other children didn't treat him differently because of his ancestry, he says, "and never even mentioned it. People in Cody don't think anything about it. I'm just another citizen of the community—until summer rolls around and the tourists come in and they start introducing me as 'the grandson.'"

Cody's grades in school fluctuated according to the time of year, and it took him six years, instead of four, to graduate from Riverside Military Academy. "Periodically I was excellent," he grins. "And other times I got lousy grades. It all depended on the hunting season which started about the same time as school. I had to go hunting first."

The trim six-footer studied prelaw at the University of Nebraska, graduating in 1936, and enrolled at Harvard Law School. "I would say that I was a pretty good student when I wanted to be," he chuckles. "Very early in high school I decided to become a lawyer. I visualized justice, equity and all that I wanted to participate in, but when I became a lawyer, I found that it was an entirely different ball game than I had envisioned, so I only practiced two years and quit."

Following Harvard, Cody enlisted in the army with a reserve commission of second lieutenant and "fought the battle of Camp Walters, Texas," for a few years. He was platoon leader and later promoted to the ranks of captain, company commander and major. In 1944, he was transferred to the 106th Infantry Division and was sent to Germany where his troops were caught in "the Battle of the Bulge." Surrounded by German artillery troops, Cody's 423rd regiment (commanded by Col. Charles Cavender) and the 422nd were stationed on the Schnee Eifel, attempting to fight their way west to the German town of Schönberg. Just before daybreak on December 19, 1944, Cavender gathered his three batallion commanders and staff in a small open field to discuss their "next line of action" when a German artillery shell fragment struck and killed the officer standing next to Cody.

After the initial volley, the American troops were assembled to coordinate an attack westward across the hilly Schnee Eifel area, but the whole command was caught in the open where artillery fire was inflicting many casualties. Colonel Descheneau of the 422nd regiment gathered the field officers together in a bunker to tell them how grave their situation was. Their food and ammunition supplies had been cut off, and the colonel concluded that the only way to save the lives of their 5,000 men was to surrender. The field officers reluctantly agreed.

Cody volunteered to try to negotiate the surrender although he and several other men had planned an escape through the woods (with the colonel's permission). He decided, however, to hand over his gun, and he borrowed some white handkerchiefs to wave as he ran an erratic path down the side of the hill into German-held territory. There he was grabbed and stripped of his "most prized possessions." He spoke no German and was unable to communicate his intent to negotiate a surrender until a young German lieutenant, who spoke English, came to his rescue and ordered his men to return Cody's watch, pint of bourbon and some candy bars. He was then taken to a major who also spoke fluent English.

John Eisenhower describes the scene that followed in his book, *The Bitter Woods:*

> Turning to the lieutenant (the major) snapped orders in German which (Cody) soon learned charged the lieutenant with conducting a patrol of nine or ten men to accompany (Cody) back to the American positions. Faced with a tense situation, the young volksgrenadier's personality instantly changed. He jabbed (Cody) in the back with his Schmeisder burp gun. "If this is a trick, Major, you're dead." (Cody) winced under the painful blow; later it turned out that his chivalrous enemy had broken two of his ribs. But the lieutenant's former friendly attitude returned. Keeping (Cody) covered, he let the American guide his patrol up the hill to Descheneau's CP on the Schnee Eifel, where they found that Descheneau had prepared everything. Weapons were broken. . . .

And many American soldiers were in tears. Cody, therefore, holds what he terms "the dubious honor" of having negotiated the surrender of the largest number of American soldiers in the European theatre; surpassed only by the Bataan surrender in 1942. Members of the 422nd and Cody's 423rd regiments spent the rest of the war in German prison camps and were awarded the purple heart for the frostbite they suffered as a result of their capture; Cody was also "unofficially shot in the leg."

Following the war, he returned to "Cody country" where he practiced law for two years and helped establish the local radio station. He was one of the founders of KODI, later serving as owner-general manager and "on the air" personality. He then went to Texas where he "got into the oil business"—the drilling end of it. He went broke after awhile, he says, because of his preoccupation with "having a good time and chasing girls." So he once again returned to Cody where he established a river float business—now run by his son—and in 1969, he married for the fifth time.

Cody first married "a girl from Nebraska" in 1937, but the marriage lasted only six months. He married again while a law student at Harvard. The union produced four sons: Bill Garlow, a CPA in Dallas; Jack Garlow who resides in Florida; Kit Carson Cody who runs the river float business among other ventures; and the youngest son, Barry, who also legally changed his name to Cody. Barry teaches coaching in Missouri.

Cody remarried after his son's mother died. His third marriage was to "a girl from California" and lasted "a couple of years." A fourth marriage also failed, but he has been "happily" married to his fifth wife, Barbara, some thirty years his junior, since 1969. Together they purchased a rundown guest ranch and have established it as one of the best resorts in Wyoming. "It was originally a dude ranch built in 1925," he explains, "and very successful. During the depression and after World War II, they just let it go to pieces. It changed hands five times and was run as a kind of off-the-road lodge and was not successful at all. As a result, Barbara and I were able to buy it for only $500 down. Everyone said that we couldn't make a go of it, but we did."

The Cody's had a difficult time borrowing $2,000 to put the ranch in operating shape but were able to raise a quarter of a million dollars seven years later to completely renovate it and turn it into a "Two Crown Best Western" and "Diamond Triple A" guest ranch. The ranch is located on ten acres of leased government land, half way between Cody and the east entrance to Yellowstone Park, adjoining millions of acres of national forest.

Cody began making public appearances for the Daisy Air Rifle Company in 1968 when a new line was introduced called the "Buffalo Bill." The promoters "insisted" that he legally change his name from William Cody Garlow to Bill Cody to do the television and radio commercials as well as public appearances all over the country. "Bill Garlow just wouldn't do," he says. Ironically, "I may have already been a Cody because my grandmother adopted me, but I never thought to check the courthouse records. So with all my marriages and the change in name, I have the Cody family book well fouled up," he laughs. "People have criticized me for changing my name, but I did it for the same reason John Wayne changed his—for a better image."

Buffalo Bill's grandson appeared on some 3,000 television shows, thousands of radio programs and various promotions during the next nine years. He also began lecturing to junior high and high school students about "American heritage" while he was on the road making appearances. He has talked to "more American youth [in person] than any other American," some 1,171 lectures in forty-two states. And he hopes to speak to students in all fifty states "before I die."

One of his school lectures was featured on Harry Reasoner and Howard K. Smith's ABC evening news with Cody carrying his "message to the youth of America" about "greater appreciation of our forefathers and America. That's my kind of pony express," he says.

Cody's talks include very little about his infamous grandfather, and he says he has "never tried to depict him. My brother Fred has, but I refuse to do that. If people call me Buffalo Bill, I tell them that he's dead and buried up on Lookout Mountain."

Malcolm Wallop, senior U.S. Senator—*courtesy Tessa Dalton*

MALCOLM WALLOP

"I don't believe in blood politics"

U.S. Senator Malcolm Wallop grew up on one of Wyoming's oldest ranches; located at Big Horn in northern Wyoming, it's the site of the nation's oldest polo field where both cowboys and British army officers "raced to the boards" on Wallop-Moncrief Thoroughbreds.

The senator's grandfather, Oliver "O. H." Wallop immigrated from England in 1882, first settling in Montana and bringing with him the first Thoroughbreds "to this part of the country." He joined his Scots cousin, Malcolm Moncrief, in the Big Horn area near Sheridan in 1888, and together they raised horses and supplied them to the British army for the Boer War.

"They were pretty colorful old gents," Malcolm Wallop says of his grandfather and his partner. "They would ride from the ranch at Big Horn to Miles City, Montana, to pick up some cowboys and ride west as far as the eastern slope of the Cascades, buying horses and trailing them back to the ranch. There they would sort and break them and do whatever was necessary until the British buyers came."

During the 1880s, Wallop and Moncrief laid out the first polo field in the nation because British army officers, who bought their horses, wanted them ridden the length of a polo field so that they could judge them. "They had horses galore," he says, "so with British buyers coming through, there was a lot of polo playing here." Cavalry units from Forts Robinson, Riley and Warren all had polo teams and often used Moncrief Field. "This was an area that was widely visited by people from all over the world [including Prince Phillip of England], but basically, the people who played polo were locals—ranchers and cowboys—and they went from here to play in tournaments all over the country.

Oliver Wallop, the senator's father, was born on the ranch and married Jean Moore, whose family owned a large "spread" now known as the Burns Ranch, and at one time owned the Bar 13 and Meade Creek. When they met, Oliver Wallop owned three ranches including the Canyon Ranch which is still in the family. "But he didn't stay here," his son says. "He was a businessman." One of his business ventures was an early flying service in the Big Horn area where he provided charter flights—from short hops to United Airline connections in Cheyenne. He began flying during the early 1920s in canvas-covered, open cockpit planes, using the polo field as a landing strip. "Dad was one of the pioneer aviators in America, and we always had an airplane on the ranch."

The aviator's son, Malcolm, also had a charter service called Mountain Flying Service during the late '60s and early '70s, utilizing a Cessna 182 and Beechcraft Baron. He holds a commercial instrument, twin rated pilot's license but hasn't had time to do much flying since he's been in Washington, other than one or two commercial flights a month to Wyoming.

The senator is the only member of the Wallop family during the last three generations to be born outside of Wyoming. He arrived "early" in 1933, while his mother was visiting her family in New York. "That was my singular accident," he laughs. "I have an older brother and two younger sisters who were born here, as were all my children." Wallop describes himself as "very shy" as a child. "In fact, I remain so to this day." His mother was ill during most of his childhood and died when he was eight. He and his siblings had attended a small, one-building school in Big

Horn but, following his mother's death, he was sent to live with an aunt in California during the school year. His older brother was sent to a boarding school and his sisters were boarded in Big Horn.

Their father was in the "army air corps" in 1941 when his wife died, and Oliver Wallop visited his children at the ranch during summer vacation. "Finally, after the war we were quite family oriented again," he says. His father remarried, "but that little segment between the time my mother died and the war ended was a fairly big chunk out of a young life. This was a marvelous place to grow up. In the summertime, there were a lot of young people around, and we would have picnics, campfire parties and we'd go up to the Teepee [a dude ranch] to dances and hayrides. We were always enthused about parties that the adults gave as well, so that we were with more young people, in many respects, than if we had lived in a more populated area."

The Wallop brothers literally grew up in the saddle trailing horses, herding cattle and taking part in every aspect of ranching. "We were a very purposeful ranch," he says. "We trailed cattle back and forth from Sheridan to the Badger Creek Ranch, some forty odd miles, and we had a mountain permit so we trailed them up there. We gathered and branded and dipped. . . . We were always on horseback. In fact, all of our hay was put up with horses." They also played polo and young Malcolm participated in every kind of sport that was available to him during his school years. He earned his letters in soccer, basketball, baseball and track at Yale; and he was captain of the soccer and track teams during his senior year.

An avid reader, he "entertained dreams of writing" while in school. He majored in English at Yale and "indulged his dreams of writing" for a brief period when he wrote children's and short stories, "but found that it was hard to eat," he laughs. "I had intended to eventually write a novel, but I never got it more than structured. It's like a model airplane. You leave it there and intend to go back to it later."

Wallop joined an army artillery unit in 1954, at the end of the Korean War. He had gone through ROTC training in college, earning a second lieutenant's commission. He served as a forward observer and briefly commanded an artillery battery before being transferred to artillery headquarters at Fort Carson, Colorado, where he was attached to the Fourth Field Command, the last U.S. army mounted unit. "It was a mule outfit," he says, "and I knew horses and mules."

He returned to the ranch in 1957, "and was restless. I tried to write for a little while, and I spent some time in England and San Francisco," he recalls. "I decided that I needed something more to do. I was in the family partnership and was the junior partner, so I did whatever everybody else didn't want to do." He then sold out to his father and brother and established a grade cattle herd of his own which he "operated" until he was elected to the U.S. Senate in 1976.

Wallop married his first wife while he was enrolled at Yale and has four children from that marriage. Malcolm Moncrief is an honor student at the University of Oregon; Oliver Matthew is studying broadcast journalism at the University of Wyoming; Paul is a veterinary student at UW; and Ann is majoring in psychology at Texas Christian. The senator's first marriage ended in divorce, and his second marriage failed during his fourth year in Washington. Life in the capital "is very difficult," he says, "and I think that, as much as anything, is the reason my second marriage failed. My wife was very unhappy in Washington."

The tall, trim rancher decided to enter politics at the age of thirty-one in 1964, when he ran for the Wyoming state legislature. It was the "Goldwater year," and although he won the primary, he lost his bid for office "by forty-two votes in the general election." Four years later, he was elected and served two years in the House of Representatives before successfully running for the state senate. Wallop then decided to take on Gale McGee, Wyoming's U.S. Democratic senator during the 1976 campaign; he defeated the veteran politician in a very novel and humorous way. "I don't believe in blood politics," he insists. "If you want to make a point, you can make it with humor. We set out to do that with a political television advertisement that would separate me from Senator McGee. He was very much for federal regulations, and I was very much against it."

While watching the evening news, Wallop found his theme. The Occupational Safety and Health Association (OSHA)

116

announced that "everyone in agriculture had to be within five minutes of toilet and lavatory facilities. People on truck farms in New Jersey wouldn't react too strongly," he says, "but it immediately implied that every little section of land had to have one on it. So what we did was to create an advertisement that said how far the federal government had gone in our lives; that now, if you wanted to go on a roundup, unless you took your portable facility, you couldn't go."

The cowboy with the portable potty strapped to his horse was a "tremendously successful political advertisement. It was one of the few political ads where people were calling the station to find out when it was going to be shown," he says. "It was electric. They showed it on the 'Today Show' and 'Good Morning, America.' We got a lot of freebies out of that because they just couldn't believe it." The more humorous the advertisement the better, he feels, because the "public is entitled to it, and I don't have to attack anyone personally. I don't like being attacked either."

Wallop is most proud of his water legislation and his bill which changed the old inheritance tax law so that a business or piece of land cannot be taxed twice within the same generation. "Families were being forced to buy back their businesses or ranches from the government whenever someone in the family died." The senator has served as head of the Intelligence and Ethics committees—chairing the much publicized Harrison Williams misconduct hearing in 1981–82; he is a member of the Energy and Natural Resources and Finance committees.

The senator rarely spends less than ten hours a day in his office in Washington, "plus a few more hour's work at home." There are usually three 8 A.M. breakfast committee meetings each week and senate sessions last all afternoon until seven or eight o'clock in the evenings. Wallop also maintains five area offices in Wyoming which schedule meetings for him when he flies home once or twice a month to confer with mayors, county commissioners, state legislators, school boards and individuals.

"I still love to hunt and fish and once in awhile I get to play golf or tennis to keep myself fit," he says. "I enjoy my life and I do my best with it. There's very little that turns me off."

Peggy Simpson Curry, poet and author

PEGGY SIMSON CURRY

"That's what made me a writer"

A homesick fourth grader wrote her first poem about life on a ranch some sixty years before she was proclaimed Wyoming's first poet laureate. As a nine-year-old, she wrote her first poem because her father moved her to town to become "educated," she says, "and I hated it. I wanted to go back home to my horse and the red fox in the meadow." That poem and a following one, written about "evening on the ranch," were published in a small local newspaper, the *Jackson County Star* in northern Colorado. And Peggy Simson was launched into a career of writing.

Her creative endeavors might have taken a different course, she says, if it had not been for the compassion of a young Adonis, a student who spurned her puppy love but saved her from humiliation. "I fell in love with a very handsome boy in the sixth grade, but he didn't think I was very good looking. I wrote hundreds of poems about his hair and his teeth . . . that's when I really became a poet," she laughs. "To complicate matters, I had this weird teacher who wanted us to tickle her neck. If you did, you got an "A" in her class. She said, 'Peg, come up and tickle my neck' and I said, 'No, tickle your own neck.' So I got a lousy grade in her class. And when I made a valentine for the boy to show him how much I cared for him, she crammed it into the box and made a mess of it. Then she took it out and asked, 'Whose this thing for?' The kids started to laugh when I said his name, and I didn't know what he was going to do. But he walked up to the front of the class and said, 'Thank you, Peg, it's beautiful.' Bless him, that's what made me a writer."

Peggy left her family and the cattle ranch near Walden, Colorado, to be "boarded" in town from the fourth grade until high school, first with the local sheriff and his wife who had no children of their own, and then with other residents. She attended her last two years of high school in east Denver where she won several in-school essay contests and sold poems and articles to various Denver newspapers.

After high school she enrolled as an English student at the University of Wyoming. "I specialized in journalism," she recalls. "I wrote special features and contributed poems to the school newspaper." She then wrote a play for her creative writing teacher and performed in the production. Classes at the university were carefully reclassified for her benefit when her writing talent was discovered, and "they really spoiled me while I was there," she says.

Peggy met Bill Curry, a fellow English major at UW. They were married following graduation in 1937 and moved to Illinois where he got his first teaching job. Within a year Peggy sold her first poem to the *Saturday Evening Post*, but she had to prove that it was her own work. "We had to get character references to prove that it wasn't plagiarized," her husband recalls. "Well, the *Post* had never heard of me," Peggy adds. "That was before I sold them short stories, and Bill and I had to go downtown to get people to testify [on paper] that it was original and my own work." Years later "one of my poems was plagiarized—right here in Wyoming—and used on the radio."

When the Currys' had been married two years, Curry was hired by Natrona County High School in Casper, but Peggy had to stay behind in North Park with her parents at the ranch because "it was August, and I was very pregnant with our son, Michael [the couple's only child]. We used my dad's car to come to Casper

120

because ours wasn't in very good shape," she says. Michael was born in Laramie, some sixty miles from the Simson ranch near Walden, "and we've been in Wyoming ever since," she smiles. "We love it here."

Peggy sent her first short story to *Good Housekeeping* magazine "and they told me it was well done but not quite for them," she says. "They said I should send it to a romance magazine—so I sold it to one. It was a silly story about a cowboy, and it contained phrases like 'cows don't breed in too much heat.' The editor wrote back and said, 'We can use it if you change some of the conversation. There's nothing romantic about cows breeding.' So I revised it and they paid me forty dollars—not bad in those days."

The author's love of the outdoors—"cowboys, horses, fishing and ranching"—dominates her fiction and poetry because she grew up with a "very close feeling for the land." Her father, William Simson, left the Firth of Clyde in Scotland with his wife and three-year-old daughter, Peggy, to become a ranch hand for the Big Horn Cattle Company in North Park, Colorado. Nine years later Peggy helped her mother cook for twenty ranch hands during haying season while she and her younger brother, Bill, grew up on the huge ranch. "I cooked biscuits and still have the recipes in my head," she says, although she admits that her memory is vague on dates and "boring details. I only collect things that interest me."

Peggy also drove a hay rake and was taught to fish and hunt by the ranch hands. "Maybe that's why I like to write from a man's viewpoint," she says. "I love horses, cattle and cowboys; and I think you become a writer by making the most of whatever you are." Asked whether she would have preferred to be a man, she says, "no, not really, but I like the man's world. I enjoy men's company, and I have a close feeling for them because I grew up with men teaching me to fish, hunt and trap. I quit trapping, though, after I met this little mink along the river one day that had gotten out of one of my traps. I had a .22 rifle with me, and I thought I could shoot him but he looked up at me with that little paw that had been caught in the trap. So I didn't have the heart to shoot him, nor could I shoot a deer. The men always took me with them because they said the deer would come around when I was there. I wrote one of my best poems about the hunt and how I felt about the death of the deer. So I guess you could say that man's world turned me on."

Peg's eyes twinkle when she recalls her thirty nights at sea with Scottish fishermen to research her first novel, *Fire in the Water*, which became a book club selection. She interrupted her college studies to rush to the Firth of Clyde to spend six months with her ailing grandmother in the town of Denure, Scotland. "I got tired of sitting around drinking tea so I decided to go out on the fishing boats," she remembers. "But the fishermen were superstitious about women being bad luck and they wouldn't let me go with them." She was finally able to convince her uncle to take her along with the crew of six on his commercial vessel, and they brought back an extraordinary catch of herring. "After that, I could go with any of them," she laughs. Her second novel, *So Far From Spring*, which she considers her best, tells the story of a young man who leaves Scotland in the 1830s to work as a ranch hand in North Park. Historical research and interviews with "old ranchers" augmented the real characters or combinations of people Peggy knew who actually inhabited the area. Her fictional ranch owner was a woman named "Monty," a very liberated woman for those times.

Peggy considers herself liberated and lucky to have a husband like Bill Curry "who has always encouraged me to do my own thing just as I've encouraged him to do his. Bill proofreads my work if he's around when I get ready to mail it off," she says. "He's been the best husband any creative individual could have."

Curry retired from teaching and served in the state legislature from 1966 until 1982, when he decided not to run, but to pursue other interests. He maintains their log home in the foothills of Casper Mountain while Peggy travels the state to teach in the Poetry-in-the-Schools Program, a service she helped to create in 1970. She also volunteers her time to teach at the blind camp each summer on Casper Mountain and has taught a creative writing class for the past forty years, first at Natrona High School and then at Casper College where her husband was chairman of the English department.

Peggy penned a textbook on writing, *How to Create Fiction From*

Experience, which has been read by writers around the world. Her three adult novels—*So Far From Spring, The Oil Patch* and *Fire in the Water,* have been translated into at least eight languages, and her juvenile novel, *A Shield of Clover,* is an historical look at ranching in the premechanized era. *Red Wind of Wyoming,* a volume of poetry about the Johnson County War in Buffalo, Wyoming, has gone through many editions and was adapted as a radio drama in 1969 by Frank Parman. She conceived the idea for *Red Wind* while sitting in the old Elbow Room Lounge in Casper with a friend during the mid-fifties. Peg had been reading *The Banditti of the Plains* when she got a phone call from a friend asking her to meet her there.

"All of a sudden the walls of the Elbow Room came alive with scenes of the Johnson County War," she remembers. "I told my friend that I saw Nat Champion, and she grabbed my arm and said, 'Peggy, that's the bartender.' You just can't explain things that happen like that."

The author's published short stories number well over a hundred. Many of them have appeared in *Boy's Life* magazine and are action-packed adventures which usually link the present with the past. Quite a few of them have been included in anthologies and in a textbook published in England. She has also written several dozen "how-to" articles for *The Writer,* a prestigious magazine for authors.

Peggy is no stranger to Hollywood. She wrote a television script and receives option payments from Walt Disney Enterprises for a juvenile story the studio plans to produce someday. Pulp westerns were her forte before World War II, and she sold stories and articles to confession and "slick" women's magazines. Western Writers of America honored her with two "Golden Spurs" in the fields of juvenile and adult fiction, making her only the second woman in the world to win two "Spurs"; Wyoming Writers awarded her two "Emmie Mygatt" awards for outstanding service to writers within the state; Kappa Kappa Gamma gave her a national award; and the University of Wyoming publicly applauded her work in the field of humanities. Her most cherished award, however, was the title bestowed upon her by Governor Ed Herschler in January of 1981, that of "poet laureate."

Tom Getter, Wyoming trucking magnate—*courtesy Tom Getter*

TOM GETTER

"I'm doing what I'm happy doing"

Getter Trucking's success could be termed a modern-day Horatio Alger story. Its phenomenal growth is due largely to the efforts of its Gillette-based president, Tom Getter, who took over the business following the untimely deaths of his father and older brother.

The trim, soft-spoken, courteous man is the second son of Glenn Getter, a Great Northern Railroad employee from Dayton, Ohio, who was transferred to the Williston, North Dakota, terminal. He met his future wife, Ruth Kittleson, in the neighboring town of Wolf Point, Montana, in the 1920s. Following their wedding, they moved on to Cutbank where he bid for Great Northern's freight-hauling contract. Working part-time during the day hauling freight by truck, he continued working nights for the railroad. "He had to trade in our car, a Willys Knight," his son remembers, "for a one-ton oversized pickup truck with dual wheels. And that served as our car and the delivery truck." The Drayline delivery service soon became a full-time job, and Getter branched out into gravel-hauling dump trucks and bulldozers in 1934, which he used to level sites for oil field drilling operations. "He then kind of got into the rig-skidding business and into trucking which he operated until the second world war, when he sold the oil field trucks." Ken Davis, a partner of Glenn Neilson who founded Husky Oil Company, bought Getter's equipment and took it to Alaska. Getter continued with his Great Northern freight-hauling business and became partners in a farming venture in the Cutbank area on the Blackfeet Indian Reservation.

Dissatisfied with agriculture, however, he sold his interest in the farm and got back into the oil field trucking business. In 1946, he was electrocuted while lifting power lines over a drilling rig, the same day his son, Tommy, was to graduate from high school in Cutbank, Montana. Although hospitalized, he died a month later when a blood clot entered his heart. Because Glenn Getter left no will, the state of Montana divided up the trucking business among the family with one-third going to his wife and two-thirds to his four children. His eldest son, Ralph, a twenty-year-old who had just been discharged from military service, took over as head of the business with his eighteen-year-old brother, Tommy, as his assistant. The brothers later bought out their older sister's interest and were given their mother's interest gradually over the years. The youngest son, Bruce, was nine years old when his father died, and he joined the firm after he completed his education.

The Getter brothers' main interests during school had always been trucks, and Tommy looked forward to Saturdays when he could "go down and ride a truck and get to go someplace with Dad." The 135-pound high school student had played some basketball and looked forward to going into business with his father.

Several years after their father's death, the Getter brothers bought out the C Brewer Trucking firm, a small business in Roundup, Montana, with a "good interstate hauling permit for Montana and Wyoming." They expanded their original three truck–two bulldozer operation to seven transports for oil field equipment hauling. Tom Getter managed the Roundup terminal and married Janet Gibbs in Cutbank before he took over the operation. Miss Gibbs was the daughter of an oil field pumper for Exxon Oil Company who had been transferred to Cutbank from Seminole, Oklahoma. The young couple's son and two daughters were born while they lived in Roundup, but they all attended schools in Gillette, Wyoming, following another expansion move in 1962.

"We lived in Roundup for seven years," he says, "and business was pretty good. We accumulated a dozen trucks. But during the last year that I was there, most of the [oil] rigs moved down into Broadus, Montana, and into Gillette, Wyoming. Business had dropped off badly, and I had to find somewhere else to go. During that period, our truck pusher came home and said, 'Man, we should move some of these trucks to Gillette. They stopped me on the street and in the cafe and wanted me to haul something.' So that got us interested in the Gillette area."

While the Roundup terminal takeover had been relatively easy because the former owner stayed on for a year to familiarize Getter with the business, the move to Gillette was a difficult one. "Some of our people came with us from Roundup, but some didn't want to make the move," he explains. "And some that did move, didn't like it here and moved back." Some 3,500 people inhabited Gillette in 1962, as did two other trucking firms, and although business wasn't exactly booming, "activity was pretty good." But getting established was no easy chore. "Coming in here cold, hiring new people, finding a place to operate from and getting customers" were the first problems to solve. "There were customers, but you don't get the best ones in a situation like that—and gain their confidence. There had been other companies that had moved in and stayed awhile and left. And some of these customers had started using their services. But when they left, it left the customers in a bind so they had to go back to these other [truckers] they had dropped. So they were a little reluctant to try a new company."

Getter rented a shop for six months before buying two acres east of town which later expanded to forty-two. A rail siding borders the property and serves as a deposit for myriad oil field pipe and mining equipment. Not long after the Gillette terminal was operating, another terminal was opened in Williston, North Dakota, when the Getter brothers purchased Associated Truckers, giving them permits to work in both North and South Dakota.

Oil field activity in Wyoming and Montana was leveling off, and new fields were opening up in the Williston Basin. So yet another terminal was opened in Dickinson, North Dakota, where oil field exploration continues. Some 120 employees work out of both terminals, leveling drilling sites, setting up rigs, tearing them down and moving them to new sites, from a mile to a thousand miles away.

Tragedy struck the Getter family again in December of 1969 when Ralph Getter, his wife and two of their four children were killed in a plane crash. "At that time, he had run the company completely," his younger brother says. "And when he died, I had no knowledge of operating the business. I was just managing the Gillette terminal. He and I had made a few decisions together, but I didn't even know our banker personally. I wouldn't have known him if he had walked in the door because my brother had always dealt with him [in Cutbank]."

After the initial shock, Getter gradually slid into the driver's seat but admits to "running scared for awhile, wondering if I could handle it. But after I built up some confidence, I could see that I was going to make it. And I feel pretty good that I was able to hold things together and keep going," he says. Judging by recent company revenue reports, business has increased thirty-fold since he took over as president. His younger brother, Bruce, who manages the Roundup terminal, is now senior vice-president and his nephew — son of Ralph Getter — is executive vice-president. His own son, Alan, is also an employee.

Four more trucking terminals have been opened since 1971, when the company expanded into hauling heavy equipment, lumber and steel; the Billings, Montana, terminal became a center location for Getter Trucking. The Casper terminal was established in 1976 and serves the Rock Springs-overthrust area as well. Two additional terminals were opened recently in Houston and Lufkin, Texas. The Lufkin terminal, located 130 miles north of Houston, services a large oil field pump-manufacturing plant and provides shipping customers for the northern-bound truck lines into Wyoming, Montana and the Dakotas. Getter anticipates opening several more terminals, including Rock Springs and Deer Lodge, Montana.

Getter further proved his managerial capabilities by running for the Wyoming House of Representatives in 1978 on the Republican ticket. Elected, he served on both the Highways and Transportation and the Mines and Minerals committees but had to resign when he required emergency surgery before the 1980 budget session. "Dick Wallace took my place," he says, "and then after I got kind of healed up, Dick and I both ran and won, so there was a Democrat and Republican from Campbell County."

He has also "worked his way up to president of the Wyoming Trucking Association" and held the wheel from 1973–75. He doesn't volunteer the information, but he has also held a number of other impressive jobs. A 1979 issue of *Drivetrain Comments*, a trucking magazine, lists some of his jobs as: director of the Idaho Motor Transport Association, director of the First National Bank of Gillette, American Trucking Association vice-president for Wyoming, member of the board of the Montana Motor Carriers directors and secretary-treasurer of Sun Cementing of Wyoming.

In his spare time, Getter dabbles in photography — mostly pictures of his family and his equipment. He also plays golf. With a twenty-two handicap, he calls himself a "social golfer" who likes to "get out for the exercise and to be around people." His favorite tournaments are the Casper "Wildcatter" and "the Oilfield Executive Golf Tournament" in Phoenix which attracts forty to fifty participants from Denver and Casper each year. He collects golfing friends instead of trophies, but he did tie for the "low net" Montana Motor Carriers trophy in 1981. He lost the toss, but the large, impressive trophy was delivered to his home in Gillette by mistake, giving him brief custody.

Getter is happy in his work and has no plans to leave his home in Gillette to personally oversee any of his other trucking terminals on a permanent basis. "I'm pretty much doing what I'm happy doing," he says. "And my time is flexible. I've always put plenty of time in the business except when I go to the legislature. Then you have to drop everything."

The trucking magnate would like to be remembered as "a friend to a lot of people. I don't want to have an enemy," he says. Finding a Tom Getter enemy would probably expend more time than counting the bolts on all the equipment in his nine terminals.

Stan Hathaway, former Wyoming governor—*courtesy Stan Hathaway*

STAN HATHAWAY

"Just a decent kind of guy"

Former Wyoming Governor Stan Hathaway will no doubt be remembered for his statesmanship, organizational ability and environmental programs, but he'd rather be eulogized as "just a decent kind of guy." The soft-spoken, thoughtful man considers it immodest to discuss his past accomplishments, a characteristic indicative of his unpretentious beginning on a grain farm in Oscela, Nebraska, July 19, 1924; the fifth child of a woman who died of pneumonia following childbirth.

"My father was left with six kids," he says. "We were all just two years apart, and it was more than he could handle. So he took the two oldest boys and farmed out the others to relatives."

Stan was just a toddler when he was taken in by a first cousin, Velma Hathaway, the daughter of his mother's sister. She and her husband, Earl, persuaded the boy's father, Robert Knapp, to let them legally adopt his son two years later while they were living in South Dakota. The family of three then moved to a 160-acre plot of virgin soil twenty miles south of Torrington, Wyoming, in 1928. "It was a raw piece of land that my adopted father broke out into a farm," he says, "and the first winter we lived in a large hunting tent. I remember it got terribly cold." During the following summer, his father built a grainery which the family lived in for a year and a half until he was able to construct a one-room house. "He was a very industrious guy," his son says. "He did all the work himself."

The farm was located three miles from the state line, and the family did most of their shopping in Lyman, Nebraska. "There weren't any roads in that country then so we didn't get to Torrington too often. We went to Lyman by a team of horses or by Model T when it ran." Hathaway recalls how pleased his mother was to move out of the grainery into the one-room house where they lived for several years while young Stan attended a rural school. During that period, the family boarded his teacher in their small home.

"To show you how people lived in those days," he says, "there was a kitchen, eating place and bedroom all in the same room. My mother put a sheet around where I slept; one around the young, single teacher; and a sheet where she and my dad slept. And on Saturdays we took our baths in one of mother's wash tubs."

Although other children called young Hathaway "teacher's pet," her presence in his home proved to be most fortunate for he contracted rheumatic fever while in the third grade and fell a year behind his classmates. With the help of his resident teacher, he was able to complete three years of schooling in one, thus enabling him to graduate from high school at sixteen. Hathaway calls himself a "fair student" although he was valedictorian of his high school graduating class. "It was only a class of twenty-five," he's quick to add.

Too small and "too uncoordinated" to participate in most sports, he was an avid reader of Dickens and other classics but admits to being "poor in math." While a junior in high school, he began entering "oratorical contests," one of which was judged by his parent's lawyer, Earl Reed. The barrister took an interest in the youth and encouraged him to study law. "I took to heart what he said, and I made up my mind before the war that I was going to be a lawyer," he says. "So I studied at the University of Wyoming until World War II interrupted my education. But I came back to law after the war."

The Hathaway father and son tried to enlist in the military when they learned of the bombing of Pearl Harbor, along with nearly every male resident of Torrington, regardless of age; but Stan was too young at sixteen, and his father too old and in poor health. Stan was later drafted into the air force while a student at the university.

Young Hathaway couldn't afford to go to the university following graduation from high school, so he worked for a year as a farm laborer for three dollars a day. "My folks were able to help a little, and my sister who was a nurse, sent me twenty-five dollars a month until after the war. I couldn't have made it without that." (He was visited by his sister, brothers and natural father several times while he was growing up.)

Hathaway asked for the cavalry when he received his "greetings" from Uncle Sam but was given, instead, the job of radioman in a B-17 bomber crew with the Eighth Air Force stationed in Great Britain. His crew flew thirty-five missions over Germany, suffered a number of crash landings and lost several crew members. Their radioman, however, received no serious injuries, and therefore, "no purple hearts."

His adoptive parents, meanwhile, had given up the farm "to hard times" and moved to California where his father worked in a shipyard during the war. Enlisted radioman Hathaway was still in Germany when the war ended in May of 1945, although he had accrued enough points to be discharged. He immediately signed up for the Pacific theatre, but the war ended in Japan while he was home on leave.

All of Hathaway's siblings served in the military during the war, including his sister who was an army nurse. When the war ended, they all decided to live together because they felt they had been "deprived of something by being split up as kids." They moved into a house in Detroit, Michigan, "where we had a ball for six months," he recalls. "None of us were yet married." Hathaway worked for a ship repair company for awhile and then his sister married a former soldier she had met overseas.

"The family started disintegrating then so my brother, Milton, and I headed West to go to college. We got to Nebraska, and

I was planning to go on to Laramie to reenter the University of Wyoming. But Milton said, 'You know, Brother, we shouldn't part like this. You ought to stay here and go to school.' We were drinking beer, and I got a little sentimental and agreed to stay in Lincoln where Milton was committed to school. So we got an apartment together, and I finished my education there."

Hathaway earned his A.B. degree in 1948 and his L.L.B. "which is called a juris doctorate," in 1950. He met his wife, Bobbie, the former Roberta Harley, at the University of Nebraska where she was in premed classes. They were married that fall. "She was going to be a doctor, and I was in law," he says, "so I told her that I didn't think it was going to work. One of us was going to have to do something to make money faster than we could in either of those professions. She had been accepted at Nebraska Medical School and gave that up to get a teacher's degree. She taught school the first five years we were married, and I might say, she almost totally supported the both of us. Starting a law practice alone—when you first hung out your shingle in those days—was pretty slow. I believe it still is, though. It took me four years to turn a profit of any kind."

Ironically, Bobbie Hathaway's first teaching job was in Huntley, ten miles south of Torrington, where her husband had attended school. She later taught at Torrington, where her husband opened his law office and later served as Goshen County prosecuting attorney from 1954 until 1962.

Hathaway was elected governor of Wyoming in 1966. "Some of my friends prevailed on me—and I gotta tell you that this business of drafting political candidates is a lot of hokey. A draft is less than a dozen people, to be perfectly honest about it. But I had a dozen people leaning on me; they thought it was a good idea. My wife and I talked it over and two weeks later we were running for governor. I surprised myself and quite a few people by getting elected." But eleven-year-old Susan and nine-year-old Sandra knew all along that their father would win.

Clifford Hansen's decision to leave the governorship to run for the U.S. Senate prompted Hathaway to try for Wyoming's head of state. He made few campaign promises "because, frankly, it wasn't the style in the '60s to make many commitments, at least not in Wyoming," he says. "The people can size you up pretty good, and they know where you're coming from on most issues." The "Hathaway years" were filled with governmental reorganization, economic development and the establishment of the Department of Environmental Quality, among others.

Hathaway was sought out to fill the post of secretary of the interior by Gerald Ford in 1975, an honor that unhappily evaporated into Washington's political atmosphere. Hathaway was subjected to three months' worth of senate investigative hearings by the interior committee before he was confirmed as secretary and had "continual exposure and harrassment by the national media." After a month and a half in office, he resigned and came home.

"The hearings were difficult in the sense that I was a pawn," he says. "But they weren't after Stan Hathaway; they were after Gerald Ford. The Democrats and some Republicans wanted a strip mining law so they held me hostage over the issue. During the process they'd hold a week of hearings, and then they'd hang me out to dry for a couple of weeks before going back to the hearings."

The Hathaway hearings broke the record in terms of length, and "they took a toll on me mentally that I wasn't aware of at the time," he says. "I'm sure I was showing some of the signs of depression which I later had a dose of. What really happened was that when I got into the job, I found that the same forces that had given me such a rough time in the hearings were going to prevent me from doing anything I considered constructive. I was completely painted into a corner because they had weakened me enough politically that there wasn't any way I could do the job," he says emphatically. "No way! The only thing that I could do was to placate the opposition and do what they wanted me to do. I couldn't do that mentally, so I wound up telling the president that I wasn't doing myself any good or the country; I didn't feel good and I was going home."

"But what really makes me feel good about all this is that the people of Wyoming understood better what happened to me than I did myself. While traveling around the state, they've expressed it with, 'Ah, Stan, it would never work, not the way you think. Not the way you do business.'"

Betty Evenson, Confessions writer

BETTY EVENSON

"I was like a bartender"

She turned up the volume and settled back into an easy chair to watch "F.B.I.," so engrossed in the television show that she didn't hear the sound of breaking glass in the front of the store, adjacent to her three-room apartment.

Suddenly, the action was taking place in her living room. A well-built, stocking-masked man was pointing a gun at her, threatening to blow off the top of her head if she didn't open the safe. She was afraid she would forget the combination, but her trembling fingers managed to unlock the safe—and the bandit made off with $400–$500 in cash, her diamond engagement ring and her fifty-cent piece collection. But first, he ordered her into the bedroom. As she held her breath, frightened of what might happen next, he motioned her into the bathroom and locked the door. Then he was gone.

She listened to the television set through the door until the station went off the air and tried to figure a way out of her porcelain prison. The window was tiny—much too small for her to climb through, but she yelled out of it each time a car went by on the lonely stretch of highway. No one heard. At seven o'clock the next morning the mailman rescued her.

Betty Evenson, then age sixty-four, incorporated her harrowing experience into a story titled *Too Many Men Knew I Lived Alone*. The facts were rearranged and the heroine's age was sliced by more than half; it was the eightieth story she had sold to a confession magazine. She wrote the stories on an ancient typewriter between customers at The Bright Spot, the only building visible for miles in the midst of the desolate Wyoming prairie. Betty ran the combination service station, lunch counter, general store and post office in Hiland alone following the death of her husband, Maurice, in 1970. But she was seldom lonely. There were plenty of tourists, ranchers, bus drivers and truckers stopping in to "unload" their problems.

"I was like a bartender," she says. "I never heard anything." But she wrote about them and sold the stories to confession magazines. Once, she wrote about a regular customer, a truck driver who told her about his love affair. "His wife happened to pick up a copy of the confession magazine in the beauty shop, and she knew that the story had been written about her husband." Betty says, cringing, "Boy, he was mad."

Another time, a husband and wife confessed to her on separate occasions. Both stories came out in the same issue, back-to-back. Fortunately for Betty, neither spouse read the magazine. Betty's life is a story in itself. The plump, five-foot-one-inch, ever smiling, past-seventy grandmother lived most of her life in the miniscule town of Hiland, but she was born in Osawatomie, Kansas, the fourth daughter and next-to-the-youngest child in a family of six children. Betty's father, Robert ("everyone called him 'Dad' ") Smith, moved around a lot due to numerous business failures—sheep ranching to furniture retailing—brought about by overextending credit to his customers. And once the Wyoming Highway Department decided to build a road through his property—right through the middle of his milk barn. A philosophical and romantic man by nature, Smith reportedly replied, "Oh well, I hate cows anyway." He then built The Bright Spot in 1923, near where his dairy barn once stood. It turned out to be the "bright spot" of his life, for the business made him prosperous. His customers were mostly "just passing through," and therefore not seeking credit. Smith's success was short-lived, however, for he suffered a ruptured appendix in 1931 and underwent surgery on his kitchen table. He survived the operation but came down with pneumonia and died.

Farsighted man that he was, Betty says, he installed an 8,000-gallon gasoline tank beneath The Bright Spot's porch. Smith also took on a partner without any cash investment; a young, single mechanic named Maurice Evenson, whom Betty soon married. "My folks decided to take a vacation trip, so we had to get married to stay there alone and run the store," she says. Together they ran The Bright Spot until Evenson's death.

Betty says of her childhood, "I was the only one of Dad's kids who liked to work in the store, and I loved meeting all the people who stopped in to buy our 'sagebrush' ham sandwiches."

She began writing "seriously" when she was twenty-five but got so many rejection slips from the editors of "slick" women's magazines that "I papered the walls of my outside toilet with them," she muses. Still filled with dreams of becoming a literary giant, she received a handwritten note from a women's magazine editor during the late 1930s, suggesting that she try the confession field. "This was after some 500 rejections, so I tried it. I sold my fifth story to *Personal Romances*. Later, I sold some to *True Story*, the élite market for confessions, and *Daring Romances*."

Betty enrolled in a creative writing class some ten years later in Casper, 120 miles round trip from Hiland. The class was taught by Peggy Simson Curry; they soon became friends and Peggy later became Maurice's fishing buddy. "My husband seemed to accept my writing more after he met Peggy," she says. "He figured that anyone who'd climb over all those rocks to fish with him couldn't be all that bad." And Betty came to the conclusion that confession writing wasn't all that good. "They're really establishment," she says. "You have to write it their way, according to their formulas, or they won't buy your work. The pay is not as good as it should be—three to five cents a word, the same as it was twenty years ago.

"Back when I started selling confessions, you could only hint at sex, and the heroine—or hero—had to suffer and repent. Sin had to kind of sneak up on your blind side when you weren't looking. Now they let you enjoy your sinning a little without undue remorse. But there doesn't have to be any sex in the story

139

to sell it, contrary to what most people suspect," she says. "Any strong emotion like hate or jealousy makes a good story. And the most common trait shared by confession writers is being able to handle emotion well."

Most articles written for confession magazines can be sold to religious publications with some revisions, she says. "I could have taken any one of my stories and turned it around to make it a spiritual experience instead of a sexual one." Betty has had quite a few experiences to draw from, other than the robbery and her trips to Europe and Cuba before Castro. She appeared on the "Phil Donahue Show" and "To Tell the Truth" as well as making national headlines, all in 1973. She was also written up in Andrew Malcolm's book *Unknown America*. Traveling reporters from the *Wall Street Journal*, the *Los Angeles Times* and *The New York Times* also wrote about her unusual existence, and the stories were picked up by newspapers across the country. Their headlines read: "Widow's Torrid Love Scenes," "She Sells Gas, Food and Sex," "Lonely Plains Cafe Hides Prolific Author," etc.

Phil Donahue decided to make an example of her. "He felt that confession stories were pornographic," she says sadly. "When the commercials were on, he let me talk about my life and my book about The Bright Spot, then quick as the camera came back on he tried to make me look like a country hick. And there was this woman in the audience who kept heckling me. I'm sure she was a plant. She was a real sour pickle, and nobody could shake her from her conviction that I had to have a sick mind to write confessions. Then a woman called in and said, 'Betty doesn't look sick to me. She looks like a woman who enjoys life.' " More than a hundred letters poured in after the show from people who agreed with the caller. "A few of them tried to get me to repent from my sinful ways," she laughs, "but the majority of them either wanted to sell, give or work with me on a story of their own."

Her appearance on Garry Moore's "To Tell the Truth" was far more enjoyable, she recalls. "I met with the 'imposters' the day before the show and filled them in on my work, like how much money orders cost because I was a postmaster. And we talked about confession writing."

The next day was Tuesday when a week's worth of shows were taped, one after another. All the contestants for the week were seated in a small room on "rickety chairs" waiting their turns to be called, six at one time. "We went through rehearsal with a fake panel who asked us questions, and we practiced putting our feet on the right marks," she remembers. "It wasn't very glamorous." One of the contestants was very nervous and suggested that they hold hands and pray backstage for a good performance. "I thought that was silly," Betty says. "God has more important things to do." After the show the imposter broke down and cried because they hadn't fooled the panel.

Betty enjoyed meeting the panelists, Peggy Cass, Kitty Carlyle, Bill Cullen and Gene Rayburn. "They were all very nice, cordial and fun," she says, "and we talked briefly about Wyoming." The panelists then went offstage to change clothes for the next taping.

After the taping of the Donahue Show, Betty had a "terrific urge" to see herself on television. "I just knew that I had made a complete fool of myself," she says. But viewing herself presented a problem. Neither show was carried at that time in Hiland, population 1. After a number of long distance phone calls, she learned that "her show" would be aired in Sacramento, California. So she and her only child, Kristi Armejo, flew there to see the Phil Donahue show. "My voice sounded like an old hillbilly woman who should have had a corncob pipe in her mouth," she says. But otherwise, she decided that she hadn't done too badly. Since that time she's been interviewed on a number of radio and television stations as well as telephone interviews with disc jockeys around the country. She has also accepted numerous invitations to speak before service clubs, writers groups, workshops and banquets.

Betty sold The Bright Spot in 1974 and moved into Casper. "That was the worst month of my life," she says of the move, but a heart attack suffered the year before, coupled with the robbery and a later burglary, proved to be too much for the spunky lady. She now writes in the kitchen of her small green frame house and dates a couple of boy friends when she has time.

"I enjoy being in love," Betty says. "I'm a romantic soul like my father. He wooed my mother with love letters but couldn't spell for sour apples."

Milton Chilcott, *Sheridan Press* publisher

MILTON CHILCOTT

"We have never been reluctant to go to court"

"You have to be a lawyer, an accountant and an electronics engineer before you can get around to the business of publishing a newspaper," according to Milton Chilcott, publisher of the *Sheridan Press*. The slow-talking, amicable, former ad salesman was awaiting court action against Sheridan's police chief in an open records violation case in February 1982, following a successful suit several years earlier against county commissioners for refusal to publish employee salaries.

Chilcott is most concerned with freedom of information and has won a number of prestigious awards for his efforts from Sigma Delta Chi, the Society of Professional Journalists. "We've won a few freedom of information awards because we've never been reluctant to go to court whenever we had to make a point stick," he says. *Sheridan Press* employees have accumulated a great many awards, as have other newspapers around the state, "but the ones we think the most of are for freedom of information because, really, that's what this business is all about. If you have no respect for the people's right to know, you don't belong in this business" unless "you're just going to run a money factory."

The case against police chief Roger Kraut stemmed from a three-week vacation when Kraut closed police records to reporters. Chilcott also butted heads with Sheridan's mayor who tried to bar reporters from city council sessions by simply adjourning meetings until members of the press left the building, he says. Another county "hassle" occurred when Tongue River teachers refused to have their salaries published until Chilcott asked lawyer Larry Yonkee to "work that out to everyone's satisfaction.

"We've had a history of that sort of thing over the last twelve or thirteen years," he says. "And unless somebody is always in there fighting, they're going to walk all over you. Everyday they close a few more doors if you let them, and I've got something else to do besides policing the flow of information. But someone has to do it." Chilcott says he dislikes taking his fellow residents to court. "Our friends, neighbors and associates—all kinds of people—are serving on city and county boards where the hours are long, the pay is nil and the criticism generous; and I don't want to take after those people . . . but I certainly insist that the open meetings law and the open records law be adhered to in Sheridan County."

The publisher was appointed lobbyist for the Wyoming Press Association shortly after he came to Sheridan from the Black Hills in 1969 and has made himself heard at every legislative session since that time. His views must have been heard because his area state senator, Malcolm Wallop, authored the open meetings and records bill in 1973, "although a lot of people didn't want it passed and a lot of people in government don't really want people to know what they're doing," he says.

Freedom of reporting is also important, and he insists that his ten reporters are not dictated to in any way. "I don't think you should stifle people," he says. "They know when they write a story that if they have their facts straight and have the courage to say it like it is, that they have the backing of the management." The publisher says he never reads anything written by staff writers until it's in the newspaper. "I'm no better than the little old lady who pays a quarter for this paper. I'll read it like she does."

144

He also insists that advertisers have no power to dictate news-paper policy; that his reporters would go out of their way to pur-sue a story if an advertiser tried to squelch it. He cited several incidents during his career that served as examples, including a health raid on Coffeyville, Kansas, markets during the late 1940s while he was newspaper business manager. Food store managers were arrested for "doctoring the hamburger," most of them regu-lar advertisers. "I never even knew about it until I read it in the newspaper," he recalls, "and that's the way it should be. It never occurred to the managing editor to ask anyone" before he splashed it across the front page. "Sometimes you just have to cringe at what you know is going to come out in your newspaper."

Chilcott got his start in the newspaper business as a "paper boy" in Manhattan, Kansas. The only child of Burton and Nellie Payne Chilcott, he attended Manhattan High School where he played some basketball, "read a lot," was interested in civics and social studies and graduated in 1935 within the top third of his class. He then attended Sacred Heart Academy postgraduate business school in Manhattan for one year where he acquired secretarial skills. "It was during the depression, and there weren't many jobs," he says. "And I received the best advice I ever got: 'Go learn to type, learn shorthand and brush up on your English.' " After the business course he "entertained thoughts of going to college, but I got married instead" at the age of nineteen. He was working for the *Manhattan Mercury* as a "front office flunky" when he mar-ried Francis Murphy from the neighboring town of Junction City, Kansas, in 1937. A daughter and two sons were later born in his home state.

Chilcott's first newspaper job prepared him for future posts because he became a summer replacement, working in every department from sports writing to advertising where he finally settled in as an ad salesman. Before World War II, he was pro-moted to advertising manager and returned to his job briefly following a stint in the navy as a yeoman, or records keeper, on aircraft carriers in the Pacific. He was an admiral's secretary in Guam when he was discharged in 1946, a job he considered "miser-able." The following year he was transferred by Seaton Publish-ing Company to another newspaper, the *Coffeyville* (Kansas) *Journal* where he served as business manager until 1951.

He was transferred again—this time to the Black Hills—where he was general manager of two daily newspapers and a weekly in the Lead-Deadwood area. The circulation of all the newspapers combined was less than the 10,000 circulation of the *Coffeyville Journal*; but working for a small newspaper was anything but monotonous. "What you've done is dealt yourself a hand where you're to be everything," he says. He became a permanent summer replacement for eighteen years. Although he still considers himself a nonwriter, he found that he could turn out editorials, sports columns "and everything else if I had to. In South Dakota I ran the place, sold the ads, collected the bills, wrote a little stuff and worked in the composing room."

The neighboring towns of Lead and Deadwood are very competitive, he says, and "I always thought they measured us, they didn't read us, to see who got the most space. We had two sets of everything to cover—high schools, girl scouts, civic clubs. . . ." Chilcott's small staff produced two evening newspapers by changing the front page for each town, but the inside news was the same. "If you had a breaking story, you had to remake the front page because of civic pride."

In 1969, Carl Rott, publisher of the *Sheridan Press*, died unexpectedly, and Chilcott was transferred to Wyoming. Sheridan's population was somewhere between 11,000 and 12,000 "depending on who you ask," and its newspaper's circulation was 6,100. The mild-mannered publisher has seen considerable change during the ensuing years. Sheridan's population has increased to 15,000, "the whole business district has changed, all the major discount houses have moved into town and Sheridan College has grown considerably." Coffeen Avenue is lined with new businesses, and a new shopping center has promoted a "clamor for rejuvenation of the downtown" business district.

The *Sheridan Press* moved out of its ancient building on the main street into a new facility in 1976. Circulation has increased to 7,200, and the newspaper is now a modern operation. Typewriters have been replaced by video display terminals (word processors), the noisy old press has been exchanged for the quiet "cold type" offset method, and a satellite dish has been installed on the roof to take the place of the traditional teletype machine. "The AP high speed wire feeds in here at 1,200 words a minute," he says. "I can remember when it was 66 and we thought that was fast. It's the wave of the future. Everything is now computerized. The old hot metal system [press] was characterized by three things: heat, dirt and noise," he says, a nostalgic look on his face. "Working for a newspaper now is like working in a bank. You've got carpet on the floors, pictures on the wall and complete silence."

Publishing a newspaper has also changed. "In the old days of newspapers, you had to have someone who was not only a publisher, but a writer, a printer or an ad peddler," he says. "Now, they call it progress, I guess, but you've got to be a lawyer, accountant and an electronics engineer before you can get around to the business of publishing a newspaper."

Chilcott aims to hire only graduates from the University of Wyoming as his reporters "because we feel we should support the journalism school," he explains. "More important, the fact that a kid goes through school at the university and gets a degree tells you that he or she is in Wyoming because they want to be. And that's a great asset. I can think of a lot of people who would not fit in this country, they just don't know how to talk the language, and golly, there is a lot of people who have some crazy ideas about Wyoming."

The "greatest thing that has ever happened" to Milton Chilcott was the "Freedom of Information Award" he received in 1980 from Sigma Delta Chi, only one of some sixteen people in the nation to be so honored, along with Chief Justice Douglas. Chilcott received about a hundred letters following the award. One of them was from a former friend who worked as a linotype operator for the *Manhattan Mercury* forty years ago. The letter said "I always wondered what happened to you and if you ever amounted to anything. Now I'm reading about you in a big shot newspaper like the *Denver Post*."

John Wold, geologist-businessman

JOHN WOLD

"I'm not ready to quit"

John Wold came to Wyoming during the blizzard of '49 as a
petroleum geologist for Barnsdall Oil Company, but it didn't
take him long to see the advantages of becoming an independent
consultant and developer in the petroleum and mineral rich state.
"I quickly decided after a couple of months that there was no
great economic future doing consulting work because of the tax
situation in this country which rewards people who make investments and improve the value of those investments by some professional expertise," he explains. "The tax structure is not fixed
so that someone working for a salary for someone else will be
rewarded handsomely."

Wold decided the best way to make his fortune was to work
for himself. He began by investing "a very modest amount of
money" that he was able to save while in the navy during World
War II, in oil and gas leases. He then put together package deals
which he sold to major oil companies. "That worked out successfully, and we built up a little oil and gas overrides and things

of that sort," he says. "I was enjoying the work but, in the mean-time, I got interested in politics."

Wold and his wife Jane became active in politics during the 1952 Eisenhower presidential campaign and were elected precinct committeeman and woman from the Westridge area of Casper. Then in 1956, Wold ran for the state legislature and was elected "by virtue of a hard-working campaign." Because the Wolds were relative newcomers to the state, they felt the need to meet the public. "I think Jane and I rang ninety percent of the doorbells in Casper," he says. "And it paid off." Wold was elected by the largest majority of any Republican running for the legislature that year. Then, two weeks into the 1957 legislative session, the House Labor Committee chairman died of a heart attack, and Wold was named to fill the post "in spite of the fact that I only had two weeks experience.

"It was a very interesting experience for me and a fortuitous one, but strangely enough, I decided that I was more interested in party organizational work than I was in actually serving in the legislature." Wold was elected secretary of the Republican party in 1960 following "a bad year in Wyoming" for his party during the previous election. "The party was in a shambles when I came in as chairman," he says, "and I had to reorganize from the point of trying to get an effective vote-recruiting organization going which would get Republicans to the polls." The new party chair-man spent a "great deal of time developing a tight organization" by publishing a party newspaper and running training schools for Republicans all over the state.

Wold decided to run against U.S. Senator Gale McGee in 1964 but lost by a "squeaker." He went back to "active party political work" and a 1968 congressional race against William Henry Harrison. The geologist-developer won the election and served two years in Congress before taking on McGee again in 1970. He lost that one during "another tough Republican year when no incumbent Democrat west of the Mississippi lost his seat in the election."

In the meantime, Wold teamed up with Paige Jenkins, "an old Wyoming uranium pioneer," in the coal business. They specialized in "putting together large blocks of coal which we turned over to major coal companies. To my knowledge," he explains, "the first major coal property acquisition that Exxon ever made, they

150

bought from us in 1965. And we worked all over the Rocky Mountains putting together about a million acres of coal leases that we sold to oil companies who were interested in moving from oil and gas in the West."

Wold and Jenkins probably handled more coal properties in terms of acres and volume of coal reserve than any other developer during the 1960s. Jenkins then felt that uranium was "coming back" and that they should "get into it" in 1967. When Wold returned from Congress in 1970, "the uranium boom was getting ready to go," so the partners "hit it pretty heavy" by putting together a number of significant uranium properties, including a joint venture with Western Nuclear and Standard Oil of Ohio (Sohio) in the Powder River Basin. They hired seismic drillers to locate the uranium deposits and found that the Christianson Ranch in the Pumpkin Butte area held the largest uranium ore reserves yet discovered. Wold later bought out Sohio and Jenkins, thus owning a half-interest in the venture with Western Nuclear.

"Then the property was getting to be so big and the demands for drilling on it so heavy, that I felt it would be smart for me to sell out," he explains. He sold his interests to Arizona Public Service in 1981. Now, with "uranium being in the doldrums," he's getting back into oil and gas, this time through the drilling business. He also has a uranium office in Austin, Texas, with uranium properties and activities on the Gulf Coast as well as other mineral developments such as talc and molybdenum. And there's a ranching business — "the old Bar C Ranch west of Kaycee."

Ranching is a far cry from Wold's roots in the East. Born in East Orange, New Jersey, in 1916, he was reared in upstate New York where his father was dean of science at Union College in Schenectady. "My father had an interesting background," he says. "His father — my grandfather — came from Norway and was a Lutheran missionary with the Sioux Indians in South Dakota during the 1870s. He died on the reservation and my grandmother took my father and his six sisters to Eugene, Oregon, where she opened a boarding house for students at the University of Oregon. All seven of her children graduated from the university in the 1880s and 1890s. I'm very proud of that ancestry because they were all professional people who, strangely enough, moved back east. One of the girls became an international lawyer in Washington, D.C., where three of my father's sisters were arrested picketing the White House during the regime of President Wilson. They were very heavily involved in the women's rights movement at the end of World War I. They were women's rights crusaders and activists."

His father, Peter Irving Wold, did his graduate work at Cornell and went to China as a professor at Ching Hua University where he taught physics in 1910–11 "at the time of the revolution when the Ming Dynasty was overthrown." Peter Wold later returned to China with his wife, Mary Helen Helff Wold, for the Rockefeller Foundation during the early 1920s. John, his brother Ivor (now a doctor in Dallas), and his sister Mary (Republican National Committeewoman from Portland, Maine, and former legislator), stayed with relatives for two years while their parents were in China.

John Wold attended prep school in Connecticut and Union College where his father was on the faculty. The Wold children grew up living on campus and young John developed his interest in geology by walking past a "dump on the way to school"; a dump comprised of discarded mineral samples from the college geology department. From that, he started his own mineral collection. But he majored initially in chemistry, math and physics during his first two years in school, planning to follow in his father's footsteps by teaching physics. During his junior year, however, he switched to geology, "and I've always been delighted that I made that turn."

He graduated from Union College in 1938 and had a teaching assistantship at Cornell University while he completed his graduate work. "Jobs were difficult to find because it was the tail end of the depression," he says. He drove his "old Model A, which cost me thirty-five dollars" down to Oklahoma where he landed a job as a petroleum geologist. In 1941, he went to work for the navy department as a consulting physicist at ten dollars a day for the Bureau of Ordnance. His job consisted of working on magnetic warfare installations "from Newfoundland to Argentina." His crew installed degaussing devices which prevented a warship's magnetic field from setting off German magnetic mines which were inflicting heavy marine losses in the Atlantic during World War II. He then enlisted in the navy as an ensign and continued his work in the Pacific where he degaussed submarines at Midway Island. Since the Japanese did not develop magnetic mines and the technology was not shared with them by the Germans, Wold grew dissatisfied with the lack of action in his branch of the navy and requested reassignment to sea duty where, following training in Florida, he spent the next four years as a gunnery officer for destroyer escorts. He then saw plenty of action on "convoy duty" from the East Coast to Great Britain, escorting high speed convoys in fourteen days across the Atlantic during the final years of the war.

Wold left the U.S.S. *Olsen* in February 1946 and returned to the States where he visited Magnolia Petroleum, the company he worked for prior to the war. He was thirty and ready to settle down and get married, but the company wanted to send him to an oil field a hundred miles from Lake Charles, Louisiana, "where I wouldn't have any social life whatsoever," he says. He then switched to Barnstall, "the oldest oil company in the country"; returned to his parent's home in New York for a visit; married Jane Peterson, a friend of the family he had met twelve years earlier; and drove to his new job in Texas on their honeymoon. After several years in Houston, the couple was given a choice in 1949 of being transferred to Midland, Texas, or to Casper, Wyoming. After visiting both towns with their one-year-old son, Peter, they decided on Casper and moved during the blizzard of 1949. Another son, Jack, and a daughter, Priscilla, were born in Casper.

John Wold calls himself "a senior citizen," although he is still very active in business ventures and his physical appearance belies his age. "I guess people say I ought to retire," he smiles, "but I'm having too much fun. I see so many opportunities, and it's fun to build things. I'm not ready to quit yet — I'm still kind of kicking."

Lavinia Dobler, children's author

LAVINIA DOBLER

"It's the logical thing for me to do"

L avinia Dobler began life as a three-pound, four-ounce twin who spent her first few months in a cotton-filled basket on her mother's oven door. Still small and feisty, her accomplishments are impressive: among them thirty-six children's books; Dodd-Mead's "National Librarian's Award"; *The Dobler World Directory of Youth Periodicals* which she compiled while head librarian for *Scholastic Magazines*; English supervisor over 700 teachers in San Juan, Puerto Rico; and patron of Central Wyoming College which stands on the old Dobler homestead west of Riverton.

In 1910, Lavinia and her sister, Virginia, were the first twins born in Riverton to homesteaders. Their parents, George and Grace Sessions Dobler, met in Lander during the first week in August 1906, when lots were being drawn to divide up more than a million acres of land (now part of the Wind River Indian Reservation) which was ceded to the homesteaders by the government on a lottery basis. Lavinia's mother, a twenty-three-year-old elementary school principal in Iowa, left home when she read about the land lottery and arrived in Shoshoni, Wyoming, on the last day of registration with her bachelor uncle aboard the Chicago Northwestern Railroad. The tracks were supposed to have been completed all the way to Lander in time for the lottery "but plans didn't go according to schedule," Lavinia says. "My mother had registered in Shoshoni, and the lottery was held in Lander, which was a cockeyed way of doing things. All those people who came to Wyoming took a chance that they might draw a number that would put them way out in the boondocks, or they could get lucky and draw a lot that would place them just outside of town."

Lavinia's father, also an Iowa native, had been working at the Shoshone and Arapahoe trading posts to pay off his educational debts following graduation from the University of Nebraska's law school. He, too, was interested in acquiring one of the 160-acre parcels which were bargain-priced at $1.25 an acre. Dobler was fortunate. The number he drew was a parcel just a mile and a half north of Riverton Township. Lavinia's mother's lottery ticket gained her a quarter section of land nine miles northeast of Riverton, close to the Wind River. She proved up on her land by erecting a one-room cabin on it with the help of her Uncle Simon and lived in it on weekends while she taught school in the town of Riverton. She married George F. Dobler in 1908 after the land was legally in her maiden name because a husband and wife could only acquire a section of land together. She speeded up the process by paying more than the going rate for her land originally, Lavinia says.

Two years later, the twins were born two months prematurely. Lavinia, who arrived last, says their lives were saved by an attending nurse who had received her training at Bellview Hospital in New York. The nurse took an eye dropper from her black bag and gave each twin a small "shot" of whiskey before placing them in a cotton-lined basket on the oven door where they lived for the next three months, although it was summer. The twins grew into tomboys who played baseball and attended Jefferson Elementary School on the south side of Riverton, but a sister, Frances, born twenty-two months later, was stricken with the "Spanish flu" in 1918, which made her an invalid until her death at age fourteen.

156

Their father was elected to the Wyoming legislature in 1916, and the family moved to Cheyenne where the Dobler twins were given the "privilege of the house" by the legislators. "We were permitted to roller skate on the marble floor under the capitol dome, the only time this had ever been done to my knowledge," she says. "There was no sidewalk in front of our house on which to skate."

Dobler was director of the First State Bank in Riverton which went bankrupt in 1924, and the family lost their huge thirteen-room house and nearly everything else except for Grace Session Dobler's homestead. The family then decided to leave Riverton for California to try to find a cure for Frances's illness. Unfortunately, she died two years later. The twins were sophomores at Long Beach Polytechnic High School in southern California and began working for rival newspapers, Virginia as a switchboard operator for the *Long Beach Sun*. The *Long Beach Press-Telegram* ran a story about her and their messenger, Lavinia. The messenger's job soon progressed to apprentice feature writer, a job Lavinia held while studying at Long Beach Junior College. Both girls continued their educations at the University of California at Berkeley—Lavinia as an English major and Virginia studying history.

"We stayed out of college one year after high school," she says, "and worked and saved enough money to eventually go on to Berkeley. Virginia had to borrow from me to finish school, and I had to borrow from the owner of the *Long Beach Press-Telegram*." After receiving their teaching degrees in 1933, the twins secured jobs in Riverton. Virginia worked in a country school with Arapahoe children, and her sister taught second grade at Jefferson School where the twins had received their grade school educations. In a short time, Lavinia was able to repay the loan to her former employer, and about that time, their mother died of a ruptured appendix.

Two years later, Virginia married a Pennsylvanian she had met at Berkeley and moved to the East Coast; Lavinia went back to work at the *Long Beach Press-Telegram*. She also applied for an overseas teaching assignment which soon materialized. Her next job was in San Juan, Puerto Rico, where she taught classes in a junior high school for two years before she was promoted to supervisor of English over 700 teachers in the San Juan area.

"We were at that time using the direct method of teaching English," she explains. "All the textbooks were in English and all the Puerto Rican children—although their native language was Spanish—were required to study their subjects in English. Teachers had been taught English by Puerto Ricans and to them 'He E's a goot boy' was considered correct grammar," she laughs heartily. "So they picked nine American teachers to teach them to break down the sounds so they could learn proper inflections."

Five years after her trip to Puerto Rico, Lavinia was attending graduate school at the University of Southern California. She later studied at Columbia University, New York University, Cape Coast and Kumasi colleges in Ghana and two schools in Nigeria. After several jobs in California, she decided to give up teaching and went to work for *Scholastic Magazines* in New York. "The only job that was open at that time was in the typing pool," she says. "And I could type ninety words a minute." She was also within commuting distance of her twin. The year was 1944, and *Scholastic's* librarian decided to enter the military service so Lavinia was asked to do some special research work. *Scholastic* then made her acting librarian and encouraged her to take library courses at Columbia University during the summer months, which they financed. "I watched a small organization grow," she says, "from three small school magazines in 1944, to thirty-two magazines in 1975 when I retired" following thirty-one years with the company. During that time she was able to build up the largest collection of children's magazines in the world.

She brought out a reference book titled *The Dobler World Directory of Youth Periodicals* in three editions and thirty-six of her own children's books were published as well as more than fifty magazine articles. She was named the Dodd-Mead "National Librarian of the Year" in 1957 for her juvenile book, *A Business of Their Own*, and her *Arrow Book of the United Nations* has sold more than 700,000 copies during the past twenty years. The librarian's award carried with it a $1,500 prize which she used as a down payment on a lakeside cottage in Connecticut.

Her favorite book, *Customs and Holidays Around the World*, written in 1962, and her first book about a glass factory in Jamestown, Virginia, are still in print and have gone through numerous editions as have twenty of her other juvenile books which are

158

Grace and George F. Dobler in 1928 in Long Beach, California,
four years after Dobler's bank went bankrupt in Wyoming

currently in print. Her latest work, *Wild Wind, Wild Water*, is an historical novel dealing with Riverton's early growing pains and lack of water in the 1906–10 era, and her feelings about the Dobler homestead which is now the site of Central Wyoming College.

She also coedited in 1981 an anthology titled *Riverton, the Early Years, 1906–1953* for the Seventy-fifth Diamond Jubilee celebration, as well as serving on the Riverton Rendezvous Steering Committee which planned the city's birthday party. Lavinia's decision to return to Riverton when she retired from *Scholastic Magazines* was a difficult one to make. "I had a lovely home on Candlewood Lake in Connecticut, and I had all those publishing contacts in New York," she says. "But I decided that I didn't want to spend the rest of my life there, so I came home." Her twin died of cancer during that period of time and they had been very close, "the best of friends."

Back in Riverton, she built an attractive six-sided log home she calls "Winged Moccasins" and endowed Central Wyoming College with $25,000 which was used to purchase sixty-nine acres of land for the school district; land now the site of the new $8.5 million Riverton High School built in 1981, and the James H. Moore Career Center.

In appreciation, the college trustees named the library meeting room for Lavinia. The Dobler Room features an attractive, rustic fireplace built from semiprecious stones and fossils donated by the Riverton Mineral and Gem Society. Other unusual rocks were also used in forming the massive fireplace which stands on the west wall. Lavinia donated a David Young painting of the Wind River Mountains to the room which resulted in a reception held at the college in her honor in August 1981, where she entertained guests by reading passages from her historical novel.

She frequently entertains friends and visiting dignitaries as well as using her abundant energy to travel and lecture to writers' groups. Central Wyoming College honored her a number of years ago as their "Writer-in-Residence" and Wyoming Writers awarded her an "Emmie" for outstanding service within the state.

Lavinia worries that she will not have enough time to do all the things she hopes to accomplish and to write all the words she wants to say. "I keep thinking that maybe a conversation I've written will help some boy or girl who is in trouble, or who has a problem," she says. "My family has always been givers. And when you live in a small town like Riverton where your parents were pioneers, you're called upon to use whatever talents you have. So it's the logical thing for me to do."

William Henry Harrison, grandson of presidents William Henry Harrison and (pictured here with) Benjamin Harrison

WILLIAM HENRY HARRISON

"There's nothing better than a retired politician"

The grandson of two presidents and a territorial governor, Bill Harrison is proud of his family heritage although it has had its disadvantages. The only living grandson of Benjamin Harrison and his first wife, Carolyn Scott, the octogenarian feels that his ancestry has been a political liability to him in Wyoming. "They accuse you of running on somebody else's name," he says. "But it's been a challenge."

Harrison's namesake, ninth president William Henry Harrison, died in office of pneumonia one month after delivering his record breaking two-hour inaugural address in 1841, in chilling winds without topcoat or hat. The sixty-eight-year-old former general was Bill Harrison's great-great-grandfather and the grandfather of Benjamin Harrison, the twenty-third president. The second President Harrison distinguished himself in Wyoming by accepting the "equality state" into the union in 1890, while he was in office. He also called out the troops to quell the Johnson County cattle war during his administration.

Bill Harrison is equally proud of his maternal ancestry which includes his grandfather, Alvin Saunders, who was territorial governor of Nebraska. The last paper signed by President Lincoln before his assassination was reappointment of Saunders as governor, a fact duly noted by Lincoln's secretary on the back of the document which rests in one of Harrison's eight family history scrapbooks. The albums contain myriad memorabilia dating back to the early 1800s. Because he knew that his family had some of Lincoln's clothing and personal effects, he began scrutinizing his family tree and found that his Grandmother Saunders' niece had married Lincoln's eldest son, Robert.

Despite his illustrious background, Harrison's childhood was disruptive at best. Born in Indiana in 1896, where his father, Russell Harrison, was head of the Terre Haute Street Railway Company, he grew up in Omaha and Washington, D.C., because his parents were estranged, although never divorced. His father left home to fight in the Spanish American War and was sent to Cuba where he hoisted the American flag over Morro Castle in spite of President Cleveland's promise to the Spaniards that no flag would be raised until they left the castle. "They tried to court-martial my father but didn't succeed," he says. "Then he went to Puerto Rico where he was provost marshall, and they gave him credit for stopping the 'WOW Insurrection' there."

Young Harrison was shunted back and forth between his mother in Omaha and his grandmother in Washington. "I was more of an introvert because of the way I was raised," he says. "I had to fight like hell to get going. . . . I moved around a lot and didn't have the opportunity to make any permanent friends or anything," and he got into a number of fights because his schoolmates teased him about his presidential grandfathers.

The Sheridan resident calls himself an average student, but he excelled in basketball. "That's why I went to high school," he laughs. He left school to join the national guard during World War I, serving in the First Company Coast Artillery Unit in Washington before being sent to Fort Myers Officer Training Camp where he wound up for an extended stay in the hospital. "We were sleeping in tents," he says, "and they gave us two small scratches in the arm for smallpox [immunization] and a shot for typhoid. Then we all went down with fever." No disinfectant was used, and the men were fed cold-boiled liver and potatoes to "cure" their fevers. By the time Harrison was well again, the war was over.

He then enrolled in agricultural courses at the University of Nebraska at Lincoln. Before graduation, in 1920, he married and moved with his wife, Mary, to a farm ten miles from Omaha. "Five years on the farm were enough to show us that ninety acres were too much for one man and not enough for two," he says. While still living on the farm, he enrolled in a special law course held in Omaha under the supervision of the Nebraska Supreme Court and taught by practicing lawyers. Three years later, they left the farm and moved to Indiana where he passed the bar exam and became a practicing attorney, as was his father. A year later, in 1926, he ran for the state legislature and won a seat in the Indiana House of Representatives while his father served in the state Senate. He was later nominated for prosecuting attorney for the Indianapolis area but was defeated because "there were too many Democrats" in his district.

The Harrison name was well-known in Indiana because Benjamin Harrison had served there as territorial governor before being elected president from Indianapolis in 1888. The president-elect moved from his family home, now an historical site at 1230 N. Pennsylvania, to 1600 Pennsylvania Avenue in Washington, D.C.

Benjamin Harrison's grandson moved his family to Wyoming in 1936, where he practiced law and waded into state politics. He had first visited the Sheridan area in 1914 when he spent the summer with his uncle, Charles Saunders, in a cabin in the Big Horn Mountains. He remembers the small town with streets paved with wooden blocks that floated away when it rained, and street cars that ran from the city's perimeter to Monarch and Acme, now miniscule ghost towns north of Sheridan.

The Harrisons bought a 2,400-acre ranch near Dayton called the IXL, a combination cattle and dude ranch that expanded to 4,500 acres by the time World War II began. Then, because of a lack of manpower, they sold the IXL and purchased the 500-acre Banner Ranch. Harrison ran for the state legislature and served in the house from 1945–49. Two years later, he sold his ranch and moved to Washington where he served in Congress for four years before running for the Senate. Defeated in his Senate bid, he served as regional administrator for the Housing Finance Agency for eight southeastern states as well as liaison officer for the agency in Washington. He then returned to Congress for two more terms.

While a member of the Ninetieth Congress, he was on the Renegotiating Board before he retired from eighteen years of public service in 1972. He had also served on the Interior and Insular Affairs, Veterans and Appropriations committees as well as the Irrigation and Reclamation Subcommittee during his ten years in the House. During that time he was in "the thick of things," he formed friendships with infamous legislators and is not shy in his reflections.

"Politics have changed quite a bit," he says, since he served in Washington. "I'm a little disappointed that things have happened with some of the members with sticky fingers and a few other things. Members of Congress are answerable only to their constituents and that means that 'you're damned if you do and damned if you don't' on many things. And too many times, particularly in the big city, a man or woman is elected by a [political] machine and you're answerable to that machine. You're forced to vote for things that you really shouldn't vote for, because you can get votes out of it or the pressure is on."

Of Richard Nixon he says: "He was a good friend of mine until he made an ass of himself. He could have prevented all that if he hadn't tried to hide things. But when history is written, I think they will give him credit as an excellent president as far as international affairs are concerned. . . . I think he's suffered enough, but it's his fault. I don't condone anything he did, but knowing him, I know that he did some good things too." Harrison remembers Lyndon Johnson as "down-to-earth and he got everything out of it he wanted. But boy, could he down the bourbon."

Harrison feels that his life "has turned out better" than he thought it would, but he would have liked to have served in the U.S. Senate. He says that the House is "more down-to-earth," however, because the "senators are too much up on a pedestal. That doesn't mean anything against them personally, but it's their position of authority and power. Members of Congress are being elected every two years, and they're so close to the people they serve." Members of both houses are not close, he says, and they don't socialize much although there are plenty of opportunities to do so. There are "groups throwing parties, trying to influence senators continually. You could go out every night and freeload and have all the drinks you want, but you can't do that and get your work done." Harrison says he only attended social functions that "would help Wyoming."

The slender, youthful-appearing octogenarian has spent his retirement gathering historical souvenirs and memorabilia together into eight scrapbooks which most museums would be happy to acquire. Among his family's collections – handed down from five generations – are valuable photos and letters, campaign buttons, political music books, handwritten results from the electoral college, a nail from the White House and bits of wood, Congressional license plates, a seashell from the Spanish American War and *New York Herald* newspapers dating back to 1841, which have somehow escaped the ravages and yellowing of time. He also has an original painting of his grandfather, Benjamin Harrison, that the White House has been trying to persuade him to give up for some time.

His wife Mary died in 1978, and he recently married a family friend, Dorothy Foster Smith, a petite, charming lady he has known for more than forty years. She's from Indiana – the state where Harrison is still a member of the Bar Association although he retired from active law practice in Wyoming in 1951. His home state has honored him on various occasions as has his adoptive state, Wyoming. On August 10, 1976, Governor Ed Herschler proclaimed "Bill Harrison Day" on his eightieth birthday.

When asked how he would like to be remembered, he says without hesitation: "As a good American and family man who tried to do his share to preserve the country. What else is there? Glory is fleeting and in politics you can be out and gone. But there's nothing better than a retired politician. You have friends and you're remembered that way."

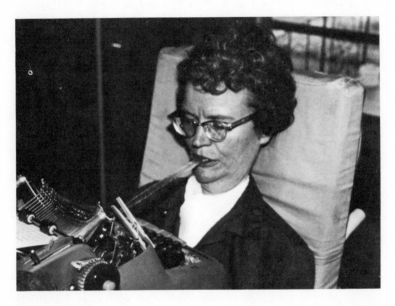

Peg Layton Leonard, author

PEG LAYTON LEONARD

"Perseverance has paid off"

Peg Leonard's courage and determination are seemingly limitless; a writer who also happens to be a quadriplegic, she has authored and edited several books, including *West of Yesteryear* and *Wyoming LaBonte Country 1820–1972*. Peg has also kept readers informed of "happenings" in her hometown and Converse County as a newspaper correspondent for the *Douglas Budget* and *Casper Star-Tribune*, as well as writing magazine articles and greeting card verse.

She types twenty words a minute with a plastic mouth wand by tapping one key at a time on her reconditioned electric typewriter. The specially adapted machine rests on a hospital table at chin level so that she can type from her wheelchair. The process is slow but worthwhile, because Peg is an accomplished writer. "Sometimes I'd like to move faster, and there is a point of frustration, but perseverance has paid off. It takes me longer, but everyone has been wonderful in helping me," she says. Her family and friends help by proofreading her work, taking notes while she conducts interviews and by inventing devices to make her writing process easier. But it's rarely been easy for Peg.

The Douglas native enjoys writing about local history, particularly since her family, the Laytons, came to Wyoming as homesteaders in 1919. Her grandfather was a realtor in eastern Nebraska when his two sons decided to homestead in Wyoming following World War I. "He told my grandmother, 'Those boys don't know anything about homesteading so I'm going with them.'" He took along a picture of his daughter, Iva, to show to local school authorities and got Peg's aunt a job teaching home economics at the high school in Douglas. Then, the subject she taught was called "domestic science."

Peg's mother also came to Douglas as a teacher, but she was on her way to China in 1923 to teach when she met and married one of the Layton brothers. Therefore, Peg says, she never made it any farther West. They were married on Christmas Day in 1924, and she continued to teach at Douglas High School. She taught a course in rural school teaching because "in those days there were so many single ranchers around that not too many girls got beyond teaching at the rural level." A few of them, however, did go on to the university to earn a degree in education. When the rural teachers course was discontinued years later, "the state department asked my mother to do a paper on it," she says.

Peggy Layton was an only child and when she started school her mother began substitute teaching. "Mom's background was such that she could teach science, math, English or languages at the secondary level. Her college minor was music, and she taught piano and organ privately." Peg was one of her mother's most talented music students, according to a former classmate, and she sang in a number of vocal groups during high school. She was also editor of her high school yearbook in 1949.

"I was a music major, but I didn't think that I had what it took to be a professional," she says. "I didn't want to teach so I changed my major. I went from the college of music at Stephens College in Columbia, Missouri, to the college of arts and sciences where I majored in radio and speech at the University of Colorado at Boulder." Because of her change in majors, she was attending summer sessions at UC as a junior when lobar polio suddenly paralyzed her from the neck down. Peg was rushed to Colorado General Hospital and placed in an iron lung before being transferred to Rancho Los Amigos, a respiratory center in Los Angeles.

"That was just at the advent of the iron lung, and of course, it saved a lot of people. I never had too many complications, and I was at the right place and had the opportunity to take advantage of the new innovations. I went from an iron lung to a shell respirator, the next step up." Peg also had an open tracheal tube for the first five years which allowed her to breathe but prevented her from talking for the first year unless the opening was momentarily covered. Her parents added a room onto their house large enough to accommodate Peg's breathing equipment, and she returned to Douglas from Los Angeles with a "rocking bed and all kinds of things." She still sleeps in the bed which operates like a slow moving teeter-totter to improve her circulation.

Her writing career began in 1958, when she wrote verse and sold it to a major greeting card company in Anaheim, California, until 1971. Poetry then inspired her to enroll in the Famous Writers School home correspondence fiction course which she worked on from 1965–68. "I learned to be a fiction writer," she says, although she was selling only nonfiction and verse. "Of course with nonfiction, the hang-up is research. You have to be a page flipper and a pencil pusher." While her mother was alive, she helped Peg by taking notes and doing research. After she completed her Famous Writers course, Peg began to free-lance and send manuscripts to *Reader's Digest* and other well-known magazines without much success. Her parents then noticed an ad in the Casper newspaper for a Douglas correspondent. "Irving Garbutt was state editor, so I sent him an application letter and he signed me up. It was advertised as part-time work for a housewife, but four of us worked at it as fast as we could. My mom and dad and my attendant, Velva Russell, and I were the Douglas stringer. We'd use my dad's polaroid camera and he worked downtown, so he knew what was going on there."

Peg's father died suddenly, leaving the two women in temporary shock. Her correspondence work was a "blessing" because it helped her work through her grief. During that time, the *Douglas Budget* editor "had seen our local features in the *Casper Star-Tribune* and couldn't understand how we could be so disloyal, so in 1971 I asked if I could write for the *Budget* instead. Then I had weekly deadlines, not daily ones so that was progress," she recalls. "It was not so harried a pace and that was better after my father's passing."

Six months after her father's death, her mother fell and fractured her hip which resulted in her permanent residence in the local nursing home for the next nine and a half years.

"It was very difficult," Peg says, "and I considered the prospects for myself. The first eight years, Mom was ambulatory. She would come home twice or three times a week with a walker, and she could stay for a meal and play her piano. After her second hip fracture, she was never able to walk again." Peg's mother died in 1980.

The fledgling writer met Ed Leonard at the First Methodist Church following his return from the army after World War II. "Ed knew about batteries and motors, and he helped wire our church and did mechanical or electrical work when needed," she says. "When something needed attention Dad would say, 'Well, we'll have to show this to Ed.' Everyone knew that Ed was a confirmed bachelor and I certainly was no candidate for marriage. But somehow the Lord intervenes and works things out. When Mom fell and hurt her hip in July of 1971, we had to go to three eight-hour shifts or live-in care. So after six or seven months, Ed decided to do something about that. We were married in February of 1972."

A letter carrier for twenty-three years, Ed took early retirement and is now maintenance mechanic for the Douglas Housing Authority and Douglas' only "high rise" apartment building (five stories). The part-time job allows him to spend more time with Peg, and they're able to take short trips and extended vacations occasionally in a specially equipped van. "I really enjoy traveling," she says. "It just adds new experiences." They found a motor home with a standard door wide enough to accommodate a wheelchair by pushing it up a ramp into the rear of the van. Ed removed the dinette table and Peg can ride behind him in her wheelchair. There's also room for all the emergency breathing equipment necessary for her survival. The van's battery and heavy alternator provide enough energy to run her respirator which fits beneath the seat of her wheelchair, and an extra twelve-volt battery is taken along as a spare. An assortment of other life-saving devices are also included.

In the event that all systems fail, Peg can "frog" for several hours. Frogging is the method of gulping air into the lungs of polio victims by stroking the tongue on the roof of the mouth. She learned the method at Rancho Los Amigos Respiratory Center, but it took five months to overcome partial paralysis of her nasal passages which let air escape from her nose instead of forcing it into her lungs. Peg demonstrates the technique by having Ed remove her plastic tracheal tube from her throat. She was able to survive without the tube for twenty-three years until 1980, when she came down with pneumonia and was hospitalized in Casper. Treatment resulted in the collapse of her tracheal tube so now she must live with an artificial one for the rest of her life. But Peg remains cheerful, optimistic and grateful to be alive.

With Wyoming's centennial in mind, she's been working on a series of articles about the state's history, and she also contributes regularly to the *Casper Star-Tribune*'s annual edition. Her interest in the former World War II prisoner of war camp that was located across the North Platte River from Douglas has prompted an update of the section she wrote about the camp in *West of Yesteryear*. Most of her information about Camp Douglas came from former soldiers who were stationed there or former German prisoners of war who were sponsored for citizenship by local residents after the war.

Peg is able to work four or five hours a day with the plastic mouth wand, and she uses a large piece of cardboard on which Ed tacks 8½-by-11½-inch sheets of research data, placed to the right of her typewriter. An engineering friend designed a device for her typewriter which rolls the paper back down the page so that she can make corrections on her rough draft. "I used to have to whistle for my mother or my helper to come and roll back the paper," she says. "Now I can do it myself."

Peg's goal is to write "novel after novel after novel."

Martin Russell, photographer and college instructor – *James Stewart, photographer*

MARTY RUSSELL

"Tinker, tailor, cowboy, sailor"

Martin Russell has "tinkered" with countless machines, "tailor made" an automatic hen house, immigrated to the "cowboy" state and "sailed" inland waterways as a fishing guide. That's just for starters. He calls himself the "original hippie" and the "world's best worm fisherman." His photography students at Casper College call him "Marty" because he's more than just a teacher; he's a friend and confidant as well. To fully understand the lovable "jack-of-all-trades," it's best to start at the beginning.

He was born in 1919 on a farm near the town of Brewer, Maine, the son of a country doctor who drowned in a fishing boat accident when Marty was seven. His mother then moved him and his older brother, James, to Boston where she was hired as a teacher. Her sons attended English School, "the oldest high school in the country," and polished off their educations at Northeastern College. James became an insurance agent for John Hancock and never missed a day's work due to illness in forty-four years. Marty, however, yielded to pressure from relatives to enroll in premed classes at the College of William and Mary in Williamsburg, Virginia. "I was there for two or three years before I decided that medicine wasn't for me," he says in his pronounced New England accent. "I wanted to be a farmer."

While studying medicine Russell became interested in photography and borrowed a camera from a friend—a 35mm Argus—the first of its kind. Although he liked the versatility of the small camera, he wasn't satisfied with the results so he bought himself a press camera which he used to "scoop" newspaper photographers all over Boston. His first and most impressive one-of-a-kind scoop was of Henry Cabot Lodge, Jr., in 1939, when the newly elected senator received his doctoral hood. Unaware that press photographers had been banned from the ceremony, Russell seated himself in front of the podium and took two pictures before he was hustled from the auditorium. "I wound up with the picture on the front page of the *Boston American*," he smiles. The photo of Lodge covered the entire page and was later run by the Associated Press (AP) which also paid him for his exclusive.

The medical student was called into the college president's office and offered a choice. Either he go to work for the campus newspaper or leave school. He opted for the former but continued to "outshoot" the professionals in the city. His next scoop, a few days later, was a picture of a fellow student swallowing a gold fish—the latest campus craze just before World War II. That one was also picked up by the AP. During the next two years he scooped photographers many times from the *Boston Globe, Herald, Traveler, Daily Record* and the *Christian Science Monitor*. The twenty-year-old student soon became a part-time staff photographer for the *Boston Globe* but refused several offers to make it a permanent arrangement. "I just didn't like the city," he says, nor any big city for that matter. He would have been happier planting potatoes. After a brief stint at Northeastern, however, he got his chance to become a farmer "downeast" in Maine on an old abandoned farm across the river from New Brunswick, Canada, in the Robertson-Calais area.

Russell started his own dairy business there but soon learned that he was allergic to cows. So he sold them and planted beans and potatoes. "I had the worst farm crop in the area," he laughs.

"But I repaired my own farm equipment and had a reputation as a good mechanic, so I started my own garage in Calais, 200 yards from the U.S. Customs House," a prime location. He designed and built the garage himself. Since there were no crops and few mechanical jobs during the winters, he worked as a lumberjack. He cut, hauled and trucked pulp, hardwood logs and Christmas trees. He also bought five trucks to haul farm produce, logs and whatever else needed to be delivered within the New England states and down the eastern seaboard. And there was snow plowing to be done on the side.

During hunting and fishing seasons, he worked as a registered guide. He sailed his fishermen along Maine's myriad rivers and lakes in a canoe and treked silently through the woods in search of game.

Although he had the first wheel alignment and balancing equipment in eastern Maine, business was "terribly slow" so he leased his service station and went to work driving a long distance gas transport truck and doubled as service manager for Federal Oil Company. Later, he went back to his service station, "but business was still terrible, so I sold my trucks in 1953 and discovered Florida," he says. For the next six years he and his family commuted from Maine to Florida as the seasons changed. He, his wife Mary and their three young children would winter in Fort Pierce, Florida, where he worked as a mechanic doing frame straightening and brake work on race cars from Daytona Beach. During the summers they lived on the farm and he operated a busy garage. "Maine in the summer and Florida in the winter, what a way to go," he laughs. But his version of paradise had to end for his children were having difficulties adjusting to different schools. So he made his choice of residences. "I chose Maine, but what to do in the winter?" he pondered.

Russell then decided to go into the egg business. "With three kids to help with the chickens during the summer while I was busy at the garage and me doing the work in the winter, I thought I'd found the answer. I remodeled an old barn to house the laying hens and I was in business." There was a need for fresh eggs in the community so he started out with a thousand birds but soon found that he had underestimated the market. He remodeled another barn. "Now we were up to 3,000 hens, and I still was unable to keep up with the demand," he says shaking his head. "So I surveyed the market and found that I could sell four times that amount of eggs if I could just produce them." With that in mind he designed the Martin Automatic Laying House. The innovative chicken coop had automatic lights, dispenser, water and ventilation, "but it had its drawbacks," he says, "because nobody wanted to finance the invention." Russell dipped into his "working capital" and became his own architect, electrician, equipment installer, plumber and contractor. The Martin hen house was a success and the automatic feeder and life support system became a model for many others in the New England area.

Business was great and the garage was "booming" during the summer months. Russell's oldest son, a victim of cerebral palsy who was unable to talk until he was eight, "really took an interest in the egg business," and Russell was happy that he had provided a means of possible livelihood for his son in later years. His second son was allergic to chickens and unable to do much of the work, but his daughter helped until she was married. Business continued to boom for a couple of years and then there was a bad slump in egg prices. "Eggs dropped to twenty-three cents a dozen and at one thousand dozen daily, I was losing ninety dollars a day," he recalls. "That lasted for two years with only a few up periods. I was making $20,000 a year at the garage and pouring it all back into the egg business. Then the rehabilitation center took an interest in my son and sent him to the University of Maine where he graduated with distinction as a civil engineer," despite his handicap. He no longer needed the egg business and Mary Ellen got married, so there was no one left who wanted to run the business. "I unloaded it when I got the chance, but I had to sell the garage and the farm."

The year was 1968; Russell encountered a state commissioner of schools 200 miles from home in a service station as he was on his way to apply for a job at a New Hampshire paper company. The commissioner offered him a job teaching auto mechanics with his choice of two Maine high schools. He also offered to help Russell obtain his teaching certification. Not long afterward, he began teaching at Dexter Regional High School in the midst of Maine. There he instigated the mechanics course

178

before the shop was built, with a classroom off the library and lab work done in the school bus garage. He worked there for the next three years while attending night classes and summer sessions to get his teacher's degree, a B.S. in education in 1970 at the age of fifty. "Then I felt compelled to start working on my master's," he says. His second son, Jimmy, was stationed at Fort Carson army base, so he decided to attend Colorado State University. After a couple of courses back at the University of Maine, he and his wife returned to Colorado where he earned his master's degree in education.

While studying at CSU he met some Wyoming state department officials who encouraged him to apply for a teaching position at the Dave Johnson Power Plant in Glenrock where Russell worked for the next two years. He subsequently joined the faculty of Casper College in the fall of 1971 as the director of a maintenance program for Pacific Power and Light Company. He taught welding, machine shop, sheet metal, metallurgy, shop math and other industrial skills in a small tin building at the power plant. After two years he moved to Casper and commuted to Glenrock. He then made his way into the mainstream of faculty life and was given the titles of job placement and guidance counselor.

Jobs were plentiful and no one seemed to need Russell's assistance, however, and he might still be sitting at his desk twiddling his thumbs if he had not mentioned to a dean in passing that the college needed a photography course. So in 1974, Russell taught his first photo class. It wasn't long before he became a full-time instructor with classes in beginning and intermediate photography, color, photojournalism and photography for criminology in the recently built photo department he helped design. His students get more than technical advice in his classes; Russell's slow talking, easygoing nature is conducive to confidence. Some students say he's like a lovable grandfather, a "real sweetheart" who never seems to get angry or out of patience. Many of his students are older than the teacher. "That's why I like them to call me Marty," he says. "I'd feel funny if they called me Mr. Russell. Besides, I tell people that I retired to get this job. I'll stay here until I'm at least seventy, if they'll let me. Being here at Casper College is my biggest dream of all—and I'm still dreaming. I don't know what I want to be when I grow up."

Charles Levendosky, Wyoming poet

CHARLES LEVENDOSKY

"Do I touch people with my poetry?"

> *In a silence so deep*
> *that winter freezes the air*
> *and motion begs forgiveness*
> *for all its furry whispers,*
> *I stand still . . .*
> — Charles Levendosky

The bearded, soft-spoken, teddy-bear-of-a-man stands still long enough to examine things most of us take for granted. Charles Levendosky sees the world through the eyes of a poet but not quite the same as other poets. "My values are 'do I touch people with my poetry?' People are the most concerned here. I don't care if an editor in New York doesn't like what I write. That means less to me than someone coming up to me and saying, 'Wow! That's my life you're talking about.'

"I guess writers away from the publishing centers are more aware of their community values which is probably why we don't have much success in the publishing world," he says with a hearty laugh. Levendosky's successes include three books of poetry – *perimeters, small town america, aspects of the vertical* – and a chapbook published in 1981 by Dooryard Press titled *Distances*, half of which describes his impressions of Wyoming; the other half an introspective look at himself. He has also had a number of poems published in literary magazines including *El Cordo Emplumada*, a now defunct bilingual leftist magazine in Mexico, and *Elizabeth*, a small New York literary magazine.

A poem dedicated to his daughter, Alytia, hung in the Casper post office while another poem rode around New York City on the walls of buses via the "Poetry-in-the-Bus" Program. Levendosky has been a poet since high school when his senior yearbook listed him as "going to be a writer." In college he started writing prose and decided that he wanted to earn a living as a poet, but being a practical man he proceeded to get a degree in both physics and mathematics.

"I enjoy physics, but I left mathematics because I felt it was too objective and had nothing to do with the concerns I worried about. So I split the difference. I went to graduate school and studied philosophy, which is sort of a leaning toward ideas and people's emotional states." He attended the University of Hawaii where he was doing graduate work in East-West philosophy when he met his wife, Charlotte Jaeger, who was also a New York City native. They were married less than a year later and returned to New York where he worked toward a master's degree in education in a special one-year program at New York University while his wife taught school.

After he graduated, they went to St. Croix in the Virgin Islands to teach. He taught math, sciences and later an honor's course in English in his spare time. His wife taught fourth grade. "We managed to save enough money by living on one salary and saving the other to go to Japan where we lived for a year without working," he says. "Our oldest daughter, Alytia, was born there." The poet took one job, however, teaching a brush up course in English to a group of students studying for their Ph.D.'s in chemistry. "I didn't expect to get paid for it; it was an easy course to teach because I was trained in the language of the sciences. It was fun and I just kind of fell into it." He spent most of his time in Kyoto writing and walking the streets with notebook in hand, although his journal doesn't contain "anything I can use for poetry," he says.

From Japan they moved back to New York City. After living in the Virgin Islands and prior to the trip to Japan, Levendosky felt that he couldn't stand his birthplace. "I hated it there. Maybe it was coming from a small island [St. Croix] where everyone knew everyone else's business – and being used to that smallness; I mean, compared to that huge, anonymous kind of crushing city that made me nervous and upset. I wanted out. I was a product of the '50s. I went to college during the McCarthy era, and I was very paranoid about being a liberal so I always carried a passport which I kept active. I was a conscientious objector. New York made me feel that there was something wrong with me. So I had to get out."

Back in New York he began tutoring students from wealthy families at a private school three times a week so that he would have time enough to write. "We lived on a marginal level for three years, but that's when I got my first book of poetry published, *perimeters*, at Wesleyan University Press." He was then offered a job as tutor for a special program designed for Martin Luther King scholars at New York University. Levendosky worked on a part-time basis for two semesters and was then hired as a full-time assistant professor of English. He taught in that capacity for the next three and a half years, and added another daughter, Ixchel, to his family.

"The crunch was on in 1972," he remembers. "They wanted to give all the professors without tenure an extra course to teach. I didn't want that because I was almost finished with my book, *aspects of the vertical*, and I needed the time. I had been making more money than I had in years and had saved enough to live for six months without working. So I quit." Two weeks later, he received a call from the Georgia Council on the Arts asking him to join their teachers education summer course as an instructor. The faculty would consist of two sculptors, two painters, two dancers, two composers, "two theatre people" and a poet. "In the six-week period we took some forty teachers from all over the country and put them through all sorts of creative endeavors, hoping we would really have some feedback from their students when they went back to teach." He worked with the program for three summers.

Levendosky was offered the job of poet-in-residence for Wyoming in 1972 by Frances Forrester who was then head of the Arts Council. He had worked in the Poetry-in-the-Schools programs in New York and New Jersey and had trained poets in workshop sessions in Colorado and Nebraska before coming to Wyoming. His new job consisted of dividing his time between the state colleges and public schools as director and founder of the poetry program. His duties were eventually split in half due to the volume of work, and he asked to be retired from his administrative duties, "all that paper work," he says. "At first, Frances would set up a gig, and I would do it. She was a good administrator and understood that an artist needs time to do his own thing. She more or less gave me a week-on and a week-off."

Children are apparently captivated by Levendosky's young Santa Claus image, his deep belly laughter and mischievous-eyed approach to poetry. He recites poems, usually not his own; some with intriguing sounds such as "S's" as in "squishy, slimy and squashy," which are found in a poem he often reads titled "Eggs" by Daniela Gioseffi. "The poem is about breaking eggs and sucking them out of the pinhole. It's very graphic. The poet buys 100 cartons of eggs and breaks them into her bathtub and gets in. It's gross, you know, but it has a lot of good sounds in it," he explains, "and sixth and seventh graders love it 'cause it gets their attention. . . . Someone will say, 'Hey, listen to all those "S's."'" He then has students write poems of their own because he feels "it's sort of like putting yourself where the poet is." He cited an example of a Crest Hill Elementary class in Casper:

"I wrote a poem about zeros and black holes, and I said 'Who knows about black holes and gamma rays?' About ten kids raised their hands, and we went into a whole list of metaphors and extended metaphors. I told them to use their imaginations and it really freed them. They went crazy with their poems and some of them were marvelous. Gamma rays turned into grammar rays . . ."

One of the things the poet likes most about his job is traveling during the winter. "Everyone gets freaked out when I say that, but I get freaked out when I'm driving to Laramie over the rim and go down to look over the valley with its ice and snow. All you can see are blacks and grays and whites. And the sky—that blows me away. I think, 'Oh my God, nothing can be as beautiful as this. Why would anyone want to leave here?' Everything seems to be simplified to essences here. In my work as a poet I want to simplify all the time. I want to simplify in order to get down to what's essential like a Japanese painter who makes three lines and there's a bird in flight.

"I've never regretted coming to Wyoming," he smiles. "The energy boom had just started when we arrived, and the two places that stood out at that time were Gillette and Rock Springs. I visited them that first year and not being a rural person, I was immediately attracted to that frenetic, often destructive energy that I understand you get in boom towns. I understand it well from urban living, and I began to write about those things right off. I felt that I could write a book about Wyoming in transition, but I couldn't compete with Peggy Simson Curry because her knowledge of Wyoming is so profound. And her sense of it is more of the past now. So I felt like, maybe, I'm a chronicler of change that's happened and, perhaps, that's my strength."

Levendosky's advice to budding poets is to write something every day. "It doesn't have to be a poem, but write something. Keep your hand in. I use letter writing as a form of my practice, and people whom I've written will sometimes send me back copies of my letters. I can recognize that my style of writing is close to my style as a poet. It's an art form, a practice of my art. I don't mean writing sonnets; I mean transcribing the words into language. Written language is the practice a writer needs. I don't care how he gets it."

The preceptor writes primarily for himself. "A Levendosky poem is uniquely a Levendosky poem. And good or bad, you can't mix it up with anyone elses."

Ruth Geier Rice, rancher

RUTH GEIER RICE

"We started with nothing"

R uth Geier Rice's life has been filled with hard work, a number of "firsts" and family tragedy. The first woman Hereford cattle judge in the nation was also the first woman county commissioner in Sheridan, and a member of the first county planning commission. During the fall of 1980, she was nominated to the Hall of Fame of the Northern International Livestock Exposition along with seven men from the United States and Canada. Her greatest accomplishment, however, was holding a large Polled Hereford operation together after her husband's death.

The small, soft-spoken lady has lived more than eighty years on a ranch. Born December 8, 1900, she moved from Iowa to northern Wyoming when she was fifteen months old. "My mother, two older sisters and I traveled by train to Sheridan where we were met by my father with a team of horses and a lumber wagon," she says. George Geier took his family to a ranch he had purchased twenty-four miles south of Sheridan. The land contained the ruins of Fort Phil Kearney which was built in 1866 to protect homesteaders from the Sioux Indians.

A younger sister and brother were born on the ranch and all the children worked in the fields, except Ruth's second sister who helped her mother with the cooking and housework. "We were outdoor children, and I followed my father," she says. "Three of us girls drove the teams and rode horses. We were father's top hands. We mowed the hay and I drove the team on the mower. My father had 500 head of cattle and we did everything, including household chores." Ruth could drive a four-horse team, abreast or "strung out" and could hitch them up alone.

Geier bought an Apperson Jack Rabbit in 1912 to drive his family to Iowa to visit friends, and they had to ford the Powder River in the new automobile. "We were lucky to get across it," she laughs, and then quotes the Wyoming adage, " 'Powder River, a mile wide, an inch deep, can't swim it nor can't wade it.' " Riding horses bareback was more to her liking. "I could skin a horse, just grab the mane and throw my foot over. I could ride most anything and handle a horse well."

The family rode to Sheridan once or twice a month to shop, do their banking and pick up lumber and supplies. "We girls would drive an old gentle team and my father would drive four horses and take in the hogs or wheat, and we'd ship our steers in the fall. My grandparents had moved into Sheridan, and we'd stay overnight with them and go home the next day, arriving about midnight."

The Geier children attended a one-room rural school near Piney Creek and were boarded in Buffalo where they finished high school. On weekends they hurried home to work on the ranch, traveling the sixteen miles on horseback when the roads were impassable. Teachers were in demand when Ruth graduated from high school, and she decided to help ease the shortage by attending a six-week summer school-training course at the University of Wyoming. During the fall and winter of 1918, she began by teaching thirty students at Piney Creek and spent her next three summers studying at the university. Ruth and her younger sister enrolled in a Virginia college in 1924; and at a "normal school in Bellingham, Washington. I finally ended my college education at the University of Wyoming in 1928," she says, "and returned home to meet John Rice, a car dealer who came out to the ranch to sell my father a truck." Rice was divorced with two children to support and had gained most of his education from "the school of life."

They were married that December and "we started with nothing," she says. "In fact, we had a difficult time paying our doctor bills. We were paying child support—I'm very close to his children and love them—but selling cars in those depression days was difficult." Her father offered the young couple some land to rent on shares, and they moved onto it during the spring of 1930. "That August our little Patty was born."

Ruth and her husband were able to acquire a small herd of registered Polled (hornless) Herefords two years later on contract with no money down, but there was no pasture available on her father's ranch, so they leased some land on the Crow Indian Reservation near Lodge Grass, Montana, for twenty-five cents an acre. They also found a 440-acre ranch ten miles out of town on a dirt road without plumbing, telephone or electricity. They rented the rundown, abandoned ranch for $300 a year and purchased it in 1935. Their son, Gary, was born that year on a night when the temperature was minus twenty-five.

The Rices experienced several years of drought and a scourge of Mormon crickets that ate up their alfalfa, garden and everything that didn't bite back. Ruth dug ditches around her garden and filled them with crude oil to discourage the crickets, but it didn't save her vegetables. In desperation she called the Civilian Conservation Corps (CCC Camp), and the ranch was invaded before daybreak by masked men spraying her property with a mixture of arsenic and lime. "John and I talked about leaving the place, but we didn't have anywhere to go," she says. During the winter of 1936, a bitter cold front set in and their five-year-old daughter, Patty, died as her parents tried to get her to a doctor in forty-five degrees below weather, using a team and sled because the roads were impassable.

John Rice was elected to the Montana legislature in 1939—the same year their daughter, Jane, was born; he served until 1943. "It gave us a break from winter on the ranch," she recalls. Their cattle herd was doing well and a prize bull was born on the ranch when the thermometer dipped to twenty-five below zero. Plato

Domino 36, champion Polled Hereford, spent his first few hours of life on the floor of their living room before a coal heater while Ruth rubbed him down and kept him alive. The calf later won the Montana Bred Championship and the Reserve Championship at the National Polled Hereford Show in Memphis, Tennessee. The bank had threatened to foreclose on their property before they left for the show, but they resisted offers to sell their prize bull. Another Rice bull was sold for $2,600, and the rest of the herd brought good prices, so they were able to placate their banker and gain an international reputation as exceptional breeders. Plato Domino 36 blessed them with offspring which brought world record-breaking prices as well as international recognition and honors.

The Rural Electric Association lighted up their lives in 1941, and Ruth was able to throw out kerosene lamps and an ancient icebox. New buildings were constructed, but they sold their ranch of eleven years in 1946 and bought the Wrench Ranch in Sheridan, Wyoming. Then they began anew, remodeling and replacing dilapidated buildings as well as increasing their herd to 500 head. Soon cattle buyers were visiting the ranch from as far away as Australia.

Their land holdings more than doubled in 1949, with the purchase of the L. Z. Leiter Estate which included Lake DeSmet and twenty-two miles of Clear Creek Valley for $50,000 down and the balance within the year. They sold ten of the twenty-six ranches at auction and retained the lake and 1,700 acres worth of coal deposits. John Rice planned to build a power plant there, but he didn't live long enough for the project to become a reality.

Rice had been invited to judge Polled Herefords in Sydney, Australia, but declined because of ranch commitments. In 1954, Ruth urged him to accept. They left for Australia in March with a Nebraska couple who were also well-known Hereford breeders, enjoying side trips to New Zealand where they visited Rice bull descendants, the Fiji Islands and Hawaii. On their return trip, they had planned to leave Hawaii on a Monday, and Rice chartered a plane on Saturday for a visit to a large Polled Hereford operation on one of the islands while Ruth and a companion did some sight-seeing. Ten minutes into the cattlemen's return flight, the small plane disappeared and was never found. Search efforts failed to find a trace, and Ruth went back to the ranch alone.

Her son, Gary, was nineteen and had just enlisted in the air force. Her daughter, Jane, was five years younger. Ruth threw herself into keeping the ranch in operating shape and continued to show her championship stock in open competition in this country and Canada. Two years after he had enlisted in the service, Gary returned home with his wife and two small daughters to help his mother with the ranch. A former air force pilot, he flew his mother around the ranch and to cattle shows and auctions. In November of 1963, Ruth lost a third member of her family when Gary's plane crashed in a freak accident. He was twenty-eight. The following year her daughter Jane and her husband, Bill Woolston, a bank employee, brought their three children to the ranch to live with Ruth and help with the chores. Woolston learned the intricacies of cattle ranching from scratch and within eighteen years was elected president of the National Polled Hereford Association, which made his mother-in-law very proud.

Following her son Gary's death, Ruth decided to disperse her large registered herd, and she stopped showing her champion cattle. Jane and Bill have gradually taken over management of the Wrench Ranch with the assistance of their two sons, and they now operate a commercial herd as well as maintaining a small herd of registered Polled Herefords.

In addition to her ranching responsibilities, Ruth served as Sheridan County commissioner from 1972–80, was president of the Sheridan Cow Belles, served on the first county planning commission, was nominated to the Northern International Livestock Expedition Hall of Fame, was the first woman Hereford cattle judge, accepted a posthumous award for her husband when he was inducted into the American Polled Hereford Hall of Fame and was honored by the American Polled Hereford Association in 1977 when it held its annual Standard of Perfection Show.

The octogenarian has written her life history for future generations and is putting her "house in order. It was not the wealth that I was seeking in my life," she says. "It was keeping my family together."

The Simpson Family, a distinguished part of Wyoming history

THE SIMPSON FAMILY

"Old saws, anecdotes, puns and parables"

Butch Cassidy was sent to prison by a Simpson—the only lawyer to convict the notorious outlaw—and the Simpson family has influenced the course of Wyoming history ever since. Among them have been a governor, two U.S. senators, state legislators, a college dean and the prosecuting attorney who let Butch out of jail on an overnight furlough the night before he was sent to prison.

Former Governor and U.S. Senator Milward Simpson has retained his marvelous sense of humor, despite a number of serious health problems that have plagued the octogenarian. The patriarch enjoys family gatherings at the Simpson ranch, west of Cody, where he and his wife, Lorna, spend the summer months before their winter migration to Sun City, Arizona. Their sons, U.S. Senator Alan Simpson and Wyoming legislator Peter Simpson, visit the ranch with their families as often as possible, usually engaging in an abundance of good natured "ribbing" and laughter.

Milward's sons have inherited his sense of humor as well as following in his political footsteps. The Simpsons obviously enjoy life and don't seem to take themselves or their accomplishments too seriously. "Politics is just a matter of lightning hitting the outhouse," his son, Alan, says. "There's no way to plan or lust for public office such as governor or senator. It just happens." The junior U.S. senator served thirteen years in the Wyoming legislature and was about to assume the post of speaker of the House when Senator Clifford Hansen declared his intention to retire. "If there was ever a time to run it was then—and I did," he says.

The Simpsons have been lawyers for nearly a century, beginning with William "Bill" Simpson, Milward's father, who successfully prosecuted Butch Cassidy on a horse stealing charge that sent him to the old territorial prison in Laramie. The night before Cassidy was to be sent "over the wall" he asked the sheriff to let him off on his own recognizance until eight o'clock the next morning. The sheriff refused but sent for Simpson as Cassidy requested.

Milward says his father told Cassidy, " 'All right, Butch, I know you'll be back,' and the next morning Butch was back. No one knows what mission he was on—being a ladies man and having some money. He stashed a lot of it away and probably had something to take care of," he laughs. Cassidy and his gang wintered regularly on the Simpson ranch between Riverton and Dubois, and Bill Simpson "knew Cassidy was a man of his word."

Just as remarkable is the fact that Bill Simpson became a lawyer by taking an oral exam in open court with three judges present, although he only had a third grade education. Crippled with polio as an infant, Bill managed to become a better than average cowboy and later opened his own grocery store in the midst of the Wyoming prairie during the late 1880s. But he longed to be a lawyer. Fortunately for Bill, he fell in love with the first school teacher who arrived at the St. Stephens Mission near Lander. "After Dad met her, he used to ride twenty-five miles from town to spark her," Milward says. She taught him Latin and proper English "and they made a pretty capable representative out of him. He'd get back on his horse on Sunday nights and head for Lander. He'd sleep in the saddle and the horse got him home." Bill Simpson also studied under Doug Preston, former Wyoming attorney general, before he passed the bar in 1892.

Milward's mother was born in 1874 in Salt Lake City because the Bannock Indians were on the warpath in central Wyoming where her parents had been staying at Fort Washakie near Lander. Women, children and old folks were evacuated from the fort shortly before she was born, because they feared that the Bannocks were going to annihilate the Shoshone Indians who were friendly to westward travelers. Shoshones then controlled the transcontinental corridor through which the wagon trains passed.

"The ninth cavalry—a colored cavalry—escorted them all to Salt Lake City," he says, "and my grandmother, who was carrying my mother at the time, was in the group that went to Utah. But she got back home as quickly as she could."

When she was old enough, Milward's mother proved up on her homestead on what is now the resort town of Jackson Hole. "Mom told us later that she had either given away or sold the lots for twenty-five dollars. It's worth a little bit more than that now," he laughs. "The street names in Jackson are all mostly Simpson names: Ida, Glenn, Virginia, Milward. . . . They're all Simpsons or people they married. And the ski area was originally called Simpson Ridge, but they changed the name to Snow King. Simpson Ridge was named after my granddaddy, John Simpson. He was one of the first settlers in Jackson in 1884. He drove cattle from the Big Thompson River in Colorado to Jackson, and my dad was born in Fort Lyons."

Milward's mother lived 100 years and was known for her quick wit which she passed on to succeeding generations. He tells of the time a visitor to the governor's mansion in Cheyenne asked Mrs. Simpson whether she and her son, the governor, were planning to watch an upcoming football game between Notre Dame and Michigan State. "We will if we can get rid of the preacher in time," she quipped. As he was leaving office, Governor Simpson was asked if he could still say that the media had never misquoted him. In typical Simpson fashion he replied, "Yeah, but I wish you hadn't said what I said."

A number of years before the governor was born, his parents lived in Lander and in Jackson, moving back and forth between the two towns because of various business ventures. "They changed until they got the right one," he says. The youngest of

195

three children, Milward was born in Jackson. His brother Glenn, sister Virginia and he were moved from Jackson to Lander to Meeteetse and finally to Cody in 1907, where they remained until Milward graduated from the University of Wyoming and Harvard Law School. The youngest Simpson son was quite an athlete in his youth and excelled in basketball and baseball. And like his father, Bill, he earned his right to practice law in an unorthodox manner.

Milward took a year off from law school to earn some "dough" to continue his studies. He tutored students in Dublin, New Hampshire for fifteen dollars a month and gained special permission from a presiding judge, one P. W. Metz, to practice law in Wyoming without a license. "I took any kind of case—bootleg—that I could get and that was the most active epic in the history of law. We got 'em all," he laughs.

His father was in ill health, and Milward helped in each of the two Simpson law offices, in Cody and Jackson Hole. "We split our time between the two," he recalls. "Mom was the chauffeur. Dad and I did the heavy work and she did the smart work." The following year, Milward returned to Harvard and passed the bar exam in 1925. Upon graduation, he couldn't "get back to Wyoming fast enough." He practiced law with his father as general practitioners. "That's the only kind of lawyer there was in those days. We didn't have tax problems then." His father then went back to Jackson "because he said it was more fun there," and Milward moved briefly to Thermopolis to practice law before returning to Cody.

The young lawyer married Lorna Helen Kooi (pronounced Coy) in 1929, after a two-year, hard-won courtship. He won her heart with flowers and cablegrams as she traveled around the world with her parents. "I don't know how he did it, but everytime we came into a port, there were the flowers and cable," she says. They had met at a wedding in Sheridan in 1927, and she hadn't been too impressed with the "best man" everyone called "Simp." So when her parents decided to tour the world after selling their coal mines near Sheridan, Lorna begged to go with them and was given permission if she promised to write down her observations of the trip in her diary every night. "I wrote volumes," she says. "They're still up in the attic somewhere."

Years earlier, Lorna's father, Peter Kooi, took over coal mining interests from his friend, Al Smith (who was running for president), and was told that he could not adequately supervise the mines from the East. So Kooi moved to northern Wyoming where he established a company town that bore his name. Lorna, her sisters and their mother divided their time between their "grand old home in Chicago" and the tiny town of Kooi.

"It was a wonderful town," she remembers. "Dad never needed a law enforcement officer, and there was even indoor plumbing. He designed the town, and they made him an honorary member of the union." Kooi disappeared from the map when the coal mines were closed down during the early '20s, as did the nearest town of Monarch (although the latter's buildings still remain). Company buildings were dismantled and shipped to another company town, Acme, and to Sheridan and Dayton. And Lorna was sent off to boarding school in Terrytown, New York. Her parents moved to Sheridan, prior to their two-year world cruise, into the house now occupied by Milward and Lorna's son, Peter, and his family.

Lorna Kooi Simpson's two sons call her "the velvet hammer." Six-foot-seven-inch Alan and six-foot-six-inch Pete agree that their delicate, soft-spoken, gracious mother is a "very sweet and wonderful lady" but she made them "toe the mark" while they were growing up. Milward says that when they got into occasional disputes over goodies, Lorna would solve the problem by making one son divide up the delicacy and the other son choose the first piece. "That was very time consuming," Senator Alan Simpson laughs.

Lorna's oldest son, Peter, says: "The permanent, long lasting, best friendship of my life has been with my brother, Al. I hope that for my own children. Al and I shared a bedroom with a couple of seven-foot-long beds because we both got so outsized so quick. I remember the time a friend of Mom's—someone she hadn't seen in years since we were nine and ten—came to the house. Al and I were about sixteen and seventeen, and six-foot-three or four. And as Mom was describing to her friend how she fed us vitamins and orange juice, we walked in the door. The friend looked up at us and said, 'Don't you think you overdid it, Lorna?'"

The Simpson brothers describe their childhood as "great." Pete remembers "our house on the southwest edge of town. I recall the sheep coming over the hill and open prairie out there with very few neighbors. And playing baseball in the backyard. Dad played baseball with the town team. He was captain and managed the team, and I was the mascot. I remember going out there with the dust blowing around, and I had on a little uniform that I thought was the greatest thing that ever happened to me. We were of the *To Kill a Mockingbird* vintage—bib overalls—and we had a great time. Both Al and I played ball in college.

"We had loving parents and a good family life. Al and I were so close in age that we shared all of that together. We got along and rarely fought, but when we did, they were doozies." The brothers vividly recall the time their father bought them boxing gloves to settle a hostility. They used them to bloody each other's noses when they were ten and eleven. "That was the last time we fought like that," Pete says.

"Pete and I were our own psychiatrists," Al adds. "We'd sit on our beds in our room upstairs and discuss our problems and our folks. We were a very close family and still are. When you gather to celebrate your forty-ninth birthday and think it's your nineteenth, you don't fit in any time span. When we come up here to the ranch, it's timeless. I go down to the creek and fish just like we never left the place. I was restless at the time [I was growing up], and more of a disciplinary problem. Sometimes I'd take off and go to work for a road crew or go to Rawlins during the summer."

"A rebel without a cause," his wife, Ann, laughs.

The lanky senator admits to weighing 250 pounds while he played first string football at the University of Wyoming. "I thought beer was food in those days," he laughs. "Then I met Ann at a high school basketball game in Greybull. She was a cheerleader and I said, 'Wow!' She wouldn't have anything to do with Pete because he had acne pimples. . . ."

Alan and Ann were married in 1954, after he had completed a year of law school and she was a student at UW. Ann's father died when she was fifteen, and her mother moved her twin daughters to Laramie where their brother was attending classes at the university. Working as a housemother, she was able to put all three of her children through college.

Shortly after they were married, Alan joined an infantry unit, and the newlyweds spent two years in Germany. When they returned home, he finished his last two terms of law school just as his father was in the process of running for his second term as governor of Wyoming. Milward lost the election to Joe Hickey, "but it was a break for me," the senator says, "because he came back to Cody and we practiced law together."

Pete, on the other hand, dropped out of law school after a year at Stanford. "It was a very abortive year," he says. "I really didn't get along well with law. I played my guitar more than I should have, and so the law and I parted company in friendly fashion at the end of the first year." The senator's brother then joined the navy and served four and a half years in the naval air force before coming back to Wyoming in 1958, at the end of his father's governorship. Pete decided he might like to teach history "because it was always easy for me while mathematics was an incomprehensible language."

He met his wife, Lynn, an aspiring actress, in Cody. "In 1959, I borrowed $350 from Al and went to New York City. By the time my money ran out I was engaged," he says with a grin. "I had only known her for thirteen days, but it was love at first sight. Lynn had gone to New York to audition for the Perry Como show at the American Theatre, so I took her away from life's fame and fortune." She now directs a theatre group in Sheridan and has a string of successful productions behind her. The couple's oldest offspring, Milward II, is a promising musician who sat in with the Dave Brubeck Ensemble in concert in Cody when he was sixteen.

In 1961, Pete took graduate work in history at the University of Wyoming, and taught out of state for awhile before returning to teach in Jackson. His family lived in the scenic paradise for more than two years while he finished his dissertation. From Jackson he taught history at Casper College before transferring to Sheridan where he is now dean of instruction. In 1979, he successfully ran an eleventh hour campaign for the state House and ruffled some feathers when his filing papers were flown to Cheyenne on a charter plane paid for by the Republican party. He now has his political sights trained on the governor's office in 1986.

A fourth generation Simpson lawyer is in the wings. Alan's son, Bill, is studying law at the University of Wyoming, which pleases his grandfather. Whether Bill also follows family tradition and enters politics is yet to be seen, but his sister, Susan, was president of her high school student body in Washington, D.C., 1980–81.

Senator Al and his wife live in McLean, Virginia, a twenty-minute drive from the capitol, in a suburb inhabited by many members of Congress and their families. "Our life in Washington is very full. It came at a good time in our lives," Ann says. "Our three children are grown and it's a new phase that's very exciting. We have a lot of social life that's available to us and, fortunately, Al has a busy enough schedule so that we're forced to rest occasionally. He has more stamina than I do, which seems to go with politics."

Ann carpools with other senate wives, especially her two friends from Minnesota who are also married to first term senators. They attend senate wives meetings once a week to work on puppets for local hospitals, but the main reason they get together "is to know each other better," she says. "If people are looking for give and take in friendship, it's difficult to do in politics. People in politics understand that so we put up with each other's way of life. I do get involved in short term things, but we return to Wyoming often, and I'm here in the summer and at Christmas, so it doesn't lend itself to getting involved in too many things."

Alan Simpson says of his career in Washington: "That's not how I'm going to spend the rest of my life. I've got lots to do. I'm a curious guy. I have no burning bosom syndrome and if I'm perfectly honest, there's no white hot flames in there saying 'What next, Alan? What are you lusting for in the way of politics?' " A number of congressmen have fallen from their proverbial pedestals during the past few years, and the senator says "there are the same percentage of alcoholics, deviates and screwballs in Congress as in the general public. After all, we're human and we represent the public.

"If you don't know who you are before you go to Washington, you'll never find it there. It's a squirrel cage. You're just on the pace and you tumble around and grab hold and do what you can — and keep your sense of humor. I learned that from my parents. We're a family of old saws, anecdotes, puns and parables. . . . terribles," the senator laughs and rolls his eyes.

Gaydell Collier, author, rancher, and bookstore proprietor—*Mary Jean Wilson, photographer*

GAYDELL COLLIER

"Wyoming Is the only place to live"

Born on Long Island, New York, and reared within the shadow of publishing giant Doubleday in Garden City, writer-rancher-bookshop proprietor Gaydell Collier was convinced at an early age that Wyoming is the only place to live, although she had never ventured west of New Jersey. A "painfully shy" adolescent, she read voraciously, particularly animal stories and books about the West. Her insatiable appetite for books and love of horses eventually brought her to Wyoming where she and her husband reared their four children in the "backwoods" without many modern conveniences. There she met Eleanor Prince, with whom she coauthored three books on horse training for Doubleday, and numerous magazine and newspaper articles. Her love of books also led her to create the Backpocket Ranch Bookshop near Sundance.

Now living on a 950-acre ranch near Sundance, Gay rises at 4:45 A.M. to work on her current novel before starting the chores with her husband at 5:30 each morning. "It's primarily a confused operation," she laughs. "We're trying to do too many things, but we enjoy them." The Colliers raise and train horses: Morgans, Drafts, Belgians and combinations thereof. They have also leased an English born Shire stallion who made the 1979 *Guinness Book of Records*. Ladbrook Invader stands nineteen and a half hands high, the tallest horse bred in the British Isles.

They've used the stallion to improve their Belgian and Draft bloodlines and are considering making him a permanent member of the ranch community. But horses aren't the only inhabitants of the Collier ranch. There are also Herefords and Jerseys, chickens, sheep, guinea hens and "untold herds of cats and batches of purebred border collie puppies." Gay milks three Jersey cows and sells the raw milk locally. She also makes her own butter and yogurt.

Staying solvent is the Colliers' main worry. Her husband, Roy, sums it up with: "Our ranch is primarily a nonprofit organization as are most other present day family-sized farms and ranches. Until there are some major changes in American society, our hopes are pretty much limited to trying to raise some worthwhile Morgans, Shires, Jerseys and Herefords; trying to leave the land and buildings in better shape for the next generation; and trying to survive."

A major problem is water, he says, and irresponsible waste and "theft" of it by industry, power plants, pipelines and "great plains farmers who are irrigating with ground water that could dry up" Wyoming and make it unfit for agriculture. Long-term planning, particularly in regard to the Ogallala Aquifer, is paramount. "Failure to neither conceive nor implement long-range planning will be the biggest single factor in turning America belly-up agriculturally, economically, socially and environmentally," he warns.

Gaydell Maier met Roy Collier at the University of Wyoming where they were both agricultural students. Gay had earlier visited the state while she was sixteen, having convinced her parents that a trip to Wyoming would be nothing short of heaven. Her parents mortgaged their home and took Gay and her younger brother, Gary, on a six-week vacation that culminated in Wyoming at a dude ranch near Dubois. Once she saw Wyoming, "that was it," she says. "I had to come back."

Following high school she attended Middlebury College in

upstate New York where she exercised horses at a nearby stable each morning before attending classes. She studied languages—Spanish, French, German and Russian—but switched to geography before transferring to the University of Wyoming where she enrolled in agriculture (ag) classes. There she met Roy Collier and was instantly attracted to the six-foot-three-inch student from Illinois who shared the same "dry sense of humor" and religion: Christian Science. They were married at the end of the first semester and traveled east for their wedding in a 1937 LaSalle which had to be kept running because the engine wouldn't restart.

Roy's penchant for old cars included a Model A Ford and a '32 Chevy Roadster. The latter was purchased when he was fifteen for $100 and sold in 1976 for $5,000. The Colliers traveled extensively with their four small children in the four-cylinder Model A, and Gay wrote about their adventures.

Roy graduated from the University of Wyoming, and Gay was able to complete her junior year before Sam, their oldest child, was born. They then moved to New York to Gay's "adopted" uncle's farm so that Roy could gain some practical farming experience and to be near her parents and maternal grandfather, with whom Gay was very close. A year later, the couple moved to Vermont where they purchased a small farm in 1960, complete with maple grove, called a "sugar bush" by the locals. They grazed a few Jerseys and rented out pasture but were unable to farm the land due to a local "depression" and lack of capital. So, in 1963, they loaded "kids, cats, dogs" and personal possessions into the Model A and '32 Chevy Roadster for the trip back to Wyoming. After some "half-hearted looking around" for employment, they settled again in Laramie in a rented cabin on a ranch. Roy received an assistantship from the university to work toward his master's degree but with four children to support, he had to give up his dream in favor of working full time for a rancher. Gay found a job at the university's Agricultural Information Center where she edited several publications as well as John Gorman's *Western Horse* book.

The cabin in which they were living was "bursting at the seams," and they moved into a larger one on the Sodergreen Ranch, without indoor plumbing except for a "pitcher pump" over the kitchen sink, and very limited electricity. Gay says: "It got pretty miser-able during winter trotting to the privy in the middle of the night – or when the kids got sick. Once in awhile one of the kids would get scared when there was a skunk or porcupine in the middle of the path, but for the most part, I think it was a pretty good experience for everybody."

Wood cutting was a regular family chore to keep the cabin warm and the "cook stove" heated. The Laramie River, which runs past the cabin, took the place of a washing machine, swimming pool and bathtub during the summer months. Without television, the Collier children turned to books, and Gay's second son, Frank, was reading Tolstoy while in elementary school. "His teachers were upset by this," she says, "and wouldn't let him give a book report on *War and Peace*."

To complicate matters, a social worker "came out from town when she heard that some people were living in the backwoods in rather primitive conditions. I guess she imagined that we were white trash from some limited background, especially since we didn't have television." Her husband adds: "Two of our kids have thanked us for raising them without a TV set in the house, a third has implied as much and a fourth never criticized us for it." When a severe snowstorm knocked out electricity and other conveniences, their neighbors suffered, but the Colliers were "unaffected" because they had a wood stove for warmth and cooking, and lanterns to read by. The "unmodern cabin" had plenty of space around it to raise orphaned lambs and other animals.

Also living on the large Sodergreen Ranch was Eleanor Smith Prince who raised and trained Arabian horses, and coauthored several horse training books with her neighbor Gay Collier. When "Ellie" remarried and moved to Bufford, the Colliers moved into the "big house" she vacated, this time with adequate electricity and plumbing, although the drains seldom worked. Gay found a job in the university library, and they were able to save money for a down payment on some land of their own. They wanted to buy a portion of the Sodergreen Ranch which was temporarily on the market, but long before they could afford it, the land was no longer for sale. "It really should have been an historic site," she explains. "We wanted to buy it and restore it."

Instead, they found some land near Sundance in the Bear Lodge area with difficult winter access. "There were no corrals or buildings on the land, and our original intent was to set up a tent while we built a corral and eventually a home, which wasn't too shiny a thought as far as I was concerned," Gay says. Before they were able to purchase the land, however, her mother died in New York, and her maternal grandfather was seriously ill. So any extra money was spent commuting to New York for the next two years to be with her mentor, her grandfather. A commercial artist, he died in 1976, and Roy's father also died during that time period. With inheritance from both estates, they were able to buy their present ranch near Sundance. Their youngest son, Fred, was a senior in high school when they made the move from Laramie to Sundance, and he delayed his college education for several years until the ranch was on a working basis.

The Collier children have left the nest and are scattered about the country. Sam is captain of a commercial fishing boat off the coast of Alaska; Frank is a radio operator for the Marine Corps in Hawaii; Jenny is an artist and bank teller in Laramie; and Fred an ag student at UW.

Running the ranch by themselves is a full-time job and more, but Gay has managed to open a small mail-order bookshop on the ranch in an old pink trailer that's parked in front of her 1880 vintage ranch house. The antique dwelling once housed Butch Cassidy for the night when he slept in the west bedroom during one of his sojourns into South Dakota.

The Backpocket Ranch Bookshop features Wyoming books, rare and hard to find editions, as well as horse training manuals, writing instruction books and others. She used her first $1,000 royalty check from Doubleday to start her bookshop, and she continues to write during the very limited time she allows herself. *Basic Training for Horses* won the Wyoming Writers "Best Non-Fiction Book Award" in 1980, and she's working on an historical novel. Gay has also written horse book reviews for the *Library Journal* since 1969, was a trustee for the Albany County Library, served on the Library Advisory Board of the Wyoming State Library, and is a "Library Friend." Her writer group memberships include Wyoming Writers, Western Writers of America, National League of American Pen Women and the Bear Lodge Writers of Sundance.

Clifford Hansen, former state governor and U.S. senator—*author's photo*

CLIFFORD HANSEN

"You'll be governor someday"

He was sent home from first grade with a note from the teacher saying he could not be educated because he had a severe speech problem: he stuttered. Trying to reassure the boy, one of his father's ranch hands told him, "Don't worry, Cliff, you'll be governor someday." The statement proved prophetic, for Clifford Hansen not only grew up to be governor of Wyoming, he served as U.S. senator and was offered the post of secretary of the interior (before James Watt).

"I always remembered that," he says, "and I thought 'I will be governor someday.' I suppose, because of my speech difficulty, I had an idea I was going to be a politician even before I knew what the governorship was."

The soft-spoken, retired legislator was born in Jackson Hole, Wyoming, in 1912, the third child of six in a ranching family. His father, Peter C. Hansen, had traveled to Jackson from Soda Springs, Idaho, during the summer of 1897 and returned the following year to homestead near the present Teton Village. He married Sylvia Wood, a teacher from Blackfoot, Idaho, and together they built a sizable ranching operation in Lincoln County where he was appointed by the governor to serve as county commissioner and "one of the first board members when Teton County was organized." Later, he served in the state senate.

His son, Cliff, grew up on the family ranch and was tutored by his mother at home the first year. "I think my mother was well aware of my speech difficulty early on and perceived that math was something that I could do, because you don't have to speak too much while you're doing it," he says. "So she encouraged me in that." His mother only completed the eighth grade, "but that was considered a good education when she was teaching school." When Hansen was sent home from first grade it "was a pretty traumatic experience for my mother, but I really didn't mind because school was an embarrassment to me."

His speech problem was so severe that he was unable to talk to adults outside his family circle and only to children when he wasn't "the focus of attention." Once he was enrolled in school, however, he excelled in his written class work. His parents sent him to a special speech clinic during the fall of 1927, just before his fifteenth birthday. The five-week course in Indianapolis taught him to speak very slowly and to think about something other than speaking. "So for every syllable I would push my fingers together and say, 'Hooooowwww Arrrrreeee Yooooouuuu?' Obviously, that would have made school impossible as far as any response from me was concerned," he says. "And I didn't go to school that year, but I had skipped some grades so I graduated with my class."

Hansen practiced the techniques he had learned at the speech clinic and gained enough confidence to try out for his high school debate team the following year. "I guess I did all right," he says, "but the judges were fearful that, if I had to talk a lot, it might bring on a recurrence of my speech problem. So I didn't make the team."

Hansen denies that it took considerable courage to try out for the debate team. "Strangely enough, after I had taken speech therapy and found that I could talk, I wanted to talk to everybody. I suppose it was like something that you weren't proficient in and suddenly acquiring some skill, you know, after having been fifteen years without courage or the ability to speak to people. When I finally found out that I could get along pretty well, I thought being on the debate team would be fine."

He didn't try out again in high school but he made the debate team at the University of Wyoming. He won a four-year scholarship to the university as a senior in high school. "It wasn't any great shakes," he says, "because there were only five girls and two boys in my graduating class, and they gave a scholarship to the top girl and boy. The other boy, I guess, took pity on me."

Hansen started out in a liberal arts program "with the idea of going into law," but it was "during the depression days when I started college in 1930—those were tough years." His father thought he should learn more about ranching so Hansen switched to animal husbandry during his second year, although he kept substituting liberal arts courses for ag classes.

Hansen says he could have gone on to law school. "My parents would have helped me. They were very generous people who did everything for their kids, but I got married that fall after I graduated." He married Martha Close from Sheridan who had also won a scholarship to the University of Wyoming. "She was much smarter than I was," he says. "She graduated from a much bigger school than Jackson."

The young couple lived on his father's ranch for the first year. Peter Hansen then gave them "some land and some cattle. And we arranged to buy a little bit and later on were able to get another place or two with his backing. We've been ranching ever since and haven't gotten very far from home." They started out with a small herd of white-faced Herefords which was the predominant breed of cattle "and continues to be in Jackson, although you see quite a few blacks [Angus] nowadays."

Hansen began his political career when he was appointed to the local school board in Jackson and "elected a time or two." He then ran for county commissioner in 1948, "the year that Franklin Delano Roosevelt (FDR), by presidential proclamation, created the Jackson Hole National Monument, a precursor of the expanded Grand Teton Park." John D. Rockefeller had begun purchasing land in the Jackson Hole area during the late 1920s, intending that it would eventually attain park status. Although various bills were proposed in Congress, nothing was done until Rockefeller wrote to the secretary of the interior in 1943, threatening to dispose of the land in some other way.

"That triggered the action which FDR took in creating the monument under the authority of the Antiquities Act of 1906," he explains. As a commissioner, Hansen was concerned with the loss of tax revenues that would result when the land passed from private to public ownershp because about one-third of the privately owned land in Jackson was included in the "monument." Hansen and the other commissioners decided to get as much publicity as possible to call attention to what they considered "a very serious situation to the county." So they persuaded movie star Wallace Beery to accompany them on a cattle drive across the land. "We would have been doing it anyway, and the forest service didn't say we couldn't. But actually, it was just a charade."

The charade resulted in a two-page photo layout in *Time Magazine* of Wallace Beery and the small band of "federal government defiers" herding cattle across the monument. The defiant act was applauded by Democratic Governor Lester C. Hunt who later appointed Hansen to the University Board of Trustees.

"That gave me statewide exposure in the political arena," he says. He had already served eight years as county commissioner as well as president of the Wyoming Stock Growers Association. He then served seventeen years on the university board and was eventually named president.

Hansen continued to ranch during his political adventures, "but my wife was actively ranching more than I was," he says. "She was the gal who kept everything together and raised our family. I saw a lot more of my family than some fathers, but not as much as I should—to have been a really good father." The couple have two children: Peter and Mary.

He then fulfilled the ranchhand's prophecy, and his own dream of becoming governor. The 1962 gubernatorial race focused on job opportunities for Wyoming youth who were making a mass exodus out of the state. Hansen and acting Governor Jack Gage spent "the entire campaign out-promising each other" in that direction. "But I had a built-in edge," he says, "because there were more registered Republicans than Democrats."

Governor Hansen had planned to run for a second term but U.S. Senator Milward Simpson was in ill health, and he convinced Hansen that he should run for his senate seat. Hansen felt that he had a good chance of being reelected governor; "it was an interesting and challenging job, but not one where you make a lot of friends." So he went to Washington in 1967, where he served on the Senate Finance and Energy and Resources committees; those he considered most important to Wyoming. Among his many accomplishments as a legislator, he is most proud of the federal government's mineral royalty amendment he successfully authored which increased Wyoming's revenue share from thirty-seven and a half percent to fifty, and the Steiger-Hansen amendment that lowered taxes on capital gains from a maximum of forty-nine percent to twenty-eight percent.

The senator had to leave Washington after twelve years because of his health. An asthmatic, he spent the last few years in the capitol sitting in a chair at night to sleep so that he could breathe. "But it's not a bad idea to quit when people think that you ought to stay," he says. "It's much better than to have people say, 'Why didn't the old fool quit?' "

Ronald Reagan offered Hansen the post of secretary of the interior shortly after the 1980 presidential election, but the Wyomingite declined with regrets. He felt that his grazing permit in Grand Teton National Park would be a liability that he and the president would have to spend considerable time explaining, although the permit was issued in 1950 and is legal. The main reason, however, was his health which has "greatly improved since I've been home and I can sleep at night," he says.

His "speech difficulty" has all but disappeared over the years "but I still stutter sometimes when I get excited. Once a stutterer, always a stutterer, they say."

213

Elsa Spear Byron, photographer and historian—*author's photo*

ELSA SPEAR BYRON

"I couldn't get along without taking pictures"

The Big Horn Mountain's Lake Elsa got its name from one of Wyoming's most prolific photographers, Elsa Spear Byron of Sheridan. The energetic, multitalented pioneer has left her mark on Wyoming in other ways as well.

Elsa is a first generation Wyomingite, born in 1896; her ancestors are all New Englanders and Mayflower descendants. Her mother's parents left Boston in 1849 and headed west to Illinois, Kansas and Nebraska—arriving in Laramie in 1881. Elsa's grandfather, G. W. Benton, was a medical missionary who was "trained as a Baptist minister, doctor and dentist."

Her father, Willis Spear, arrived in Wyoming with his family in 1874, from Connecticut by way of Indiana and Missouri, and eventually settled "on the next place to my Grandfather Benton at Big Horn," she says.

Willis Spear married his neighbor, Virginia Bell Benton, and they settled on 260 Big Horn acres near Sheridan. Elsa, her two brothers and sister grew up on the ranch which expanded rapidly to include millions of acres of land, most of it leased from the government. Two years after Elsa was born, her father and his family started the Spear Brothers Cattle Company "and Papa traded off some land for some grazing land on Dutch Creek to the east." The Spears then leased over a million acres of the Crow Indian Reservation in Montana as well as five ranches on the Powder River north of Arvada, and several others north of Clearmont.

"Then they could trail cattle about a hundred miles, either on their property or on leased land," she says. "There was 400 miles of fence that was 90 miles north and south, and 20 miles east and west. They ran 57,000 head of cattle although the company only owned 36,000 head and pastured the rest."

Elsa and her siblings grew up on horseback, although she and her sister rode sidesaddle. "That's what my mother rode all her life. When I was four, my father bought me a red saddle and I rode an old roan horse that my mother used to ride. I've often wondered what happened to that saddle," she says laughing. "We rode to the ranches all the time and I went on the roundups a lot. I liked that."

The drought of the early 1920s nearly destroyed the northern Wyoming cattle business. "Everyone around here went broke and had to ship their cattle to Texas to feed them," she recalls. "So Papa decided to build a dude camp on our place that had such a wonderful spring. He could pipe water from this deep pool; it bubbled up from the bottom and stayed thirty-four degrees all the time." The Spear-O-Wigwam is still operating as a dude ranch.

The Spear children attended the Lone Star School located half a mile "up the river" from the present Bradford Brinton Memorial Ranch in Big Horn. The family then moved into Sheridan where they built a large house off Coffeen Avenue. The house kept growing until it contained twenty-three rooms and four bathrooms on three floors. "I don't know why Mama thought she needed so much room, but we always had relatives living with us, both hers and Papa's. There was somebody coming and going all the time."

The Spears were a musical family. Elsa took piano lessons from the time she was six, and other members of the family played guitar, banjo and mandolin. "We played together a lot." The family also did quite a bit of traveling. "Papa had to go to Washington, D.C., every two years to make a sealed bid for his reservation lease, and he thought that we children should go and see everything. So we were there for six months. And we had such a good time and took in everything" including musical matinees after school and plays starring famous actors such as John Drew and his niece, Mary Borden. "She was such a grand actress." They also moved to Pasadena, California, for a few months while Elsa was in seventh grade because her mother was in "poor health. She always felt better at a lower elevation," her daughter says.

Elsa graduated from Sheridan High School in 1914 and returned to Washington to attend the National School for Domestic Arts and Sciences that winter, accompanied by her mother. "We boarded with some friends," she says. There she studied the "theory and practice of cooking and all kinds of fancy work in sewing and millinery. We had to make hats from scratch, and I used to make them to wear with different dresses."

Two years later, she married Harold Edwards from Colorado, an office manager for the Sheridan County Electric Company (now Montana-Dakota Utilities). They built a home in 1916, and moved into it before it was finished. Elsa still lives there after more than sixty-five years; her five daughters grew up in the same frame house on the west side of town.

Elsa has been interested in photography all her life. Her mother purchased a "plate camera" in 1900 and had taken photos and processed them while her children were growing up. Elsa remembers helping her mother develop the pictures in wooden frames which were placed in the sun. "You would lay back half of it to see if it was dark enough and close it up again," she says. "And we used blueprint paper so all you had to do was wash it with water." She still has many of her mother's plate photographs although some of them have been broken over the years. A number of the plates turned up in a Sheridan antique shop recently, and she thinks they might have been borrowed by her mother's friend and never returned, but found and sold after the friend died.

The pack trips to her father's Spear-O-Wigwam provided the petite photographer with endless picture-taking opportunities. She made sixteen annual pack trips of two weeks' duration while her daughters were growing up, hiring a housekeeper while she was gone. "That's the way that I got my pictures from all over the mountains," she smiles. During one of the pack trips "some dudes" decided to name one of the trout-stocked lakes for her, "Lake Elsa" stuck and is recorded on Big Horn Mountain maps.

When she returned home, she enlarged her pictures in the kitchen where she had a trapdoor cut in the ceiling to raise the head of the enlarger high enough to make huge prints by projecting the light on the floor. Some of her photos include the Cheyenne Indian survivors of the Custer Battlefield whom she photographed in 1926 on the battle's fiftieth anniversary. Among the Indians who posed for her on the battle site were Red Cloud, grandson of the infamous warrior, and Plenty Coups, a Crow chief. Another of her pictures was enlarged to eight feet wide by twenty feet long in Denver and used as a background for an Indian camp display in the Cheyenne museum.

Elsa tinted her black and white prints with oils to make them more attractive and sold them to many sources including the Northern Pacific and Burlington Northern railroads. "I think my greatest thrill was when I was walking up the street in Chicago and saw four of my big pictures framed in the window of the Northern Pacific office on Jackson Boulevard in the '30s," she says. "They did a lot of advertising and used a lot of my twenty-by-thirty-inch pictures to try to get the dudes out here."

Elsa's biggest production, however, was her lamp shade and letter basket business. She made the shades from "cream colored developing paper with a velvet varnish coating to make them look like parchment, utilizing a special film which she colored from the reverse side with oils, reproducing many of her Big Horn Mountain scenes on the lamp shades. She used a similar process on the letter baskets. Her biggest customers were a "cedar root hotel furniture manufacturer" located in Sheridan—they shipped her shades all over the country with their lamps—and the General Custer Hotel in Billings ordered thirty-four lamp shades in all shapes and sizes for their two downstairs lobbies.

She also filled orders for individuals from various parts of the world. "I can't remember all those places I packed and sent them to—China, England, Scotland—to people who ordered them." She didn't advertise, but the orders came from people who had seen her work. After forty years, she had to give it up because she was allergic to the photographic chemicals. "My fingers were split wide open for five years," she says, "and it took them a long time to get them healed."

Since the late 1960s when she gave up the processing end of her photography, she has occupied her time with numerous organizations including the Daughters of the American Revolution (DAR); the Sheridan County Historical Society; the Trail's End Museum; the Mayflower Descendants, both state and national organizations; and the Sheridan Range Writers and Wyoming Writers. She has served as officer for the DAR and the Historical Society for many years but finds it increasingly difficult to get to the meetings although she still drives. "I spend so much time here with all this now," she says, motioning to an assortment of books and sixty-five years worth of memorabilia which surround her in her home. "I've got such an assortment of things—pictures, films, historical stuff—that I'm trying to decide what to do with." She also takes orders for the Historical Society's books, receiving four phone calls within an hour for delivery.

Elsa has raised two families in her home. She was divorced from Harold Edwards in the early '30s and remarried in 1938 to another electric company employee she calls Mr. Byron. "He had seven children and two of his boys were in a children's home after his wife died in Denver," she says. "So we brought them to live here with us." After five daughters, she acquired some sons of whom she's also proud.

Elsa is the only surviving member of a pioneer family who contributed to Wyoming's heritage, and she's tried to keep the memories alive with her historical writings and photographs which have been widely published. Although she lost the center vision of her right eye in 1980, she continues to take beautiful photographs of her home state. "Goodness, I couldn't get along without taking pictures," she says. "And I have two girls who are good at it, too."

219

Duane Shillinger, Wyoming state prison warden—*author's photo*

DUANE SHILLINGER

"They've gone against the old convict codes"

State prison warden Duane Shillinger looks upon his charges with a benevolent eye. The former counselor views prisoner rehabilitation as a means of not only putting them on the right social track, but as a method of defusing potential problems in the Wyoming penitentiary. Education, maximum freedom and personal contact are the main ingredients in his psychological brew. With the exception of a five percent escape rate in 1981, his methods appear to be successful.

"The inmates, themselves, have changed some of the traditional ideas about prison life," he explains. "They've gone against the old convict codes: 'You gotta' be tough, you don't interact with the establishment, you do things to disrupt life within the prison,' and so forth. The real energy comes about because there's a cry for change. [The prisoners] felt it was necessary, and I wonder how many other institutions have heard that kind of cry from the wilderness?"

Shillinger worked as a counselor at the prison for three years before he was promoted to administrative assistant and deputy warden under Leonard Meacham in 1975. During his twelve years at the penitentiary before assuming the post of warden, he had considerable contact with the inmates and knew each man by his first name. He still spends several hours a day "inside the wall" conducting formal inspections and visiting with the inmates who greet him like an old friend. The warden says he enjoys his work "tremendously. I guess the thing that's been a real impetus to me is the challenge to do something constructive with the prison. I've always detested the idea of people coming in here and being forced to do nothing but learn how to live in a penitentiary. The state can do better than that. I think there is something that can be done as far as opportunity—stimulating people to pick up a new life-style.

"There's a term called sensory deprivation. If you take everything away from a person and allow him to do nothing but remain in a cell or be confined to the same environmental situation day after day, he's going to react to that. And he'll generally react in a negative manner. He'll possibly try to destroy his environment; he'll create disturbances—yell and scream—and a number of things that are terribly upsetting to the staff and those people who must live with him. So for the maximum effort out of the inmate, they should be given something constructive to do. Traditionally, it's been something of a taboo to allow people in segregation to have a lot of privileges, and those traditional institutions have a lot of trouble in their segregation units."

Inmates at the Rawlins prison may now earn an associate of arts degree by attending classes taught by visiting faculty members from Riverton's Community College. The educational system has come a long way since the warden was first employed at the state pen. Shaw High School, the prison's original academe, provided prisoners with two high school equivalency (G.E.D.) instructors who were inmates in the beginning, "and now there's state appropriation grants" which provide full-time remedial education programs as well as advanced courses in a variety of subjects.

The recidivism rate at the prison averages fifty-five percent. Nationally, the rate of inmate return is eighty-five percent. "It's a life-style," the warden explains. "The fellows have learned to survive in a somewhat asocial manner. It's easy for them to survive in a penitentiary by being asocial which they've learned out of necessity – if they haven't learned how to replace some of it with socially acceptable behavior, for whatever reason."

Shillinger describes a typical inmate coming into the prison as twenty-three years old with a third grade education, a mouthful of decayed teeth, a hernia and a wife who is ready to divorce him. "Generally, when these fellows hit the institution, they've reached a pretty low depth of failure in all areas of their lives," he says. The inmate is initially counseled and encouraged to use his prison time in a constructive manner, "not to just sit around smoking dope or sniffing glue or learning to gamble or getting involved in the penitentiary hustle. So we try to convince the person that going to school would be the best thing and getting involved with the dentist and taking care of the hernia; all this with some counseling constitutes his program. It's almost like a contract. We've identified these problems with him, and he sets out to resolve them if he possibly can. When he gets into school a new door opens and maybe he finds that learning is fun. He thinks 'I've learned to read and write now, and I've always wanted to read blueprints' or something out of a welding manual. Maybe he wants to get involved in one of the construction trades; that would be part of the program."

Prison counselors are responsible for reviewing prisoners on a regular basis. "I would like each inmate to be interviewed and reviewed at least once a month so we know where he is," he says. "Some of the management problems – those who are destructive to themselves or to other people – are vulnerable and become victims of other people. They need monitoring and may find themselves in various stages of critical management [protective custody]. They would be in a segregation unit in a cell that they leave only when we want to release them, and that's on a schedule."

Shillinger doesn't believe in solitary confinement for extended periods of time. "I really ask the question, 'How useful is it?'" he says. "It might be worthwhile overnight, an hour or two hours, but it isn't something that I would like to use on a consistent or routine basis. I believe that people, because we are gregarious, are dependent upon each other. I think they should learn to live with one another and respect each other."

Inmates in the old prison, first occupied in 1901, were segregated by behavior, not by crimes committed. Segregation in the new facility is basically the same but the accommodations have improved considerably. Prisoners have more privacy in the new prison, which was already filled to near capacity and obsolete when they were transferred from the antique prison during the early fall of 1981, when a number of inmates escaped in transport. Cells in the old prison were four-by-six-feet, dank-smelling cubicles with metal bunk, small sink and lidless toilet. Prisoners in protective custody were hidden behind a variety of old blankets and sheets with peep holes to hide their identities. Now, bars have been replaced by windowed doors and "protected" prisoners have uniform coverings on the outside of their cells so guards can check on them. Those housed in minimum, medium and maximum security cell blocks are allowed to socialize outside of their cells on weekends and are allowed to wear civilian clothing and retain personal possessions such as television sets, radios and musical instruments. Some minimum security prisoners have had pets.

One of the warden's biggest headaches is recruiting and keeping security guards. The attrition rate is extremely high, he says, and the average length of employment is four years. Contributing factors to the high turnover is low starting pay, tension, poor working conditions, and when "short-handed," some officers have had to work three consecutive shifts. Officers working in segregation have been subjected to physical abuse: "Food thrown on them, urine, garbage, and whatever else is available." There are some seventy-five correctional officers who are "lucky to receive twenty hours of preservice training before they're put to work," he says. "They get that training here at the prison from a staff development officer." A high percentage of guards have some law enforcement experience, but quite a few are recruited locally from Rawlins and some from national employment agencies. In addition to the security guards, there are three federal instructors; less than twenty administrative positions; employees who work in counseling, rehabilitation, medical and industrial services; totaling more than 130 employees.

The penitentiary is a city unto itself with self-sustaining shops where inmates work during the week. "When you look at it, our

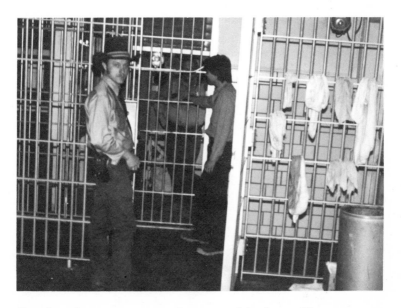

Guards in the protective custody section of the former Wyoming state prison — *author's photo*

population consists of felons who have committed various types of crimes, and our total community is lawbreakers. The frequency of crimes in here is much lower than the community at large," the warden says.

The print shop produces a monthly, informative in-house magazine, *The Con-versation*, which is written and produced by the inmates. Freedom of the press is strictly adhered to; Shillinger permits uncensored criticism of prison practices. One reporter who calls himself "The Shadow" wrote a column about his keepers:

> Some [guards] are pretty humorous to look at, even entertaining! But most of all, are they properly trained to cope with the situations that the prison atmosphere commands? . . . I believe that there must be some changes in the hiring practices of the prison staff. Sure there are some well-educated persons here but then and again there are a lot of rumpkins too. For heaven sake bring up the requirements, better the staff, and most of all, get rid of the hayseeds that bring down the quality of the administration.

The head of the administration, Duane Shillinger, is a native Wyomingite with a vested interest in the success of his liberal rehabilitation program. The stockily built warden was born in Sheridan in 1938, the son of Virgil and Merna Arbogast Shillinger. The eldest of three children, he was a "B" student, quiet, didn't participate in sports nor get into any trouble, according to his mother. He graduated from Sheridan High School in 1956 and enlisted in the navy where he spent four years in Virginia, England, and Morroco, Africa, as a radio operator. He also married Darlene Buchhoulz, whom he met in high school. Shillinger then attended Sheridan College where he majored in counseling and psychology before transferring to the University of Wyoming, working part-time in service stations and an orphanage in Laramie for disturbed children. He began working as a prison counselor in 1967 and worked his way up to warden in 1979, after two previous wardens quit in as many years. Shillinger works six and a half days a week and it's a twenty-four-hour job. The phone rings constantly, frequently in the middle of the night, leaving the warden with little time to spend with his wife and three children.

The new prison has been called "a boy's camp" by observers

who feel that Shillinger's methods of operation are too lenient, but the warden believes that his almost-500 prisoners shouldn't be treated like "hunks of flesh. There are two kinds of prison management," he says. "Reactive management where you wait for a fire to start and try to put it out. Pretty soon there are so many fires that you can't put them out. Or there is proactive management where you strategically examine the total operation and decide how best to manage each element in a wise, economical, practical and efficient manner."

Phil McAuley, senior editor-reporter—*author's photo*

PHIL McAULEY

"Never talk about a story"

Phil McAuley's life has been as varied and colorful as anyone
interviewed for his *Casper Star-Tribune* column or *Wyoming
Horizons* magazine. The award winning editor was nominated for
the Pulitzer Prize for his breaking story on Charles Starkweather,
Wyoming mass murderer, but he feels that doing his job "is reward
enough."

The senior editor-reporter was born in New York City, March
2, 1927, the second to the youngest of eight children. His father
immigrated to this country in 1910, following imprisonment in
Dublin, Ireland, for participation in one of many revolutions,
leaving his wife and three children behind until he could "afford
to bring them over." His mother narrowly "missed the boat" — the
Titanic — in 1912 and came to America aboard the *Majestic*.

"My parents never intended to stay," McAuley says in his New
York-Irish brogue. "My father owned property in Ireland, but
after my sister died in New York, my mother refused to go back
to Ireland and leave a child buried here alone." His father died

when he was five, and he earned money by "shining shoes." His two older sisters found jobs and his mother became a chambermaid at the Deacon Tower Hotel in New York City during the depression. She brought home magazines left in hotel rooms by guests and her young son began reading the British magazine *Punch* and *The New Yorker* before he started first grade. "So I became a good reader," he says, "but I was terrible in math."

McAuley tried to enlist in the Marine Corps when he was sixteen, but the recruiter opened the birth records book and "caught" him. The following year he enlisted in the navy where he learned the basics of news reporting from a war correspondent on board a ship cruising between San Diego and Iwo Jima. Less than two years later, he was discharged from the service and returned to New York where he worked for awhile in construction before enlisting in the geodetic survey, a domestic branch of the navy which searched for ships wrecked off the East Coast during World War II. "We wore navy uniforms and went searching for wrecks around the Florida keys," he explains. "The waters hadn't been surveyed in the years since 1940, and a lot of ships had been knocked off the coast of Florida." Sailors also searched farther north with wire drags and charted the location of the wrecks for salvage attempts.

While in the geodetic survey in 1946, he decided that he should further his education and went back to New York where he was employed as an iron worker to earn money for college. "I wrote away to about two dozen colleges," he recalls. "The Ivy League schools immediately upped the tuition [after the war] to keep trash and working people like me out." He was accepted by several smaller schools, including Missouri Valley College where he enrolled as an undergraduate student in economics. The G.I. Bill helped to pay his way because he was contributing to the support of his widowed mother.

"The first year was the hardest," he says. "Once you got beyond that, there was a big drop-off, and then you could transfer to just about any college your second year." He transferred to the University of Missouri "and then the G.I. Bill expired and I expired with it." He later went back to earn his master's degree, but during the intervening years he worked in construction and newspapers; among the dozen newspaper jobs during his career were the City News Bureau of Chicago and the *Sedalia* (Missouri) *Times-Record.*

He married Theresa Wradec in 1951, "a Slavian girl from Sugar Creek, Missouri, from a family of thirteen children." McAuley remembers telling her mother at the wedding: " 'Don't worry, Grandma, I promise you, no wife of mine will ever work.' But she's been working every bloody day since with time out for babies." Theresa McAuley has worked as a secretary in various school systems as well as for oil companies.

The McAuley's came to the Rocky Mountain states in 1954, with their one-year-old daughter, Clare; the newsman was looking for work. He tried the *Denver Post* and the *Rocky Mountain News* but was told that there were no openings. The advice he was given was "go out into the hinterland, start stringing, make a name for yourself, and when something breaks, come in." So he wound up in Casper, Wyoming, planning to stay just "until something broke in Denver, but I found that Casper was everything that I ever wanted in Denver," he says.

The bearded writer started out at sixty-five dollars a week as a general assignment reporter and his wife found work at a printing company for forty dollars a week. Together they homesteaded on Casper Mountain and bought "a little cabin and winterized it. The payments were fifty dollars a month, and I paid for it by cutting wood." McAuley and deputy sheriff, Roy Street (now deceased), would cut two cords of wood, split and deliver it for thirty-five dollars a cord. Then they would cut two more to make their payments, each "buy a bottle of whiskey and head for home. We'd make more money cutting wood than we would all week at work," he laughs.

The reporter "went through all the chairs" at the *Star-Tribune* as first state editor, city desk editor, news editor, managing editor and finally senior editor and editor of the Sunday magazine. Along the way, he wrote some sports news although he isn't particularly fond of athletics and did some oil reporting as well as general news. But his favorite subject is people. Personality profiles filled his thrice weekly columns—"McAuley's Wyoming" and the recently conceived Sunday magazine, *Wyoming Horizons.*

Although McAuley professes to "not think much" of collecting journalism awards, he's proud of the "Associated Press Managing Editors Award" he received following his breaking coverage of the Charles Starkweather murder spree which culminated with Starkweather's capture in Douglas in 1959. McAuley was the first reporter to write about the massacre, and with the award came the nomination for the Pulitzer Prize. The Pulitzer went to a woman who wrote about the Little Rock school crisis, however, "and in retrospect, I think they were right," he says. "It had a much bigger impact than the slaughter of people. I've never been much for awards. I think that doing your job is reward enough and getting paid for it." Besides his editing and writing jobs in Casper, he free-lances for *Time Magazine, The New York Times* and he once wrote for *Newsweek.*

Recent changes in the newspaper business have left the veteran editor with mixed feelings. He's proud that his newspaper can "literally get a news story on the front page in six minutes" from telephone call to paste-up. "That's incredible, but we've tried to get into too much soft news, featurized stuff. I think it's coming back to hard news, because it has to. I've also contended that an inch of hard news is worth a yard of feature. The newspaper business remains the same: to inform, educate and entertain. Occasionally, you get all three."

McAuley feels that because pressure is exerted by broadcasters, newspapers can't compete and are headed back "to the days when it was the heyday of journalism when the bright writer was in demand. Right there in Denver, they're headed for the biggest newspaper war in years," he says. "With the Times-Mirror syndicate buying out the *Denver Post*, they're putting on a 100 percent increase in the editorial budget alone. The *Post* is going AM [morning edition] and the *Rocky Mountain News* has surpassed the *Post* in circulation, so there will be two papers battling it out in an enormous market. They'll also be concentrating on good writers."

The senior editor advises students to look for a profession other than journalism because "a bad situation exists. The business is contracting all the time. There's an enormous amount of kids who jumped into journalism because of (Woodward and Bernstein) and they all want to be investigative reporters. Nobody wants to write obituaries, which is an art in itself. When I was trained, a person appeared in the newspaper three times during

his lifetime: when he was born, when he married and when he died. That was really drummed into me." Nobody wants to serve as an apprentice anymore, he says. "I'm really concerned for these kids. There will always be a market for the printed word, but the new generation coming up has been weaned on the tube. Why should there be anything on newsprint now when they can see it on TV? [Broadcasters] can grind it out with a few good leg-men, a couple of editors, and put it out over the TV cable. That way, they don't destroy a forest overnight and there's no distribution problems."

The *Star-Tribune* moved into a multimillion dollar facility on the west end of Casper during the fall of 1981, with the latest electronic gear available to the statewide newspaper. Despite the "six-minute news delivery," he is concerned about the "sloppiness" caused by electronic word processors. "There's no proofreaders anymore," he says. Reporters compose their stories on video display terminals which feed into the composing room to be pasted-up, without editors to scan the copy for errors. "Essentially, it's made us not only newsmen and newswomen, but printers as well. This new process is speed up, speed up, speed up."

McAuley taught journalism during the 1965–66 semester at Western Washington State University where he advised the student newspaper and did some public relations work. He also worked weekends and nights at the *Bellingham Herald* newspaper, "but I didn't like it," he groans. "Number one: it rained, rained, rained. Secondly, I wasn't ready for boneyard. It was very easy work, but the world of academia is pretty much of a boneyard to me." So he returned to the *Casper Star-Tribune* as managing editor.

His daughter, Clare, has followed in her father's footsteps and has worked for a number of newspapers. Following graduation from the University of Wyoming, she wanted to work for her father, "but I wouldn't let her," he says, because he doesn't believe in nepotism. His son, Michael, has worked in the oil fields since he was thirteen.

Beneath his gruff newsman's exterior lies a well camouflaged heart of gold, according to a former associate. McAuley has experienced and written about more aspects of living than most people would care to partake, including trips to his parents' war-torn homeland. When asked about future subjects he'd like to pursue, he says: "Never talk about a story or you'll talk it out. There are literally dozens and dozens of them that I want to write, and I intend to do them."

(Note: Phil McAuley left the *Casper Star-Tribune* in April 1982 following a policy dispute with the publisher.)

Jean Goedicke, artist

JEAN GOEDICKE

"It's best not to tell too much"

The Jean Goedicke Art Gallery is tangible evidence of the esteem in which the watercolorist is held by her colleagues. The Wyoming native was honored in June of 1981 by fellow artists in Casper who named the new wing of the West Wind Gallery for her. Jean has dedicated her life to art, fledgling artists and counseling the jobless. Ranking high among her numerous achievements and rewards, however, was serving as surrogate mother for her nephews.

"Jeanette" Goedicke was born in the Lost Cabin area near Lysite, Wyoming. Her parents, Ernest and Florence Walker Goedicke, were employees of J. B. Okie, wealthy cattle baron who found Jean's mother working in a drugstore in Jamaica while his family was on a world tour. Florence was the adopted daughter of an English army officer who married her mother after her father, Leonard Barrett (brother of Elizabeth Barrett Browning) drowned before his daughter was born. Florence's adoptive father, Alfred Walker, was stationed in Jamaica where she, a younger brother and three sisters were born. The J. B. Okies hired Florence as governess for their children and took her to Lost Cabin in 1904. She later imported her siblings following the death of their mother and desertion by their father.

Ernest Goedicke was hired to landscape Okie's property – called the Big Teepee – at Lost Cabin. He arrived from Omaha where he had "laid out Kurg's Park" as a landscape gardener following his family's immigration from Saxony, Germany. He married Florence Walker in 1906, and the two of them homesteaded on Copper Mountain near Depass the following year. "Jeanette," their oldest child (named after the first Mrs. Okie), was born in 1908, followed by five brothers. The youngest boys, twins, died at an early age.

The family moved to the D-Ranch in 1911 on Bridger Creek where Jean's father farmed, raised livestock and operated the Holt post office, before moving to his brother Otto's place nearby where they went into the cattle business. Ernest Goedicke erected a one-room shack on the property to be used as a school, and a neighbor child was "borrowed" to make them eligible for a teacher during the months of June, July and August. Florence taught her children during the winter months and "was proud that they were up to grade level" when the teacher arrived in June. When Jean advanced to the seventh grade, a full-time teacher was hired by the Goedickes and lived at the ranch.

In 1921, the Goedicke brothers borrowed several thousand dollars from an Omaha man to purchase a herd of cattle, but disaster struck when a "hard winter" set in, killing the entire herd. Bankrupt, the family loaded up their possessions into a wagon and buggy during the summer of 1922 and moved into Riverton where Goedicke grew a truck garden. The following year, they bought two lots with one "papered shack and a chicken house" for $600 and began to remodel it.

Jean's father then found a job as postmaster and storekeeper in DuNour at the Wyoming Tie and Timber Camp. Every three or four weeks he would go home to buy lumber and leave instructions for his wife and children "to put a window in here and plaster a wall there," Jean says. "And finally the day came when they could take off the roof to put it over the whole house. The rain came and we had to cover our piano that we had gotten with some other furniture in a trade for some horses."

She inherited her creative talent from her father who did some "romantic paintings" and played the flute. Jean remembers the time he sat playing his flute in the doorway of their homestead at Depass when a herd of wild cattle cautiously approached the cabin. "They came closer and closer until they were within ten feet," she says. "Then my father had to laugh and as he took his mouth from the flute, they turned and left."

The shy, soft-spoken girl started high school in Riverton and "was scared to death of algebra. I got through the first half of the year and failed the last half so I knew that I was too stupid to go on to college," she says. But the superintendent convinced her that she could pass algebra and geometry, and she was later able to hand in "almost perfect papers." She graduated from high school in 1926 and arranged for a teaching job on a ranch on the edge of the Arapahoe Indian Reservation, qualifying for it by attending summer school at the University of Wyoming. But she taught only one year because she was plagued with feet and ankle problems, and was told by doctors that she needed a more sedentary job. "I thought you could teach school and be seated," she says, "but you can't. I had to go to Mayo Clinic many times [over the years] for surgery."

During the "Great Depression" she worked as a clerk, stenographer and "kind of social worker," she says, "although I wasn't qualified for that kind of work." When the depression finally began to ease and the relief programs ended, she took a state merit test and was hired by the Employment Security Commission (ESC) in Casper. Her job title in 1938 was "computer" or clerk who refigured claims for worker's benefits. She continued to work in the contribution section until 1955 and progressed from junior to senior clerk, and junior to senior accountant after completing night classes at Casper College. She also took courses in Spanish, English and art, and sold a few of her paintings.

In 1955, she transferred to the Employment Security Service and became supervisor of special services to the handicapped which later expanded to include older workers, youth, minorities and prison "retirees." The Employment Security Commission arranged for her to take counseling courses at Casper College, and she earned her associate of arts degree by attending night school. Many of the required classes were extension courses from the University of Wyoming, so she began spending her summer vacations at UW until she earned her bachelor's degree, and eventually her master's. She also attended a number of noted artist's workshops around the country and took advantage of counseling workshops funded by the ESC, from coast to coast, to extend her trips to include visits to local art galleries, theatres and museums.

Although she never married, Jean became a mother to her nephews in 1960 when her brother, Fred, gained custody of his sons following his divorce. The boys joined Fred and Jean in her small, white carpeted home in East Casper, bringing with them a dog, cat and five hamsters. The following year, Jean and her brother bought a larger house to accommodate two growing boys and their accessories. Her annual xeroxed Christmas letters to friends were filled with humorous anecdotes derived from her surrogate motherhood.

Jean frequently accompanied her brood on fishing trips, but her tackle box was filled with watercolors. Her favorite spot from which to paint was the tailgate of her station wagon or the hood of her brother's jeep. She also became interested in geology; she took a college course and joined a local group to go on organized "digs," becoming their official photographer and artist.

Wyoming's Mobile Symposium was the brainchild of Jean Goedicke and fellow Casper artists in 1970. "We were meeting at Frances Forrester's house and decided that we should be getting some of the money from the National Endowment on the Arts," she explains. "We had a little brainstorming session and set up a whole program in one evening. We figured that we would conduct a traveling symposium of five of us to go to the small towns around the state to have workshops and demonstrations. In other words, we wanted to get things moving in Wyoming. And we did."

The workshops were held on weekends with Frances Forrester teaching oils; Peggy Simson Curry, creative writing and poetry; Mike Hanna, children's workshops, painting and clay; and George Trimble and Jean Goedicke taught watercolor and drawing. Getting artists started was their primary function including inmates at the state penitentiary in Rawlins and the girls' school in

Sheridan. The artists did an excellent job activating tiros around the state for eleven years until the Reagan administration budget cuts severed their financing. Jean and George Trimble have continued, however, as "Friends of Artists" without outside funds.

Jean sold her first painting during the early '30s while she worked for the "relief agency" in Riverton. "It was a picture of the Tetons in an old rough frame," she recalls, "and it was terrible." She prefers to sketch and paint her pictures on location, but weather and circumstances often prevent her from doing so. She takes 35 mm slides to use in her studio in conjunction with numerous sketches she does at the scene. She has taken hundreds of slides during the years since her retirement in 1972 from the Employment Security Commission and has traveled to such exotic places as Jamaica, Hawaii, New Zealand, Guatemala, Australia, Spain, Mallorca, Italy and Mexico. Many of her finished paintings from these areas have been shown in one-woman shows in a number of states and have traveled in art exhibits. Many others have been sold, even before they were framed.

The Casper artist was the "driving force" behind the Artists Guild's West Wind Gallery which came into existence in a former church and fire station on West Fifteenth Street. She and other artists sought out plumbers, electricians, painters and workmen to donate their time and talents to renovate the building as a showcase for area craftsmen and visiting artists who conduct workshops there.

Jean joined the Artists Guild in 1941 and was recently responsible for obtaining their tax-exempt status. She also is a member of Casper's "Scotch and Watercolor Club," the Western Artists Association in San Francisco and the American Watercolor Society.

Among her many accomplishments, she was listed in *Who's Who in American Art* in 1976, was a featured artist in *In Wyoming* magazine, is past president of the Wyoming State Gallery Advisory Board and has served as judge of many art competitions.

She describes her own work as "mostly realistic, though I never carry paintings too far with too much detail. I suggest things, leaving the viewer to interpret in his own way—to arrive at his own interpretation. It's best not to tell too much."

Ed Bryant, science fiction writer—*author's photo*

ED BRYANT

"Fiction by omission"

Science fiction writer Ed Bryant didn't like growing up "in the wilderness" at the foot of Sybille Canyon on a ranch between Laramie and Wheatland, so he escaped from his environment by reading. "I felt a great sense of isolation," he says, "and I looked for companionship in books. I read everything I could get my hands on." Bryant looked for the "most exotic and colorful destinations" he could find fictionally, which started out as fairy tales and mythology, later evolving into science fiction (SF) and fantasy. "Those were my favorite books and I read them voraciously through junior high school."

While in seventh grade, his family "moved into town" where he and two younger brothers attended school in Wheatland. "I hit the peak of my science fiction and fantasy reading while I was in high school, and it stopped dead while I was in college. But I started reading it again when I got out of school, and that's when I started writing seriously."

Bryant graduated from Wheatland High School in 1963 and enrolled at the University of Wyoming as an engineering student. "But that didn't work out." So he switched to a general arts and science program. "The semester before graduation, I was informed by the department that I would have to declare a major—I had enough credits to graduate, but I needed a category to put on the diploma—so I became an English major," he explains. "I had discovered that I had some faculty to bring words together, though at that time because of the general lax standards of English departments almost everywhere, I had no idea that I was really as bad a writer as I actually was."

The slender, bespectacled student immediately began work on his master's degree at UW with a Ford Foundation scholarship. He then attended a six-week workshop in Pennsylvania, taught by experienced writers and editors. Bryant attempted to "coast through" the workshop by rewriting stories from high school and college which the workshop teachers "tore apart." His problem was overwriting. "All the verbiage was there, but none of the content," he says, "so the first practical advice given me was to pare down my style to the very minimum that I could get away with."

Taking the advice, he wrote an original story at the workshop and sold it to an editor who was collecting material for an anthology for Doubleday Publishing Company. "So that was a tremendous, positive stimulus to continue writing. On one hand, in 1968 dollars, I had earned 150 of them, and the assurance that the story would be published and appear in libraries and book stores. It was a great ego reward. On the other hand, I wanted to find out whether it was a fluke and I was just a one-story writer."

For the next year, Bryant was a one-story writer. He coauthored one piece which sold, but it was two years before he began to sell his work on a regular basis. In the meantime, he worked in his uncle's stirrup buckle factory in Wheatland to support his writing habit.

"Probably because of my initial reading background, I began to write science fiction and fantasy stories," he says. "It wasn't a conscious thing, that's just what I wrote. And I would find myself writing all sorts of stories that would go off to The New Yorker and Atlantic [Monthly magazine] during the early 1970s. And I was having all sorts of rejection notes from editors saying, 'We like this but it is too science fictional for what we tend to run.' So I'd send it off to the science fiction markets and they would say, 'This is too literary for the sort of things we're using. Can't you do something with some spaceships in it?' " Bryant considered himself in a "bind," but he kept writing and sending out his stories until he found a particular editor who liked his work and was willing to "bend the rules a bit" for him.

Bryant categorizes his work as "supernatural and even horror fiction. The best way I can describe it is fiction by omission," he says laughing. The award-winning author omits hardware in his stories such as "bright, shiny machines" or spaceships. And he's never set any of his stories or books on another planet. "Everything I set has been relatively close to home, either in geography or in time." A number of his stories have taken place in Wyoming, including one titled *In the Shade*, which occurs in Wheatland and focuses on the impact of the power plant and the people it displaces.

"It's supernatural fiction," he explains, "and the main character is a witch who's helping a friend whose mother keeps disappearing from the senior citizen's home. The question is why? Aside from the fact that people are being displaced by progress, the story is about a new type of ghost I think I've invented."

The long-haired author has written and sold more than 100 stories and six books since his first sale in 1968. His first book, *Among the Dead*, is a collection of short stories published in 1973. *Phoenix Without Ashes* came along in 1975, a novel based on the pilot television series "Star Lost." Then in 1976, he published *Cinnabar*, another collection of short stories; and the following year, *2076, the American Tricentennial*, an anthology he edited of other writers' original poetry and fiction. Jelm Mountain Publications of Laramie brought out another collection of his short stories entitled *Wyoming Sun*, which preceded *Particle Theory*, published by Pocket Books. He also wrote two screenplays.

Bryant supplements his income by working with the Poetry-in-the-Schools Program in Wyoming although he now lives in Denver. "I've cut it down to twenty speaking days or four weeks each year," he says, "because it takes whole blocks out of my writing time. But it's important to me to get out to situations such as teaching in the schools, especially if it's a school in a town where I've never been before. In some respects, I'm forced to live by my wits—even after all these years I'm not that polished a teacher in the schools—and I'm forced to survive by my wits because it's a new classroom, a new administration, a new community; and I have to adapt whatever I know about writing."

Some schools provide extracurricular benefits which add to Bryant's writing expertise. He recalls one student whose father owned a gold mine in Nevada. The writer later found himself 450 feet inside the mine shaft without "OSHA or safety devices." The student's father told him, " 'Remember to keep your head inside the cage or one of those two-by-fours will take it off at the shoulder.' And it would have," he says, shrinking deeper into the sofa. "But that was great fun. And those things happen to me all the time when I'm out in the field to teach. That's important to me as a writer." Bryant also likes to participate as a workshop panelist and does one-time speaking engagements.

He reads other writers' work as often as he can and ferrets through trade publications to "see what's happening" in his profession. "I try to keep up with what's being published, announcements of forthcoming anthologies and magazine projects," he says, "and sometimes you see your chance to make a sale." One of his "favorite sales" occurred in 1980 while he was riding in an elevator with a well-known literary agent who happened to mention an anthology he was collecting. Bryant asked if he could submit some of his work, and the agent replied that he was unaware the writer worked in the supernatural field. Two story submissions later, the agent accepted one which appeared in *Dark Forces*, which was published by Viking Press. Bryant found his work among that of such famous authors as Stephen King, Joyce Carol Oates and Isaac Asimov. The anthology was included in several book club selections and printed in a number of foreign languages. "And I wouldn't have known about it except for pure dumb luck."

Two of Bryant's stories won the Nebula Award, in 1979 and 1980, the "Oscar" of science fiction writing. But he's not content to rest on his proverbial laurels. He continues to grow as a writer and produces work for the science fiction reader who is predominantly male, Caucasian, and between the ages of twenty-five and forty. Primarily young professionals, "who aren't directly involved in science or technology," his readers "have a healthy interest in those things."

Since the first science fiction magazine, *Amazing Stories*, appeared on newsstands in 1926, the readership has tended to be young, middle class, white men. Within the last fifteen years, however, more women—the number has more than tripled—and members of minority groups have begun to read and write science fiction and fantasy. Another group that appears to be coming upon the SF scene, according to Bryant, are the gay writers who will be able to sell their fiction themes which "generate from gay society, and this will be a very lucrative market. It reflects a growing acceptance of types of behavior different from the reader's previous experience," he says.

The bachelor writer laughingly says he'd be a rock star if he were not in love with his typewriter. "But one thing that I'd really like to do, something I've wanted to do for years," he says, combing back his long, brown hair with his fingers, "is to write a science fiction novel about Wyoming in the near future: my version of 'Land of the Lost.'"

Emmie Mygatt and Roberta Cheney at writers' conference—
Cheney Collection

ROBERTA CHENEY

"We must have laid a good foundation"

Wyoming Writers owes its existence, in part, to a Montana native, Roberta Carteek Cheney. The historical writer lived in a number of western states before moving to Sheridan with her psychologist husband, Truman, in 1968. There she met Emmie Mygatt, a transplanted easterner, whose creative writing class at Sheridan College had evolved into a group called the "Range Writers." The group was later responsible for the formation of the statewide writing organization.

Roberta heard of the Range Writers shortly after her arrival in Sheridan, but when she inquired, she was told that she would have to wait until the group's revered mentor, Emmie Mygatt, returned from New York to "okay" her membership. "I guess they were a little leery of someone who barged into town and said, 'I want to belong to a writer's group,'" she laughs. But before long, she and Emmie were inseparable friends and the "mother superiors" for the fledgling authors. Roberta and Emmie later collaborated on a book titled *Hans Kleiber, Artist of the Big Horn*

Mountains, which won the Western Heritage Award as the best Western art book of 1978 from the "Cowboy Hall of Fame" in Oklahoma City. They also edited and contributed material to *Road Map for a Lone Writer* in 1972, a guidebook for isolated writers that was written by the Range Writers. Some 400 copies were sold before the booklet was picked up by an eastern firm and republished under the title *Your Personal Writers Workshop.*

When the Range Writers had grown to more than twenty-five members, they decided to sponsor a writing contest within the state; expecting, perhaps, 10 entries. Instead they received an avalanche, some 200 from all over the state. "We were amazed at the neophyte writers who came out of the sagebrush," Roberta says. "And it was a thrill for me to find that all those people were interested, although they had so little encouragement and chance to talk shop—or to advance with their writing." Because of the response, Range Writers decided to hold a workshop at Sheridan College in 1973, inviting professional writers from other states to lecture on various aspects of their craft. The two-day conference was attended by writers from surrounding states as well as Wyoming. Equally important was the formation of a statewide group during the workshop, Wyoming Writers. Vandi Moore of Woods Landing was selected as the first president and annual workshops and writing contests have been held ever since.

Roberta instigated the annual "Emmie Award" which honors member writers within the state. The first recipient was her friend, Emmie Mygatt, for whom the award was named. When Emmie died of leukemia in 1977, an Emmie Mygatt Memorial Fund was also established to give scholarships to writers participating in workshop sessions. "Emmie always said, 'If you start something that can't go on without you, it wasn't worth starting,' and it's obvious that Wyoming Writers has gone on, so we must have laid a good foundation." Of her late friend she says: "Emmie was a tremendously inspiring person to work with, so unselfish and willing to help others," a sentiment echoed by many others.

In 1975, the two friends had decided that a Wyoming Writers anthology should be written—a potpourri of fiction, poetry, non-fiction and photography which Roberta and Emmie spent six months editing. They were gratified to receive another avalanche of manuscripts from writers across the state. The book was published by Big Horn Books, a now defunct Wyoming publishing house, and it sold some 1,500 copies.

In order to be "refilled by a more professional group," Roberta accompanied Emmie to a Western Writers of America (WWA) convention in 1969 and became a member of the prestigious worldwide organization. She later held various WWA jobs such as national contest chairman for the "Spur Awards." Another year she served as a nonfiction judge. In 1978, she took over the reins of the organization and found the presidency a "big job. You just try to keep the ship from tipping over," she laughs, "and keep things on an even keel. I answered hundreds of letters that year and tried to keep the wheels greased. It's a very rewarding job, and it gives you the opportunity to meet a lot of influential people as well as giving yourself some status."

Sheridan Range Writers hosted the Western Writers of America convention of 1972 under Roberta and Emmie's direction. "All those starry-eyed people who were just beginning to write got to rub elbows with the old pros who were successful," she says. "And they in turn were inspired and enthused by the western flavor and the people who helped with it." WWA members returned to Wyoming in 1980 to attend the Casper convention.

In addition to her writer organization accomplishments, Roberta used her talents to help create the Sheridan Fine Arts Council in 1977, which includes performing and visual arts. She met with Lynn Simpson, Betty Ward, poet Jane Johnson and sculptor Bunny Connell for several months to lay the groundwork for the Arts Council to give Sheridan "power" when requesting federal and state grants to fund their programs and activities. The group also looked for a building to house their various disciplines and found the carriage house of the Kendrick mansion. Lynn Simpson now directs the community theatre group there. Roberta was a member of the drama group board as well as the community concert and worked with her husband in the Episcopal church.

When Dr. Truman Cheney retired from his psychologist's post at Sheridan's veteran's hospital in 1978, the couple returned to Roberta's family ranch site, sixty-five miles from the Wyoming border near Cameron, Montana. Although Roberta and her younger brother, Raymond, had sold off some 7,000 acres of their family's landholdings, Roberta kept the old ranch house and outbuildings along with four or five acres where her children and their families come to visit on a regular basis. The Cheneys remodeled the big ranch house and converted the milk and ice houses into cabins for their children, along with the bunkhouse and laundry buildings that had been used for decades when her parents, George and Pearl Storey Carkeek, were actively ranching years before.

Her children, Karen Shores, a professor of ballet at the University of Utah; Maureen Curnow, associate dean of the College of Arts and Sciences at the University of Montana; and Larry Cheney, an animal nutrition consultant in Colorado, bring their families (Roberta's seven grandchildren) and friends to stay in their cabins at the ranch. Roberta cooks for her entire brood and does more housework during those visits "than I've ever done in my life," she says. "But I feel that in these days of world upheaval, my goal is to help these three young families to hold on to some values."

The Cheneys also entertain frequent visitors during hunting and fishing seasons because they live at the foot of the game trail in the Madison Mountains. "Everyone stops in," she smiles, "and I love it. I'm never lonesome, but I'm not getting much writing done."

Roberta and her brother grew up on the ranch and attended a one-room rural school on Bear Creek where she completed her first eight grades in six years, placing her in high school when she was twelve. Her grandmother moved temporarily to Bozeman, Montana, to board Roberta, her own daughter (Roberta's young aunt), and several other girls so they could further their education. An outgoing child, Roberta found the outside world quite different from the sheltered, "secure" life she had experienced "back at the ranch surrounded by loving parents, uncles and aunts."

She graduated in 1928 from the Gallatin County High School and got her first job cooking for a hay crew on the River Ranch that summer. She cooked for ten men, three meals a day for seven dollars a week. With her first paycheck she bought a taffeta formal to wear when she attended the University of Montana at Missoula

Roberta Cheney, Wyoming writer and historian – *Cheney Collection*

that fall when she was sixteen. A member of Kappa Delta sorority, she graduated in 1932 with a B.A. degree and began teaching high school English and biology in the small town of Lavina, Montana. "Fifty years ago there weren't too many opportunities open to women," she says. "You could teach or be a nurse. And I run when someone gets sick. I always wanted to be a teacher, but then I found that I didn't really like teaching because you spend half of your time in discipline, and the students don't seem to want to learn. That really annoys me."

Roberta met Truman Cheney, who was teaching and coaching in the neighboring town of Cline. They were married in 1934 and lived in Cline for two years before moving on to Melstone where he served as superintendent of schools. She began writing professionally after they moved to Helena, Montana, where Cheney was appointed state vocational guidance director. During the next seven years, Roberta wrote newspaper and magazine articles and was in partnership with her oldest daughter, Karen, in a ballet school. Although her mother claims to have two left feet, Karen does not and still dances professionally, on occasion, with Ballet West.

Roberta's husband's jobs also took them to Townsend and Buhl, Idaho; Reno, Nevada; Portland, Oregon; Sturgis, South Dakota; and Sheridan, Wyoming. Cheney earned his doctorate from Oregon State College at Portland during the 1950s, and he began teaching psychology and guidance counseling at the University of Nevada at Reno. In Reno, Roberta and her two youngest children attended classes, and she still praises her creative writing instructor who encouraged her to continue "writing seriously."

After Maureen and Larry graduated from the University of Nevada, Roberta and Truman moved to Sturgis, South Dakota, where he served as a psychologist at the Fort Meade Veteran's Hospital. While there she wrote her first book, *Names on the Face of Montana*. She's been writing steadily ever since. Her work includes numerous free-lance magazine and newspaper articles, one fiction sale to a children's magazine, and she coauthored a book titled *Music, Saddles and Flapjacks* as well as *The Windows of St. Peters* and *Big Missouri Winter Count*. She also coedited the Western Writers of America anthology, *Women of the West*, and recently produced a revised edition of her Montana place-names book.

The outspoken writer did graduate work in creative writing at Columbia University of Nevada and Oregon State College and is listed in *Who's Who in American Woman* and *Contemporary Authors*.

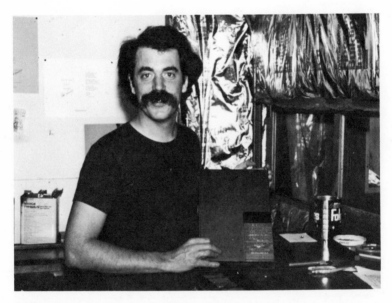
Tom Rea, printer and poet—*author's photo*

TOM REA

"I want to publish the best books I can find"

Letterpress is a dying art, but a few dedicated printers are keeping the process alive by producing exquisite, limited edition poetry books. Tom Rea of Story, Wyoming, is one such printer and poet who, with his wife Barbara, has successfully produced five books of poetry at their "Dooryard Press," with considerably more in the offing.

The young couple became interested in the printing process in 1977, when they attended a writers conference in Port Townsend, Washington. There they met Sam Hamill, editor and publisher of the Copper Canyon Press, who shared a house with one of Tom's college friends, and liked his poetry. The following summer, Tom and Barb returned to Port Townsend through a Poetry-in-the-Schools Program for the northwestern states and became Hamill's apprentice printers through yet another grant from the National Endowment on the Arts.

"That entire summer we learned to print and at the end we got to print my [poetry] book, *Man in a Rowboat*, on their press under Copper Canyon's name," he says. Learning the basics was "a real peon's job with just the thinnest pieces of spacing going in between the letters. You have to work with it and clean out the drawers to begin with, so you realize the size of things that you are going to have to work with. It was really enlightening, and it served a dual purpose by introducing us to the increments that we were going to have to recognize."

Tom and Barb began setting type for poetry books and were instructed by Terese Hamill, Sam's wife. "She just sort of immersed us in her work, and she's a good teacher," he says. "Every time we'd have a question, she'd stop whatever she was doing and pull down two books off the shelf and say, 'Well, the first time I did it, I did it this way; and then I realized that it didn't work well, so I did it this way.' So she always had examples from her own experience, and she was very patient and verbal. She never said, 'I did it because it looked right'; she always said more unartistic things, something we could deal with. Terese gave us everything she had."

The Reas returned for three consecutive summers and learned to design books; print, clean and ink the press as well as binding chapbooks by sewing the backs. "Sewing the book is really simple," Tom says. "Then there is a writers conference in the middle of the summer, and they always do a printing workshop, so poets can get to set their own poems, letter by letter, and it's a good learning process." Barb adds: "Because we were there, we were expected to be teachers at the same time we were learning. And we had to come up with the answers we were being asked. So when I did have the answer, I felt much more confident. I had to teach printing during the writers conference while Tom was teaching poetry."

The novice printers also learned to do broadsides, poems printed on one sheet of paper. "And that's a different way of printing than bookmaking, so that really stretched my mind about all the various things you can do with the process of printing. It's like detective work," Tom says. "If you can visualize how you want it to look, you can figure out how you can get it done. And I was really impressed with how Sam and Terese could make all those great books."

258

The Hamills have produced a great many books for young and unknown poets under their Copper Canyon imprint through state and federal grants, but now that funding has been drastically cut, they've charted a different course. "Sam used to believe that he was put on earth to print books for people who have never been in print before," Barb says. "And he's done a lot for a number of young writers while becoming a better printer, which is what we want to do. And now that they have a good national reputation, they've been asked to give lectures all over the country. It's a natural progression. So in 1980, they stopped doing young poets and started doing established ones, including Ezra Pound. They're doing beautiful limited editions of poetry books and a few pamphlets."

Barb and Tom bought their 1918 vintage press in 1979 from Ralph Moorehead in Sinclair, Wyoming. They had written to every printer listed in the *Directory of Mining and Manufacturing in Wyoming*, inquiring whether they had a press for sale. "We asked for letterpress and a lot of people have gotten rid of them because they're so slow. Offset is much faster. But we kept getting letters from people saying, 'Oh, if you had just written to us three years ago. We sold it for scrap metal' or 'If you had just written to us six months ago.' That came from the *Buffalo Bulletin*. Finally came an answer from Ralph Moorehead, a retired engineer from Sinclair who said 'I can let you have my twelve-by-eighteen platen press for $500.' We wrote back and said 'We're coming to Wyoming in March, and we want to see your press.' We did and bought it. Then we picked it up the next June," Tom says.

Tom was completing his master of fine arts degree in creative writing at the University of Montana at Missoula, and Barb had earned her bachelor's in anthropology the year before. They returned to Wyoming to find a house to fit the press; they found one with a double garage which Tom converted into a print shop, later adding another room, in Story, southwest of Sheridan.

When they returned to Sinclair to load up the press they expected three, maybe four sections, but "there were fifty or sixty pieces all lined up in his garage," Tom remembers. "He had very detailed instructions, however, and had written backwards as he took it apart so that we could put it back together again and assemble it from top to bottom. He even took polaroid pictures to show us how to assemble the press. He was a very nice and methodical man. After taking the press apart, he got it out of his basement by sliding it up some ramps, so it was all ready for us when we arrived."

Barb's two brothers-in-law helped them put the press together by "thinking as hard as we could," he says. Since that time they've produced four poetry chapbooks: *The Map Maker's Lost Daughter* by Lee Bassett, *Distances* by Charles Levendosky with artwork by artist George Vlastos, *Sleeping on Fists* by Alberto Rios and *Mapping My Father* by Ripley Schemm. They also produced a trade edition of Peggy Simpson Curry's book, *Summer Range*, in offset, with plans for another Bassett and Levendosky in 1982. Tom doesn't publish his own work because "a writer needs an editor," he says. "Some people publish their own work and it suffers for that reason. They publish too much and they can't tell the good from the bad."

The Dooryard Press is self-supporting "more or less," according to Barb. "We usually have enough money from one book to another to buy materials for the next book. And we do a little bit of job work [from local merchants]. We haven't taken anything out of the press account so it would keep going by itself, although I did take out ten dollars for coffee beans."

"Trade books should be sold in bookstores and chapbooks [those without spines] should be sold in person to those who know letterpress and what it's worth and are willing to pay for it," Tom explains. "We should charge enough to make it worth our time, but we're not in it for the money, although it would be nice to make some." The Rea's first chapbook cost $3.50, the last one $8; the printing and paper quality have improved with each one, and all have sold well. "We've even been able to pay our poets something."

Tom supports his family by teaching English Composition at Sheridan College two nights a week and conducts the Poetry-in-the-Schools Program in his area. He also gives poetry readings and participates in writers workshop sessions in a humorous and direct manner that appeals to all ages. Judging poetry contests is another pastime.

260

Tom didn't write poetry until he migrated to Wyoming in 1972 to help his Uncle Bart Rea build a cabin on Casper Mountain. Born in Pittsburgh, Pennsylvania, in 1950, the third son of a banker, Tom was a good student, "and somewhat of a bookworm, but I didn't really like poetry," he says. "I read mostly novels, and I tried to write fiction in college and a few years afterward, but I never really wrote poetry until I met Charles Levendosky at Casper College in 1974, when I signed up for his class. Charles really encouraged me to start sending off my poems to publishers, and a year or so after that, he got me into the Poetry-in-the-Schools Program—which was nice because it made it sort of official that someone was paying me to teach."

Tom also began substitute teaching in Casper besides working for a survey crew, a counselor at a halfway house for alcoholics and a bookstore where he met Barbara Scott. The couple were married in 1976, the summer they moved to Missoula to attend the University of Montana. Tom made forays back into Wyoming occasionally to teach Poetry-in-the-Schools and then took a year off from the university to teach poetry in the Montana school system while Barb earned her B.S. degree. He returned to school in 1978 to work on his master of fine arts degree in creative writing while Barb worked in a book bindery. The following year they bought their press and home in Story, gradually acquiring the necessary accessories to print their Dooryard publications.

Tom has since been honored as "Poet in Residence" at Sheridan College, become the proud father of two children and acquired a printer's ink transfusion; he'd rather produce books than teach or most other things he can think of. "I feel committed to it," he says. "And I don't feel like a press that comes and goes, like so many others have. I hope to do something similar to what Sam Hamill has done. I just want to publish the best books I can find."

Alice Bubeck, owner of KVOC, Casper —*author's photo*

ALICE BUBECK

"People have been very good to me"

Alice Bubeck never dreamed, as a home economics major at the University of Illinois, that she would marry the man who created sound effects that sent chills up her spine as she listened to the "Inner Sanctum" radio show or made her laugh when "Fibber McGee and Molly's" closet contents crashed to the floor. Nor did she envision herself behind a microphone, years later, ad-libbing her way through commercials and interviewing guests in Casper, Wyoming, on her own country-western music radio station, KVOC.

The attractive, blond Kentuckian has always loved country music. "My mother's people were all farmers from Louisville, and farm people like fiddling music," she says. "So we kids just kind of fell into it." Alice and her sister were moved around the country by their traveling tire-salesman father and their mother, finally settling in Chicago where she attended college. "I was a Phi Beta Phi who used to sit up in the den on the top floor of the sorority house with the other girls to listen to the radio every Wednesday night," she says, "doing our nails and putting up our hair in curlers and listening to "Inner Sanctum." I never dreamed that I would marry the man who was doing the sound effects."

Harry Bubeck started out as a page at NBC in Chicago and worked his way up to sound technician, then into programming and production, finally becoming West Coast NBC radio manager before buying his own radio station in Casper. As a sound man, he created Fibber McGee and Molly's closet, a noisy half-minute clatter for which he used his mother's old pots and pans to make the noise—and later Alice's. The comedy radio show was a hit of the 1940s.

After twenty-five years with NBC, Bubeck bought KVOC in Casper, but he first went into radio advertising and surveyed the market to determine which areas were most promising. Casper, Wyoming, and Fort Collins, Colorado, radio stations surfaced on top of the list, and Bubeck made a down payment on the station located "out in the country across the street from Casper College." It was housed in a former hamburger drive-in with "an old white picket fence around it at Wolcott and College Drive." They purchased KVOC in 1964 and remained in that location for four years until they built a modern station atop Fifteenth Street hill near Beverly.

Harry Bubeck suffered a disabling stroke as he sat at his desk, a few months after buying the radio station. Aged fifty-two, he was paralyzed on his left side and has become progressively incapacitated since that time. The Bubecks were granted a Federal Communication Commission (FCC) license, however, because they hired a manager to run the station.

Alice had spent her married life raising two daughters and three sons and participating in "PTA, scouting and church." Radio broadcasting was not part of her schedule until 1970 when she decided to take over the "Coffee Klatch" program which aired each morning. The show's previous hostesses kept getting married and moving away, or didn't like the job to begin with.

"I was so frightened the first time, my mouth dried up, and I could hardly talk," she remembers. "My husband told me to take home a tape recorder so he could coach me, and I could play it back on the air the next morning." She was caring for her husband at home and his bedridden mother, so some nights she was too tired to tape the next morning's program and finally decided to brave the microphone in person. "I explained to the [listeners] that I was new at it and if they would go along with me I would do the best I could – or I would quit. They must have thought I was crazy, but I finally became more relaxed and my salespeople got me a client or two." She now has as many sponsors as the FCC allows for a half hour show, and they've been with her for years.

Alice schedules her guests a couple of weeks in advance – local people or those who are traveling through central Wyoming. If there are no guests, she reads from various magazines and newspapers and comments on current topics. When guests are present, she sits down with them before the show and asks pertinent questions. "But I don't ask embarrassing questions," she explains. "I admire Barbara Walters quite a bit, but I feel that she asks a few too personal questions and she digs."

The youthful senior citizen changed the name of her morning show from "Coffee Klatch" to "The Women's Magazine of the Air," but she doesn't confine her subjects to women. "I have as many men, if not more, who listen in," she says. "Shops all over town are tuned to KVOC, and the men have gotten used to my voice. I get a kick out of passing construction sites, when I'm on tape, and hearing my voice. After the July 1978 hailstorm, new roofs were going up all over town, and the boys on the roofs would wave to me as I drove to work and back," she laughs.

Alice ad-libs her commercials after going downtown to view merchandise on Saturdays. "I really enjoy that. I visit with my people and hear about all the new babies, weddings and divorces." During the week she arrives at the station at 8:45, does her talk show from 9-9:30 and her fifteen-minute "Swap Shop" show at 11 A.M. Between programs she sits at the station switchboard to answer calls and goes home at noon to "keep Harry company." She returns at 2:45 and works until 5:00 P.M.

"I don't write any of my [advertising] copy," she says. "I just do it. I would rather go downtown and see something to talk about than have someone just tell me about it. I get to see all the new things in town and see how the town is growing. And it gets me out of the house."

Alice took her husband on a "Love Boat" cruise on the Princess

Line from Los Angeles to Puerto Vallarta several years ago, and on a recent cruise from San Juan, Puerto Rico, through the Panama Canal for Christmas. "I'm keeping it a secret," she said before the Christmas cruise; she was anxious to surprise Harry.

Her husband needs an attendant at all times, and KVOC is Alice's main diversion. Her youngest daughter was killed in a car accident in 1975, shortly after her wedding, and four other children are scattered around the world. Her surviving daughter, Pat, lives in Venezuela with her husband who is general manager of a Ford Motor Company assembly plant; her son, Bryan, works for Haliburton in Libya; Roger owns an employment agency in Chicago; and her youngest son has worked as a "disco jockey" in Phoenix.

KVOC plays Alice's kind of music. "I like songs that tell stories," she says. "Repetition bores me. So much of it is one sound or one word, and they run it into the ground. I like to relate and cry in my beer. I've got problems the same as [the singers] have." Her favorites are Kenny Rogers and Loretta Lynn. "I like the way Kenny sings 'Ruby, Don't Take Your Love to Town,' and the cry in Loretta's voice when she sings. I'm sympathetic."

KVOC was a "middle of the road" music station when the Bubecks bought it in 1964, "but my oldest son thought country-western might be a good direction to take," she explains. "We had a little problem with the younger members of the family liking rock, but the older members liked country and there was no country station in town." The switch to Kenny Rogers and Loretta Lynn proved to be a smart move.

The country station has been so successful that the Bubecks were able to buy another station, KLO in Ogden, Utah. Alice hopes to acquire several more. "It keeps you alive, it really does. And I enjoy working with all these young people. They're really patient with me," she laughs, "and I enjoy being around them." High school students often come in off the street looking for jobs at the station, she says, without prior experience. But Alice thinks they should first enroll in broadcasting school. "We've had some young people here in the station who've gone to those schools and they're good. The high school kids don't know what to touch and what not to touch around the equipment, and it's high powered and could electrocute you in a minute," she says.

266

The station purchased eleven new canary yellow cars as an advertising gimmick in 1979, which Alice says worked quite well. KVOC was the only country station in Natrona County until the local FM station, KATI, decided to make the transition from rock to country in 1980. An immediate outcry arose from Casper's youth and went unanswered until another FM rock station cropped up in 1981. KATI did an about face, and Casper once again has one country AM station, a middle-of-the-road music channel (KTWO), but two FM "rocks."

Alice is proud of the "Outstanding Citizen's Award" she received in 1979, from Casper's Ramada Inn, and is very fond of the city in which she lives. "People here have been very good to me," she says. "The whole town has, and I guess that's why I'll never leave. The people are wonderful.

"You know, I've discovered something about Wyoming people. They need each other. We live out in the wide open spaces and when you break down on the highway, they stop to help each other. And in bad weather, people pitch in and help each other. Wyoming is quite an experience for us after living in Chicago most of our lives."

Leo Sprinkle, who studies psychic phenomena—*courtesy of Leo Sprinkle*

LEO SPRINKLE

"They are preparing us for the new age"

D r. Leo Sprinkle saw his first unidentified flying object (UFO) in 1949, while a student at the University of Colorado at Boulder. He and a friend had just left a symposium on general semantics – "How People Talk about Reality" – and were asking each other to describe whatever they saw, while trying to define whether it was the "first or second level of reality" when they saw it.

Just before sunset, they spotted a "round, metallic object about the size of a fingernail at arm's length. There seemed to be a glint or reflection on the outside edge, and we could see it glimmer about every second as if it were turning," he says. "I tried to turn it into a helicopter or an airplane, but it wouldn't go that way, so I thought it must be some kind of homing device or air force object. I didn't want to talk about it to other people; I didn't even want to think about it."

His second sighting occurred in 1956, while he and his wife, Marilyn, were driving home just after sundown. They saw a noc-

269

turnal light glowing bright red over the Flatiron foothills of the Rockies. He stopped the car, and they got out to watch as the brilliant object began to hover between them and the foothills. His wife described its movement as "back and forth," but Sprinkle called it a "dipping motion. We watched it for several minutes while it hovered and moved and then gradually moved toward the northern edge of Boulder and disappeared. So after two sightings, I couldn't deny that something unusual was going on."

When Sprinkle finished his doctoral studies in counseling and guidance at the Univerity of Missouri in 1961, he was hired as an assistant professor of psychology at the University of North Dakota. "One of the first things that I did was to check out a UFO case that I had read about, because I had changed my views," he says. "When I was an early graduate student, I had scoffed at my wife for being interested in ESP and UFOs. She had tried to get me to read some books on the subject, but I wouldn't have anything to do with them."

After his second sighting, however, he began to read everything that had been written on the subject, and he checked into the reported case of a "guardsman air force pilot who claimed to have been involved in a dog fight with a UFO near Fargo, North Dakota." He was still not convinced, but joined several organizations such as National Investigations Committee on Aerial Phenomena (NICAP) and Aerial Phenomena Research Organization (APRO) for which he became a consultant. Until that time there had been "rather general studies done of people's characteristics and attitudes" who claimed UFO encounters, so he began learning more about specific attitudes and traits. He found, as other investigators have discovered, that a wide range of characteristics involved the "old, young, rich, poor, well educated and poorly educated. Some experienced psychotic or neurotic symptoms, but no more than the average population," he explains.

Sprinkle began his study of psychic phenomena in 1964, while a professor of guidance and education at the University of Wyoming. He expected to take five years to complete his study, but he's still compiling data. "I decided to survey a hundred people who claimed psychic impressions of UFO phenomena—those with the most interesting claims—and use hypnotic techniques to help them recall more about their experiences. I now have over 200 people who have participated in the survey." Participants begin by filling out a six-page questionnaire which requests information such as age, educational level, occupation, whether they've seen a UFO and how they interpreted the sighting—whether they've experienced a "loss of time" in conjunction with the sighting, whether they have psychic ability (a common ability reported after being abducted), etc.

Those surveyed who claim UFO abduction participate in Sprinkle's hypnotic sessions and are given psychological and personality evaluations by a trained psychiatrist who is paid $150 a session by Sprinkle himself. At first, he found his subjects in newspaper reports, then from telephone calls to APRO headquarters in Tucson, Arizona. Dr. Sprinkle has traveled all over the country at his own expense to interview those who claimed sightings and abductions, including the classic, most publicized case of Betty and Barney Hill. Although he wasn't in on the original investigation, he has interviewed Betty Hill on a number of occasions and is impressed with her sincerity and recall.

Sprinkle has thoroughly investigated a number of Wyoming UFO cases, including that of Carl Higdon, Rawlins oil well driller, who was abducted while hunting elk in the Medicine Bow National Forest in October of 1975. Higdon encountered a strange "man" who took him on board a spacecraft from a clearing where the hunter had tried to shoot an elk, but his bullet traveled fifty feet and fell to the ground. Higdon told Sprinkle under hypnosis that he felt his legs and arms were clamped to a lounge that resembled an astronaut's chair, and that a helmet with wires protruding from it was on his head. The alien, "Azo I," as he called himself, told Higdon that the helmet was "reading" him. The craft then began to move away from Earth, and he found himself in what appeared to be a space tower with a brightly lighted object that resembled a Christmas tree, which hurt his eyes. Under hypnosis the second time, he recalled being taken into the tower where he saw others who resembled humans.

Higdon was taken up to a large room in an elevator and examined under bright lights, which made his eyes water and caused him to cry. He was then told, "We'll take you back if you're not one of them." Higdon doesn't know the meaning of that statement, and he was found in his pickup truck around midnight babbling, "they got my elk," by friends he didn't recognize. Three days in a hospital, x-rays and examinations by doctors turned up nothing other than the facts that he had no drugs or alcohol in his system. And that some tubercular spots had disappeared from his lungs.

When questioned at length, Sprinkle found that Higdon has some American Indian ancestry, a characteristic found in a high percentage of "abductees." He has also learned that a large number of those who claim they were abducted are from the lower-middle income group in this country, although a higher percentage of professional people in Central and South America have reported UFO experiences.

Sprinkle himself is from a lower-middle income family. Born in Rocky Ford, Colorado, the son of a barber "who was also a butcher," young Leo began working in the "seed fields" at four-teen, when not in school. The second son of four children, he read incessantly and participated in basketball, football and track while in high school. He studied psychology, sociology and history at the University of Colorado, where he worked in the residence hall kitchen four and five hours a day, washing pots and pans. Graduating with a B.A. degree in 1952, he married a music major who wrote down the notes to the songs he composed on his ukulele. He then served in the army for two years in Germany, before returning to the University of Colorado where he began work on his master's degree in personnel service.

He completed his thesis in 1956 and worked as instructor-counselor and acting director of psychology at Stephens College in Missouri, before starting his doctoral studies at the University of Missouri. Ph.D. in hand, he was hired as an assistant professor of psychology at the University of North Dakota in 1961.

Since that time, Sprinkle has taken part in a number of UFO symposiums, two of which were held in Brasilia, Brazil, and London in 1979. He has lectured at various colleges, universities and parapsychological symposiums besides serving as consultant to network television shows: "That's Incredible," "20/20," "Tomorrow Show" with Tom Snyder, "In Search Of" with Leonard Nimoy plus a number of local shows in Laramie, Cheyenne and Denver. A member of the *Playboy* magazine UFO Panel, he also served on the *National Enquirer* UFO Panel from 1972–80. Sprinkle is a member of fifteen professional societies dealing with psychology, hypnosis and parapsychology in addition to his post at the University of Wyoming where he holds the title of director of counseling and testing, and professor of counseling services.

To finance his UFO investigations, Sprinkle conducts group regression clinics around the state, charging twenty-five dollars per person for a six- to seven-hour session. Using Dr. Helen Wambach's methods of "past life therapy" he hypnotizes participants who bring sleeping bags to recline on, and sack lunches to take part in the reincarnation experience. The psychologist finds that nine out of ten people are able to successfully recall impressions of former lives. At the conclusion, they are asked to fill out questionnaires about their experiences, a copy of which is forwarded to Dr. Wambach in San Francisco.

Dr. Sprinkle's list of "papers" and publications is long and impressive, with subjects ranging from parapsychology to hypnosis and self-improvement programs. A health and exercise "nut" himself, he plays basketball three times a week and engages in other forms of self-improvement because he wants to make sure he's around when the "U-Folks" decide to land or communicate directly with Earthlings. Sprinkle still gets a fair amount of good-natured ribbing and some cynical remarks, but he no longer hears "Hey, Leo, seen any little green men lately?" The social climate is changing.

If the "U-Folks" haven't shown up by 1995, when he retires from his job, he plans to work full-time in UFO investigations. "I feel that I'm kind of a shepherd to help people who are going to be frightened when they learn whoever is behind the UFO phenomena is around," he says.

There is scientific evidence that aliens visited Earth as long ago as 10,000 years, and Sprinkle doesn't think that they are monitoring us in preparation for invasion to take us slaves. "They could have done that a long time ago," he says. "It's worse than that. We've got to learn, to grow up. It seems as though they are preparing us for the new age. We're about to graduate and become cosmic citizens."

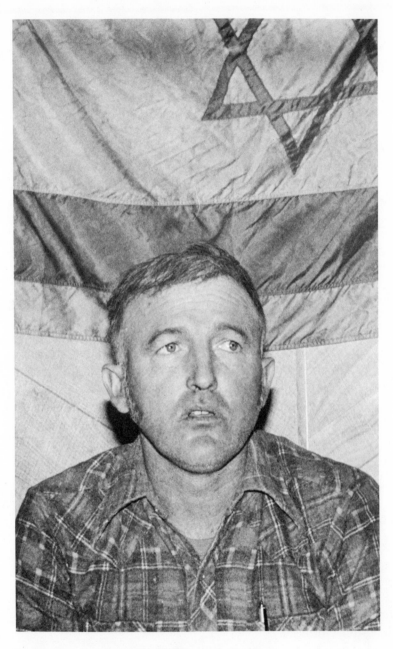

Pat McGuire, abducted by UFO—*author's photo*

PAT McGUIRE

"106 species of aliens observing earth"

Pat McGuire's well was said to be the largest one this side of the Mississippi when the 750-horsepower pump was installed in it in 1976. The 16-inch, 350-foot well could furnish water to the entire town of Laramie, he says, pumping 8,000 gallons per minute; and it irrigated his 2,500 acres of malt barley, hay, certified seed and pasture. It took considerable determination, hard work and know-how to put it there on a piece of land that everyone knew had no water. But McGuire built the drilling rig himself with the help of a Wheatland machinist, after being turned down by countless drilling contractors from around the country. Seven years after he began, the well was completed and the farm put into production. Five years later, however, the McGuire farm was all but abandoned; the infamous "UFO showcase" had rung down its own curtain.

Pat McGuire grew up on a farm in the Wheatland area where he attended high school before buying some land north of Laramie in the Boswell area with his father and two brothers. The dry land was to be used for cattle grazing. In 1971, he suddenly acquired a burning desire to drill a well on his property and raise some crops. Everyone told him that it was nonsense. There weren't any deep well aquifers in the area. He might be able to drill a small well to water the cattle, but there certainly wasn't enough available for farming. His family wouldn't go along with him so he bought them out, and for reasons unknown even to himself, he selected a spot and marked it with three rocks.

No one would drill the well for him. He called drilling companies as far away as California and Texas, but nobody was interested. He finally found a drilling contractor who started the hole but gave up, moved off and left. So he persuaded a Wheatland machinist to help him build a drilling rig according to some plans that McGuire had drawn up. The project took a year to complete and the drilling began. Before it was completed, however, another drilling contractor "showed up out of the blue" and finished the well for him at a depth of 350 feet.

The farmer then bought a 750-horsepower pump from Denver and began planting and irrigating his crops, up to ten circles of barley at one time. His wife and eight children then moved to the ranch from Wheatland into three old trailers until they could afford to purchase a double wide mobile home. It wasn't long before they found that their isolated ranch, some thirty miles northeast of Laramie, was frequented by extraterrestrial craft which put on dazzling aerial displays over the McGuire property.

The first time a UFO appeared, McGuire ran out of his trailer and got within about a thousand feet of the ship before it turned off its lights and disappeared. The following night he heard cattle bawling. "There were 900 head of them out there and the dogs were really barking, so I ran out and found a dead cow. I assume that they operated on her and just dropped her there," he says. "She didn't even struggle, and she was a good three-year-old. I didn't believe in UFOs then and the first time I saw one, I thought it was a weather balloon from the university."

Spacecraft began appearing regularly over McGuire's property, and he watched them through his twenty-power spotting scope from his kitchen window. A number of times they would land, and he and his family would hear them walk up the porch stairs, open the door and move around the rooms—but they couldn't see them. "Sometimes they would knock on the side of the trailer to let us know they were here," he says. The short, stockily built farmer took infrared pictures of the spacecraft one night and Los Angeles television station KABC had the film analyzed at the Jet Propulsion Laboratory in Pasadena, California. The jet lab enlarged the film 250 times its original size and found that "an extremely bright object has burned a hole in the film," according to a letter to McGuire from KABC. The result was a special show on KABC, and a subsequent feature that appeared on "That's Incredible," which aired during the fall of 1980 on ABC.

When a second cow-related incident occurred on the McGuire farm, he called in the sheriff's department—and after a brief investigation was told that he should contact Dr. Leo Sprinkle at the University of Wyoming, but it was almost two years before Sprinkle had time to go out to the McGuire farm. The farmer observed a huge ship "the size of a football field" hovering over the herd and found a bawling calf the next morning a mile from the rest of the cattle. The cow had vanished. He thought the first cow had been the work of a Laramie "sex" cult, but now he felt that it was the work of aliens. "They could have taken a cow on the other side of the ridge," he says, "but they wanted us to see them."

A cow mutilation occurred on the Benick ranch fourteen miles southwest of Laramie and forty-five miles from McGuire, in September of 1980. Ranch manager, Ron McDonald, felt that the death of the eighteen-month-old Angus heifer was unusual and not due to predators, as did McGuire who investigated as soon as he heard the report. An APRO investigator was also on the scene taking photographs. Wyoming state veterinarian, Dr. Herman Hancock, conducted a brief examination of the cow four days after her death and concluded that it was the work of predators. The teats, anus, tongue, genitals and some hide had been removed in what McDonald and McGuire felt were razorlike incisions. They also agreed that predators never eat the hide or the ears of an animal. Some 8,000–10,000 cattle mutilations occurred in the United States during the 1970s, according to Dr. Sprinkle.

Once McGuire had been tested and hypnotized by Dr. Sprinkle, mysteries occurring on the ranch began to unravel. Under hypnosis he recalled being abducted by aliens in 1973, as he was hunting in the Tetons where he had served as an outfitter and hunting guide for fourteen years. He describes the aliens as six feet tall, slender with pale white skin, large heads and eyes, appearing as if they had been cast from the same mold. They wore one-piece black outfits of a jerseylike material, belted in black with a silver "star of David" belt buckle. The aliens were bald and spoke to him both verbally and telepathically, he says.

They said that he had been abducted before, and they had told him where to drill his well and that they would "provide the water. They said it was to be their showcase," he says, but isn't sure what that means. McGuire was also told that there are 106 species of aliens observing Earth, and that they travel in eight different dimensions. "Some of them just come to check soil samples, and I imagine that they're the ones who leave burn spots," he says. "They told me that I'm supposed to let people know that they're here."

McGuire observed spacecraft often hovering over his fields, watching him work during the day for up to two-hour intervals. Other times a "red ball of fire" would hurtle over the top of his crops and "terrify" the animals and his hired men. Employees would usually pack up and leave without a word, "and I don't blame them," he says. One night while he was alone, he heard someone moving about his trailer and he raised up in bed but fell back paralyzed from the neck down. Earlier that evening, he says the aliens were shutting off his sprinklers, one every fifteen minutes. "At first it was fun, but after awhile it really got to me so I went out and thought I'd take a shot at them—not to hurt them but to tell them to cool it. What I was really trying to do was to give them another chance," he explains. "By that time they left [the sprinklers] run, so I thought they got the message." But it was McGuire who got the message when he woke later to find himself paralyzed. Later, under hypnosis, he recalled "their further instructions" while he lay screaming in his bed.

One of the more bizarre aspects of Pat McGuire's life is the "Israeli connection." He was told by his abductors that he has worked to "save" the Israeli people in former lifetimes, and that he was needed to lead them to Cairo during the 1973 war with

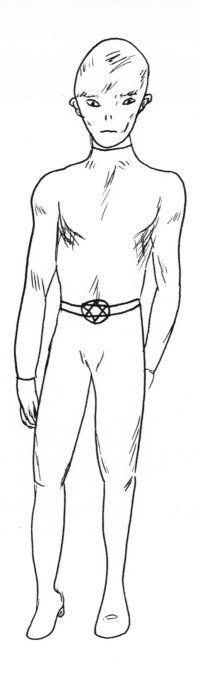

Pat McGuire's impression of space aliens after hypnotic sessions (redrawn by Jean Mead); clothing was a black, jerseylike material, and there was a Star of David on the silver belt buckle.

Egypt. McGuire describes his "out of body experience" with graphic detail as the general who led his troops in American and English made tanks against the Russian supplied Egyptian third army. "We were so close to Cairo that we could see the buildings," he says. "And then the American 82nd Airborne parachuted troops down to stop us." Under hypnosis, he told Dr. Sprinkle in a different voice than his own: "Those sonsabitchin' Americans are stoppin' us. Let's run over them. They've only got rifles," and he ordered his troops to "start engines." At that instant, however, he says that he was zapped back into an alien craft and was told that the war was over for him when he protested that it was still going on.

McGuire later encountered a paratrooper from the 82nd Airborne Division on leave in Laramie and told him that he knew of the American intervention in the war. He was then told that it was a military secret ordered by Henry Kissinger, and that no one was supposed to know. The farmer later told his story to a member of the "20/20" ABC news team and the reporter called Washington, came back "white faced" saying he "wouldn't touch it with a ten-foot pole because it would ruin the Camp David Accords." McGuire says the aliens can intervene to a certain extent and were attempting "to prevent the annihilation of the Jews. They had to step in and help them out," he says.

He was also told that the aliens, who wear the star of David, are against abortion because there are "all those souls waiting to be reborn." McGuire is Irish-Catholic, and the theology stems more from the Mormon religion although they do not believe in reincarnation.

When news of McGuire's successful well and UFO contact became known in Laramie, stories concerning his sanity immediately began circulating. (He was tested by a psychiatrist and psychologist and found to be normal during Sprinkle's evaluation of him.) But worse than being called "crazy" were the instances of vandalism which occurred as a result. The farmer feels that three separate groups were responsible for the destruction to his crops and farm equipment, totaling some $200,000 between 1976 and 1980. "They'd take the bolts out and spray a chemical on the shutoff valve so the sprinklers wouldn't shut off," he explains. "So the sprinklers would just go around and twist the heads off.

It would take about a week to fix, and you couldn't catch up with the watering, so you lose your crops."

McGuire, when contacted by phone January 31, 1982, was losing his land, divorcing his wife, and says he was told by the aliens that his land is going to become a Jewish settlement—and that he was to run for public office.

Jean Jones, book publisher—*author's photo*

JEAN JONES

"Jelm Mountain Pub"

Admittedly temperamental and gregarious in nature, Jean
Jones left home and husband to begin a life of her own
in the publishing business after thirty-six years of marriage. "I
wasn't getting any feedback, and I was literally starving intellectually at home," she says. So she left, after earning her master's
degree at the University of Wyoming, to teach school and build
a book publishing company, Jelm Mountain Publications in
Laramie.

Jean was born in Modesto, California, in 1919, the daughter
of Frank Huntington Russell and Allene Kelly Russell; a third
generation Californian. Her father quit school in the ninth grade
and eventually became a practicing dentist in Nevada. Her
mother's family was in "real estate" and persuaded the Russells
to return to Modesto where they were given some property, and
Russell became a dental technician.

His outgoing daughter, Jean, was the third child of five, who
grew up near the grape vineyards and orchards so prevalent in

the fertile San Joaquin Valley. "I guess I was pretty much of a tomboy," she says. "I competed with boys in everything that I did. I never played with dolls, but I played every kind of sports" including football. She also read lots of biographies and "true stories that challenge you. One of my favorites was *Helen Keller*." The tall, slender, dark-haired girl "elected a liberal arts course in high school that included foreign languages, music, art and lots of English and history" before she attended Modesto Junior College and San Jose State where she earned her B.A. degree in 1942.

"I immediately got married, which surprised me more than anyone else, because I had decided that I didn't care too much about marriage," she says. "But this fellow came along and was very persuasive. So I graduated on the eighteenth of June and drove clear across the country to Virginia where we were married the first of July." Jean met Troy Jones at a San Jose YMCA dance where he and other soldiers socialized in the evenings. "He was a nice dancer, was very intelligent and we had similar interests." They dated every night for three weeks before Jones was transferred to Virginia where he entered officer training school. Two month's worth of correspondence followed before she graduated from the university and they were married.

"Troy progressed in rank faster than you would think possible, partly because of the war problems, but he was also the oldest of seven children and the sole support of his family most of the time because his parents were not well. He just popped right to the top and came out a major at the end of the war," she says. Jean secured a teaching job at the army base "and the salary was awful—$90 a month and $900 a year." She taught fourth grade until it was apparent that she was pregnant; and Russell Jones was born at Walter Reed Hospital before his father was transferred to the China-Burma-India theatre of war in 1944. Jean returned to California's central valley then to teach school while her mother cared for her baby.

Jones returned home in December of 1946, and the family moved to Amarillo, Texas, into his parents' home so that Jean could "take care" of her mother-in-law who was dying of cancer. Following his mother's death, Jones became a building contractor and constructed a large "beautiful home in Amarillo" for his family. When his father died a short time later, they took in his six brothers and sisters. "We had a huge house and rented out the upstairs rooms," she remembers. "I was running the whole house and taking care of all the kids—we had two of our own and never less than thirteen people at a meal. And I got very involved in church service where we spent all day Wednesday and Sunday." Jean taught Sunday School classes and began to put her writing talent to work by authoring a bible school textbook and contributed regularly to teachers and childrens religious magazines. She wrote and sold both fiction and nonfiction pieces as well as "fun things like crossword puzzles and games."

"I did a couple of biographies of Jonah and Paul," she says with a broad smile, *Jonah Had a Whale of a Time* and *Little Missionary with a Big Job*. Paul was a tiny man, but what an impact he had on the world!"

Involvement with the Southern Baptist Church led to Jones building a church of the same denomination in Laramie in 1959, located on the corner of Ninth and Hancock. "And we discussed what a delightful place Wyoming is," she says. Because her husband was having health problems they decided to move to the "cowboy" state in 1962, where they purchased a small guest ranch on the Laramie River, thirty miles south of the town of Laramie, and five miles from the Colorado border in the Jelm community. Their four sons ranged from a senior in high school to a first grader when they settled into the ranch.

"So I was running a guest ranch as a business, and by that time, needing a lot more stimulation than I was getting intellectually," she says. The ranch consists of "200 acres of rock and river— marvelous trout fishing and the finest dry fly stretch in the world." She then decided to return to school and commuted with her sons to Laramie where she earned her master's degree in guidance and counseling in 1969. But after a year, she decided that she would rather be teaching school and had a number of rural elementary teaching jobs during the next few years.

In 1974, her second son, Keith, a student at Baylor Law School, was editing the *Law Review* and discovered, while home on vacation, an "old timer" in Laramie whose work he wanted to publish. Jean agreed to finance the venture and her son edited Conrad Hansen's work, a booklet titled *I Live Again*, the restoration of a Model T Ford.

"We had a party for Connie and sold all the books and made enough money to pay our expenses. We gave the rest to him. And then in 1976, I decided to do some more of his stories, and that's how I got into the publishing business," she says.

During the period she was writing religious articles in Texas, from 1952–62, Jean says she felt that she wasn't getting any "feedback" from her family. "None of them would ever read anything that I was writing. And I was literally starving at home. But that made me realize that if you can't look to the people around you for support, it's time to get the hell out and on your own to do it." She and her husband separated several times before they were divorced in 1978, following thirty-six years of marriage.

Jean had started her small publishing business while still living at the ranch, using a spare bedroom to do her "layouts" before sending them to the printer. She had gotten bids from several printers before finding one in Michigan who would produce paperbacks and a few hardbacks for her for an average cost of one dollar each. "And they do beautiful quality work," she says, displaying a number of her most recent successes such as *Wyoming Sun*, written by science fiction author, Ed Bryant, a Wheatland native now living in Denver. And *Pachee Goyo*, written by Rupert Weeks, a native American, which Jean edited and hopes to sell in Germany.

Her second book was a collection of Conrad Hansen's short stories titled *I Remember: Stories of Wyoming*. She then met Emma Rice who had self-published her *High Altitude Cookbook* and offered Jean a flat fee to distribute the ones yet unsold. "And we sold her out and had a reprint made," she says. Her fourth book in 1977 was a bilingual poetry book—English and Spanish—written by Dick Fleck, a teacher at the university. She also began distributing existing books of other Wyoming writers to fill out her book catalog which she presents to prospective buyers.

Jean's first business location was at 304 South Third Street in Laramie, a small store on the main street which she rented on New Year's Day in 1979. After installing her desks and typewriters, she printed "Jelm Mountain Pub" on the window which prompted the entrance of many Laramie residents who wanted to "check out the new beer joint."

"Anyway, it was a marvelous location," she says, although she was feeling very lonely because she had "just left home." One of her sons and his new wife wanted to help his mother in her new venture, but Jean felt after a time that "it wasn't working out." So she turned the bookstore over to them and moved her publishing business to the Wagner Building where she produced three to five books per year. "The overhead there was eating me alive," she says, so she moved into her current location, a house just off Third Street, across from the A&W drive-in.

Her son and his wife decided to give up the bookstore in the spring of 1981, and Jean took it over and remodeled extensively, turning it into a book shop and coffee house. Live entertainment is featured as well as slide shows, and a "seminar-type discussion on Indian Affairs," among other activities. The coffee house is open from eleven o'clock in the morning until eight o'clock in the evening, and Sunday afternoons. Jean spends considerable time overseeing the operation as well as her publishing business. "I close down the store at eight and come back here [the publishing house] to finish up about ten at night," she says, "and that goes on 7 days a week, 365 days a year, except when I can escape."

Her next project is a color photography book for which she will write the text, and she plans to "finish my doctorate degree when I find the time." She also wants to return to England to do some research.

Jean Russell Jones calls herself "a late bloomer and my family is one of longevity," she says. "I was talking to my eighty-seven-year-old mother [who lives alone in California], and she was worried that I'm working too hard. I told her that this is the first time in my life that I'm working to capacity. I'm working for myself, and I'm doing all the things that I love doing. I'm not about to have a breakdown or throw in the towel."

Don Anselmi, Democratic committeeman for Wyoming—*courtesy
Don Anselmi*

DON ANSELMI

"I'm going to live until I die"

Super salesman Don Anselmi has suffered his share of adversities, most of them within a five-year span, but he rebounded each time, determined to live life to its fullest. A proven success in the business world, he'd rather be fishing off the Alaskan Kenai Peninsula or hunting white-winged dove with his black labrador in northern Mexico. National Democratic Committeeman for Wyoming since 1980, he has survived two political scandals, a divorce, the loss of his younger brother whom he idolized, the death of a valued employee and loss of public esteem.

The pyknic businessman probably inherited his "spunk" from his father, John Anselmi, a native of Rock Springs and son of an Austrian immigrant, who peddled fruit "up and down the railroad tracks" in southern Wyoming. During one of his trips he met a school teacher from Hanna whose father had been killed in a mine explosion. They were married and produced five sons; the eldest, Don, grew up to achieve financial success and undeserved notoriety. His business achievements are phenomenal but

"I never would apply myself in school," he says. "I was a free spirit before they even coined the word." School was never as important to him as hunting and fishing.

The Rock Springs superintendent of schools hunted and fished with his father and advised John Anselmi to send his "happy-go-lucky" son to a boarding school because he was "frittering his life away." So Don was sent to the Abbey, a Catholic school in Canon City, Colorado. "But I only stayed two years," he says, "because it was too tightly structured for me." He graduated from Rock Springs High School in 1946 and wanted to join the army but "flat feet" kept him out. "There was nothing else for me to do so I went to school in Laramie," but that only lasted three months. "That wasn't for me either."

He then went to Jackson where he worked that fall as a hunting camp packer. "We packed their camps in and their game out," he explains. When winter came "feeding those cattle in the snow didn't please me either, so I quit. I went back to Rock Springs where I sold beer and dry cleaning, and the guy who owned the cleaning plant asked me to collect some money for him." Anselmi collected ten dollars from a customer who happened to own the local credit bureau. He was so impressed with Anselmi's collection techniques that he offered the young man a job in his agency. Before long, Anselmi was taken into the business as a partner.

The Korean War then broke out "and they were drafting 4-Fs," he says. "So I enlisted in the air force." Anselmi attained the rank of corporal and was assigned the job of counseling servicemen on their insurance needs because he had sold some insurance while in the collection agency. He received his basic military training in Texas and was sent to Victorville, California, when a new base was opened up. It was his second residency on the West Coast for his father had briefly operated a diner on Sunset Boulevard in what is now Beverly Hills during the 1930s. But business was bad during the depression so the Anselmis returned to Wyoming.

Discharged from the air force in 1952, Anselmi returned to Wyoming where he went to work for his father in a car dealership in Rock Springs. "I didn't think that I could sell cars," he remembers, "but boy, I took off like gangbusters. My father was a top salesman, and I found that I could sell just about anything, too." John Anselmi and his partner decided to sell their business in 1956, along with a finance company they founded, and they told the younger Anselmi that he could take some of the cars on consignment to form his own dealership. Within three years his business was "booming," but two things made him decide to sell out to his largest competitor; "tight money in 1959 like now," he says, "and interest rates were sky-high." He also felt that his employees were letting him down. "I was in Idaho, steelhead fishing and elk hunting for ten days and when I returned I found that none of my fourteen employees had sold a car." So he sold the business. "Then I had nothing to do," he frowns.

He found something to do. He was a delegate for John F. Kennedy in 1960 and took his family to the Democratic convention in Los Angeles. He had married Dora Giovanini—a girl he had known all his life—in Rock Springs seven years earlier. They had three sons by the time the 1960 convention took place and their daughter, Gina, was born that September. Anselmi had asked state party chairman, Teno Roncalio, if he could represent Wyoming as a convention delegate, to which Roncalio reportedly replied, " 'My God, everyone in Wyoming wants to be a delegate.' " Anselmi was elected an alternate and took the place of his county's delegate when the man was unable to attend the convention.

He then decided to work for the Kennedy administration and took his family to Washington where "we knew a lot of people but everyone was running over each other as in any change of administration," he says. "Friends forgot each other, and I told Dora, 'this is not for us.' They returned to Rock Springs where he set up his own New York Life Insurance Agency and sold $1,100,000 worth of insurance during his first twenty-three days in business. "So the last five days I went fishing," he says.

He then acquired a summer home in Jackson and worked as a volunteer fund raiser for a home for handicapped children. He also became a partner in the Outlaw Inn, Rock Springs' utopian motel complex. Two managers were fired before the Outlaw opened its doors and Anselmi found himself in the manager's chair, assisted by Lauren Brown, whom he hired away from the Marriott Hotel chain. Brown was Anselmi's "right arm" and died of cancer while "everything else was going wrong."

Anselmi continued to be "relatively active in politics" and was asked by Roncalio in 1965 to run for party chairman. He lost to John Rooney, however, by one vote due to a snowstorm which kept some of his committed votes from materializing. "I thought it was the end of the world," he recalls. "As it turned out, it was the best thing that could have happened to me because the Democrats got wiped out in 1966. It wasn't John Rooney's fault. Lyndon Johnson was in and the Great Society programs weren't that popular, especially in Wyoming."

Anselmi then became Rooney's vice-president and was elected chairman of the Democratic party in 1970, where he served until 1978. "A state chairman can't do much really," he says. "There's no such thing as a strong, cohesive party organization – Democrat or Republican. Our state, primarily, tends to be independent. We might register as a Democrat or Republican, but people cross party lines back and forth. The Republican party is in a better position because the majority of registered voters are Republicans, but no thinking person in this country votes straight down the party line."

Money is always a problem, regardless of party affiliation, and party chairmen must also grapple with the problems of finance. Anselmi admits to donating considerable time and money to his party, including the use of his airplane, telephone and his pride. "I've never gotten anything out of politics except a lot of grief," he says, and with good reason. The first scandal occurred in 1974, an election year, following the furlough of an inmate from the state prison in Rawlins. He was "wired" by a justice department strike force team and sent into Anselmi's office with a self-fabricated story about some stolen shotguns from California. As was later learned, Neil Compton, who was attached to the state criminal investigative division, had arranged for the man to be released so that he could confront Anselmi with a "gun-running conspiracy story." The party chairman later submitted to a lie detector test and appeared before a Los Angeles grand jury before hiring Jackson lawyer, Gerry Spence, to handle his libel suit against the *Los Angeles Times*, *Denver Post* and the Associated Press which carried "the trumped up charge" to the public. Anselmi won the case in 1975, but settlement terms prohibit the revelation of the amount he received. "It wasn't enough to pay the lawyers what they deserved," he says, "but it was a moral victory." Anselmi lost another case, however; he and his wife were divorced prior to the trial.

Ray Whittaker, a Casper lawyer and Democrat, was also implicated in the gun-smuggling farce, and he held out for "a much bigger settlement." The reputation-damaging episode was politically inspired, Anselmi says. "The grand jury investigated and found that Compton was a liar. Now he's cut and run, leaving everyone to live with it."

The youngest Anselmi brother died in a 1978 hotel fire in Chicago; the tragedy compounding the chairman's grief, and the real reason he says he quit his political post. "Tom had a deep appreciation for the arts and taught at the University of Arizona. He loved music and poetry—he even made his wife a violin—and he had a pretty tragic ending for someone with such a beautiful outlook on life." Anselmi says the dark clouds hanging over his head were "continually raining."

Nineteen seventy-eight was also the year that he remarried his wife, Dora, and the time period when the grand jury investigated alleged corruption in Rock Springs following a "60 Minutes" television invasion of the area. The Democratic party was once again "embarrassed" during an election year, he says, and he retired as party chairman. "By embarrassing me, they rationalized that they could destroy any Democratic candidate and embarrass the entire party. Had I not been the state chairman, and just a motel owner, there would have been no reason to take after me."

Anselmi was elected National Democratic Committeeman in 1980, and he continues to do charitable work in his home state. The Anselmis spend considerable time now in their condominium in northern Mexico on the beach so that he can fish and hunt white-winged dove. "My plans are to enjoy life," he says, "and help my kids get started on the right foot. I'm going to hunt and fish and do things we enjoy. In other words, I'm going to live until I die."

Arline Cohen, chairwoman of the Wyoming Arts Council—*Dick Wittliff, photographer*

ARLINE COHEN

"If my life were not totally hectic"

Arline Cohen is an achiever who is totally dedicated to her creative endeavors, including the chairmanship of the Wyoming Arts Council where she has served since 1976. She has gotten a great deal of satisfaction and pride from her volunteer efforts with a number of civic organizations as well, but she's most proud of her three sons: two doctors and a lawyer.

"Would it sound corny to say that I feel very lucky to have raised three boys who turned into young men who are leading productive lives?" she asks. "I'd hate to think that I was living my life through my children." Her sons are second generation Cheyenne natives; Arline and her husband were both born in the capital city and lived just a block from each other, although they didn't meet until she graduated from college.

The youngest of three Pasternak sisters, Arline was "very introverted" and spent a lot of time reading as an adolescent. In high school she played piano, sang in the "Triple Trio" and participated in sports. Writing was another talent she pursued by working as a reporter on her school newspaper and yearbook. That talent eventually led to legislative reporting for the Intermountain Radio Network from Cheyenne during the late '70s. She also worked on college newspapers at the universities of Wisconsin and Colorado at Boulder where she majored in sociology.

She graduated from UC in 1950 with a B.A. degree and met Lawrence Cohen, the boy from down the street who had spent most of his youth in an Indiana military academy and then twelve years in medical school. They were married that fall, and Cohen practiced pediatrics in Cheyenne for nineteen years. While rearing their sons—Craig, Robin and Brent—Arline served as den mother, took some art lessons, played her piano and sang soprano in the local chorus.

"When I became a mother I thought 'What can I give my children besides materialistic things?' " She decided that it would be music. "It was one of the most important influences on my life as an adult . . . to play, sing and enjoy." So she consciously set out to lead her sons into the world of music. "They all studied piano and went on to other instruments and had fun in bands . . . and they played guitar, wrote music and sang. They've all gone in different directions with their music, but I feel that, maybe, I've succeeded with that one thing."

When her eldest son was fifteen and the youngest eleven, her husband decided to go into public health service, and the family moved to New Orleans for nine months so that Cohen could get his necessary degree at Tulane University. "It was marvelous," she says, "the best of several worlds because my husband was in school—and he had been there before. We had many friends in the academic circle, and he had many social friends he had known in college who were influential in New Orleans." Her sons felt that moving to Louisiana for a short time was "the end of the world, but it was a great experience for them," she says. "It made us all appreciate the things [in Wyoming] that we had taken for granted."

The petite blonde immersed herself in social activities and began working as a tour guide at the New Orleans Historical Museum. "I missed Cheyenne, of course, and I couldn't believe that the telephone wasn't ringing for me and that nobody cared what I was doing," she remembers. "But the fact that I could go to hear a major symphony every Tuesday night made everything worth-while."

Arline had been involved in volunteer work since shortly after her marriage. She had taught at a school for exceptional children, worked in the community concert, was president of the Symphony Guild and had been elected president of the Laramie County Arts Council when she was appointed by Governor Ed Herschler to the Wyoming Council on the Arts in 1976. "My first job was treasurer," she says. "I felt that I could learn best how [the council] worked by learning the financing end of it. . . . I've spent so many years doing volunteer work for organizations that were always struggling for money; in almost every art endeavor I've ever worked, we were always struggling to raise money and going to business people to ask for donations. It was so dreary. And then, because of the National Endowment for the Arts, we automatically receive a large sum of money. And it was so wonderful to be able to give it to different organizations that I have worked with—to be able to say 'Here's several thousand dollars. . . .' They have to deserve it, of course, and present a good grant [applica-tion]. So I just felt that I was doing something worthwhile."

The Wyoming Arts Council was established in 1969; its main function is to fund the various art organizations throughout the state including disciplines such as dance, literature, visual arts, music and a recent project, folk art. One of Arline's pet projects is the artist-in-education programs which places artists in various schools. "In Jackson we had a violin teacher, in Casper a dance instructor and in Cheyenne a cello teacher," she explains. "And just recently, we hired an architect for the schools. We also have Poets-in-the-Schools. . . . I think it's a wonderful opportunity for those children to be able to work with professional artists."

The council received $302,000 from the National Endowments of the Arts in 1980 which was ninety-eight percent of its budget. An additional $82,000 came from the state legislature's appro-priation for adminstrative costs, "but they only gave us $5,000 for our budget," she says. The Reagan administration's "original Stockman budget cut" would have reduced the council's funding by nearly half, "but we've had our people lobbying like crazy in Washington, and we think that we will probably only be cut by thirty percent," she said in August of 1981. "We can live with that. We'll just be more particular where we spend our money. I think Wyoming has a fantastic opportunity to go to private sources and corporate funding; we would like to think that our legislature would give us more money since we're the wealthiest state [per capita] in the nation. We feel that they should devote more money to the arts. Right now, Wyoming is ranked thirty-eighth as far as state funding goes and we spent eighteen cents per capita. That's not very much when we consider how wealthy Wyoming is. We have an optimistic feeling about the legislature though. In the last few years that I've worked with them, I find that the newly elected legislators are interested in the arts and anxious to help us; whereas, our legislature—let's face it—is a very conservative group."

The council usually receives between forty-five and sixty grant applications each year which amounted to four times the available funds in 1981. Chair grants, emergency funds of $500 each or less, are also given each year, some fifteen of them in 1980, at the discretion of the chairman and depending on the budget, she says. The council's past record of funding nearly eighty percent of all grant applications brings a smile to the face of its chairman. Her job includes acting as a liaison between the council and the six-member administrative staff as well as working closely with the executive director, John Buhler. Recent endowment cuts have threatened the size of the council staff which, she says, would be unfortunate "because they're all so important." Council members number ten around the state and are appointed by the governor.

A new project which Arline and the council members have been working on for some time is a "Governor's Award Project" which would "designate persons who have worked hard and helped to further the arts. I hope it will also name some outstanding artists," she says. "We've gotten permission from the governor and a $5,000 grant from Union Pacific. . . . Most other states have been doing this for some time, and I'm so glad that Wyoming is going to."

Arline's journalistic talents prepared her for dealing with the state legislature, not only in her Arts Council capacity, but when she became a legislative reporter in 1976. "I just fell into the job," she laughs. "Someone else was supposed to do it but decided not to at the last minute." She was "out to dinner with the radio station manager" when he offered her the job. "I thought it was for the local station; I didn't know that it was for the fourteen Intermountain News stations. . . . Not really having enough journalistic background and not really knowing what it would involve, it was a case of 'ignorance is bliss.' " Without prior training she "just blundered right through it."

Her most embarrassing moment occurred when she interviewed "a major member of the legislature" without turning on her tape recorder. But knowing many of the legislators "was a great help. A lot of people gave me interviews because I had known them for so long," she says. Arline had to take a cram course in various pending legislative bills. "The mineral severance tax had so many aspects to it and the federal mineral royalties—when I was interviewing someone I would think, 'I hope I don't make a stupid mistake.' Besides knowing about the content of bills, I think that interviewing is one of the most difficult things to do. It takes years to learn. And it was interesting to me to see who the really good legislators were. A lot of them I couldn't figure out how they got there."

In her spare time, Arline gardens, has organized an art show at a savings and loan company in Cheyenne and has gone into her first "very own business venture." She produced—found an artist and funds—for a limited edition advertising poster for the Cheyenne "Frontier Days" celebration, much like the ones created for the Santa Fe Opera. She only broke even on the venture but is pleased with the results.

Arline credits her husband, who is head of the State Public Health Services, with being "very supportive" of all her various projects and involvements. "When I was a legislative reporter," she says, "he was wonderful about helping me with the groceries and dinner." And she looks to him for advice.

"If my life were not totally hectic," she sighs, "I'm not sure how I would live. I'd like to try, but I probably wouldn't like it."

Paul Wataha, former mayor of Rock Springs, Wyoming—*courtesy Paul Wataha*

PAUL WATAHA

"Did it really happen?"

*Never before have so few attempted
to speak for so many with such
devastating results.*
—Winston Churchill

In the aftermath of the devastating assault on Rock Springs,
Wyoming, by "60 Minutes," October 23, 1977, residents of the
energy city were still in shock when the CBS television program
once again steamrolled over the state with a subsequent attempted
smear of Governor Ed Herschler and other high ranking Democratic officials. Of the more grievously injured victims, Rock
Springs's mayor, Paul Wataha, suffered a heart attack from stress;
and Democratic politicians in Sweetwater County suffered defeat
as a result of the CBS program and the grand jury's extended
investigation of alleged governmental corruption.

"I think that the last couple of years has been sort of a healing
period in Rock Springs," Wataha says. "People who knew what

was going on now look back and feel that they've been had. And they realize that the grand jury and '60 Minutes' were witch hunts. They were out to do a job on the Democratic party in Wyoming, including the governor who was running for reelection. Rock Springs and Sweetwater County have always been Democratic, and I think that they felt that if they could destroy the community, they could get the job done; it was all coordinated and it wasn't accomplished overnight. It was well planned."

Wataha was portrayed by "60 Minutes" as a corrupt mayor who took bribes and payoffs from underworld figures and allowed prostitution, drugs and gambling to run rampant in hs energy-impacted city. Clyde Kemp, the town's former safety director, had been fired on the grounds of ineptness and was one of the mayor's prime accusers. Interviewed in August of 1977 by "60 Minutes," the former mayor recalls: "Dan Rather [the interviewer] was a very friendly man prior to the time that the camera lights came on. When the filming began he was like a rattlesnake, completely changed. I showed him the evidence on the firing of Clyde Kemp and the questionnaires that the police department had, and other documents. Kemp was a former employee who was mad, and he became one of their witnesses. He testified and they gave him more time [on camera]; more than I was given because the only response they gave me was when I called him a liar. It was extremely unfair."

As a result of the allegations brought by Kemp and former state criminal investigator Neil Compton, on "60 Minutes," Wataha brought suit against Dan Rather, producer Paul Lowenwarten, William Luzmoor III and Arnold Morch of Media West, Inc. (KRKK radio); Charles Richardson and the Rock Springs Newspapers, Inc.; E. D. Stone, the *Glendo Grapevine*; and Clyde Kemp. (The Glendo newspaper went bankrupt, and Stone wrote a letter of apology.) Five of the suits were settled out of court. The suit against "60 Minutes" was dropped following the mayor's heart attack, which incapacitated him for three months. The doctors "would not let me continue," he says. "We knew that they would go all the way to the Supreme Court, and yet two of their key witnesses, Mr. Kemp and Mr. Luzmoor, settled out of court. So I felt that my case was extremely strong. We had all the evidence we needed on any of their charges that they made, but I couldn't go ahead with it. That was one of the most painful decisions I ever had to make."

Following the CBS broadcast, the mayor requested that the grand jury convene in Rock Springs "to clear the air." Wataha wrote to Larry Yonkee, the special prosecutor and said that "we would like for him to come in and investigate," he says. "They did come in and what was supposed to be a statewide grand jury turned out to be a Rock Springs grand jury, because they spent over a year in the community. Their investigators were coming out of the woodwork. In addition to their own men, they got the internal revenue and the F.B.I. into it. I was like a jack-in-the-box, up and down. They read my rights to me hundreds of times and took statements from me," he says. "We cooperated and gave them anything we had that was open."

Dan Rather concluded the first "60 Minutes" program with the statement that the mayor was being investigated by the I.R.S. and the F.B.I. "This was not true," Wataha says. "About two weeks later, two internal revenue agents came in and told me that they had received notification from their Washington office to pull an investigation on myself and [Democratic state chairman] Don Anselmi because of the "60 Minutes" program. They examined me back two years and went through every receipt, every savings account for myself and my sons—everything I had. At the end of the examination, I wound up owing $150 for an item they felt should have been capitalized. So I had a clean bill of health." Wataha also received clearance from the F.B.I. and the grand jury because "there was nothing to indict on. We provided them with records that showed over 200 arrests for prostitution from 1975 to 1978. And 200 arrests is a lot when you don't use entrapment. But the press blew it all out of proportion in future writings.

"I don't believe in entrapment, setting someone up to break the law and then arresting them. So we didn't use it. There were some prostitutes, but we didn't arbitrarily take a paddy wagon down and load them up, saying 'You have on high heels and a bright dress so you're a prostitute.' We had to catch them in the act of prostitution or solicitation before we could take any action. And '60 Minutes' used that." The mayor created a special

303

task force with the county to work undercover to curb both pros- titution and narcotics. During one of their raids they picked up a young woman who was in town for a bowling tournament from Cheyenne and booked her on the charge of prostitution. "She worked for a very respectable law firm but they thought that she was dressed like a prostitute – if a person can determine what one dresses like," he says. "I was very fearful for a long time that she would sue the city, but luckily she didn't."

Wataha hired Clyde Kemp, a former police officer and truck driver, as safety director for the city of Rock Springs during the summer of 1977, and he fired him three months later. The job entailed supervising the activities of both the police and fire depart- ments. "Kemp had the police department in such disarray that they asked for a meeting with me," he says. "They were ready to walk out if we didn't do something."

Neil Compton, special state investigator, was also a "60 Min- utes" witness. The mayor had asked for his professional services twice and was pleased with the results the first time, "but the second time I wasn't. He wanted me to fire all of the radio opera- tors at the police department because he said they were peddling narcotics in the radio room. I said, 'I can't do that without evi- dence' and he said, 'I'll get it for you,' yet weeks passed before he admitted that he couldn't come up with the evidence. But if I had listened to him . . ."

For months following the "60 Minutes" invasion, the mayor was harassed by reporters and cameramen as well as federal and state investigators. "I would leave my [accounting] office at night and there would be television cameras behind the brush – the bushes across the street – and they were taking pictures of me get- ting into my car. All kinds of things like that happened. They were mostly from Denver and Salt Lake City." The Cantrell-Rosa shooting, July 15, 1978, intensified community paranoia and added fuel to allegations of governmental cover-up because Rosa had been scheduled to appear before the grand jury within a few days. "Everyone was paranoid," Wataha says, "because of the methods of the grand jury. I can understand what the men were going through, trying to enforce the law but wondering, 'Who do I trust?' or 'Who is trying to set me up?' It was horrible."

Rock Springs uses ads to refute stigma

ROCK SPRINGS — Full page advertisements denouncing the stigma left by media and state grand jury probes into the city of Rock Springs are ready to appear in Wyoming newspapers.

The advertisements refute statements made in the grand jury's report and defends the city from what the advertisements call "a hatchet job" by the grand jury and CBS's "60 Minutes." They are also sharply critical of methods used by grand jury investigators, calling them "amateurs, keystone cops" and "creators of paranoia" whose investigative techniques "went out with Hitler's Nazi Germany."

The advertisements begin by listing reasons for which the city might have been "singled out" for scrutiny. The reasons include retaliation by the urban media for libel suits filed by a Rock Springs resident, a partisan political vendetta against the heavily Democratic community, jealousy over the town's prosperity and the search for sensationalism by newsmen misled by "local malcontents, anti-establishment cultists and political opportunists."

Further broken into two parts, the advertisements detail the accomplishments of the city government — the new recreational, civic, sewage and fire department facilities — and refute point by point statements made by the state grand jury

The defense of the grand jury statements, which implied that city officials failed to curb crime in the city to the full extent of their embodied powers, begins by saying Rock Springs citizens are now free to defend themselves because "while the grand jury was in session, it was not safe to speak up, because those who did were immediately the subject of investigation and threats of indictment."

The advertisements continue, "It soon became apparent the grand jury investigators were anything but fair and open-minded. No investigators called on the city officials who asked the grand jury to come in, or on other responsible citizens who knew the community. Instead, the investigators beat a steady path to the doors of the known malcontents, anti-establishment cultists, political opportunists, and those with private personal axes to grind. These were, in large part, the same individuals who steered the "60 Minutes" crew around the city and showed them only what they wanted to see.

"It was a stacked deck from the start — stacked against the City of Rock Springs."

The city's attempts to deal with prostitution are detailed in the advertisements in response to allegations by the grand jury report that the practice was allowed to flourish in the city. Also defended is the arrest of grand jury special investigator Cecil Cundy on charges of drunkenness, disturbance and resisting arrest.

The advertisements sharply attack actions by Bill Luzmoor, general manager of KRKK radio station in Rock Springs, who is also the subject of a libel suit by Rock Springs Mayor Paul Wataha, and investigative techniques used by grand jury investigators.

"...they were consistent in one field, that of violation of civil rights," the advertisements read. "They apparently contended that the Rock Springs police should dispense with constitutional guarantees of probable cause and arrest any woman who looked like what they thought a hooker might look like.

"They appeared at midnight and in the early hours of the morning, at the homes of Rock Springs citizens, and demanded that they come to the motel room of the investigators for questioning and for lie detector tests."

The motive of the investigators is also criticized.

Also included are statements praising the grand jurors themselves.

From the *Casper Star-Tribune*, December 22, 1978

Wataha knows the problems and assets of his hometown as well as he knows the top of his accounting office desk. He was born and reared in Rock Springs, a third generation native; attended city schools with his older sister and younger brother; and earned his accounting degree at the University of Wyoming. Soon after he set up his accounting office, he became involved in civic affairs and helped organize the Junior Chamber of Commerce. During the primary election of 1957, his fellow jaycees prevailed upon him to enter the mayor's race and conducted a last minute write-in campaign against five well-known "honorable" candidates. Wataha, then thirty-one, won the election and served in that capacity for the next twenty-one years, for seven consecutive terms. "In 1974, I announced that I wouldn't run again," he says. "I wanted to retire from public life. I felt that I had done my share." But voters again wrote him in, and he won the primary and general election. In 1978, after the "60 Minutes" attack, he wearily retired from public office "permanently."

The mayor first took office in 1957 during the "throes of a depression." The coal mines had closed down, and houses were selling for $3,000–$4,000 because everyone was leaving town. The city was bonded to capacity and he was faced with no money in the city budget for improvements of any kind. Then the petroleum industry "started taking over" in the early 1970s, bringing in new people. With the optional sales tax in 1973, Wataha was able to complete a $3 million sewage treatment plant and make a number of civic improvements. He also merged the city and county airports, backfilled the coal mines which crumbled beneath a block of houses in the southern section of the city and instigated low cost housing when the energy boom struck. He left office with $4 million in the city treasury and a debt-free town.

The City Recreational Commission, composed of prominent Rock Springs citizens, named the sixty-acre "Paul J. Wataha Recreational complex" for their former mayor following the "60 Minutes" invasion to thank him for his marathon service to the community. The facility contains a golf course, club house, tennis courts and ball fields. Wataha is quick to praise other public servants who helped him complete his projects—including Cliff Hansen, Stan Hathaway, Ed Herschler and Dominick "Snooks" Ferrero.

Wataha guided his town through an energy impact nightmare during the mid-seventies when Rock Springs's population jumped from 11,700 in 1970 to 25,500 five years later. His skillful handling of the impact problems prompted speaking engagements in a number of western cities where he shared his techniques and tribulations. Since retirement from public office, he has cut down the volume of his accounting business, spends more time with his wife, Dorothy, and three sons—all college honor students—and is working on a book about Rock Springs and his ordeal. "When I go through all my things, I see headlines that I still can't believe," he says. "And I catch myself thinking, 'did it really happen?' But it happened."

Gerry Spence, top trial lawyer—*author's photo*

GERRY SPENCE

"The law profession is full of pansies"

The nation's top trial lawyer says the law profession is full of "pansies" who have been defrauded of their educations. Gerry Spence, self-proclaimed gladiator of the legal arena, commands the respect and attention of some 10,000 trial lawyers each year with his candid appraisals of his profession.

Between lectures the Wyoming cowboy-lawyer has managed to win some of the biggest court judgments in history. His fees run in the neighborhood of fifty percent "after expenses" and his more notable cases have gained his clients court judgments in the millions of dollars. The 1979 Karen Silkwood trial in Oklahoma City resulted in a $10.5 million settlement against the Kerr-McGee Corporation, which followed another multimillion dollar judgment against the Squibb Company in a Casper synthetic hormone-birth defect case.

More recently, his 1981 Miss Wyoming–*Penthouse* magazine trial awarded his youthful client, Kimberly Pring of Cheyenne, $26 million in damages although that amount was later cut in half and appealed by the magazine.

The high fees allow Spence to take on cases of "vast social significance," he says, which usually don't even cover his expenses, such as the Singer case in Salt Lake City, scheduled for trial in September, 1982. Singer, a polygamous Mormon, was shot in the back by a deputy sheriff when Singer refused to comply with a court order demanding that he send his children to school instead of teaching them at home. "The Singer case asks the question, 'Are parents the mere custodians of their children or do they have some say as to how they are trained and educated?' " Spence said before the trial. "If the case doesn't tickle the attention and the soul of every American parent, then America is deaf."

Spence turns down some fifty cases for every one he accepts. One of his most publicized cases that demonstrated his incomparable ability was the Ed Cantrell trial when he successfully defended the Wyoming lawman who shot undercover agent Michael Rosa between the eyes while he was seated in the backseat of a patrol car. Cantrell so convinced Spence of his innocence of the murder charge that the lawyer put him to work on his 35,000-acre cattle ranch while Cantrell awaited trial. Spence also sent his fourteen-year-old stepson to cow camp with Cantrell for the summer. The grueling three-week trial culminated in the jury bringing in a verdict of not guilty after only two hours of deliberation, and Spence was given a standing ovation by courtroom spectators. Cantrell went home to take a nap while the jury deliberated—totally exhausted. Spence, however, slept fitfully for several weeks afterward because he experienced reruns of the trial; something that usually happens after each case, according to his beautiful second wife, Imaging.

Another case, sandwiched between the Silkwood and Cantrell trials, concerned the bombing murders of Spence's friend and fellow attorney, Vincent Vehar, his wife and son. Spence served as special prosecutor in the case against Mark Hopkinson, a convict who ordered the murders from his minimum security prison at Lompoc, California. He also phoned in the torture slaying of Spence's chief witness in the case just as the Silkwood trial ended, and Spence was to appear on "The Today Show" to talk about his successes.

Spence suffers from a compulsion to succeed which is rooted in his childhood. The eldest of three children born to a chemical engineer and fanatically religious mother in Laramie, Spence and his siblings were taught about "all kinds of sin" which he later rebelled against. He graduated from high school at sixteen and "tried all those sins that I was taught man ought not to commit, and I later came back to the teachings of my mother, but in a different way." The barrister neither drinks nor smokes, "but not because it's a sin as she saw it, because it wouldn't allow me to perform adequately in the courtroom." Spence also runs twenty miles a week to stay fit.

The six-foot-two, 220-pounder, whose trademarks are a twenty-gallon hat and Lucchese boots, graduated as valedictorian of his law class from the University of Wyoming, "not because I was so bright, but because I was so frightened that I might fail—and I was intimidated by my professors." After graduation he moved to Riverton where he asked the county attorney for a job "because I needed it so badly," was refused and subsequently conducted a successful campaign the following year to unseat the prosecutor. Spence then proceeded to close down all the "little yellow houses" of prostitution in the county and all the gambling dens. At twenty-four, he was the youngest Wyoming prosecuting attorney in history and never lost a case in the eight years he was in office.

"I was very much despised. I was a blue stocking kind of crusading prosecutor—indeed I was," he says with a grin. "And it was a very unpopular thing to do to close down all the little yellow houses in the county. The people thought that if you closed down prostitution the sheepherders would come into town and rape the women." One day someone showed his displeasure by shooting a hole in the window of Spence's car. Ironically, the first fee Spence received as a lawyer was a used Ithace pump shotgun. "When I first started in Fremont County I had the world's largest peanut business," he laughs. "I got $5 for a deed, $15 for an abstract, $5 for a farm lease, and $50 to $100 for a divorce. I worked five years before I got my first $1,000 fee."

A young lawyer has a "hard row to hoe," Spence says, "and soon somebody owns him. He starts out working for a bank, and he's owned by the establishment. If he goes to work as the county or city attorney, the politicians own him—or try to. Or he gets a retainer from an insurance company and pretty soon the insurance company owns him. There aren't many unowned lawyers in this country to go to, and the good ones are almost always owned by the big money."

Spence was "owned" by insurance companies until he was forty, then he turned his back on big business and became a champion of the people. "I suddenly realized that my talents were being used to deprive people of their just dues," he says. "When you see people coming into the courtroom with lawyers who can't match you in skill and experience and go home with nothing as a result, you see the system fail. That's what's wrong with the legal system and it makes me feel bad.

"Albert Kreiger is a friend of mine who represents the Bonanno family of New York–the godfather of godfathers–and I said 'Albert, how can you do that?' Albert has received national and state awards many times simply because he is one of the great, honest, decent, qualified, competent lawyers who has made a contribution to jurisprudence. How can a man of this quality represent the Bonannos? First of all, the Bonannos want someone they can trust. Albert's answer is 'Every time I defend a constitutional right of the Bonannos, I save one for you. And every time the Bonannos' rights are lost in court because they are the Bonannos, the same right is lost to you.' That's what the system is all about; to determine who is guilty and who isn't. . . . There's a little killer in all of us, but there's also the lover in you and me. But for one, the other can't exist. And when one gets loose–when a man kills his wife–I'll represent that person because the jury needs to understand the facts."

Spence defended a Mexican itinerant worker for seven years through three court trials, finally securing his release. The man shot and killed his Caucasian wife, "who treated him like a pet sexual gorilla," in a room filled with social workers and a deputy sheriff. Spence defended the man on the grounds that society was the killer; that the city of Rawlins was guilty because of its attitude toward "penniless Mexican people" and had allowed his client to grow up "covered with lice and barefooted in the snow; a child who watched his mother make love to railroad workers across a boxcar to gain enough money to feed her starving child." The defendant was finally found not guilty by reason of insanity (following two mistrials), declared sane not long afterward and

312

released from the state mental hospital in Evanston. Spence wrote a textbook based on the case.

"I think people are basically good, and I believe in their honesty," he says. "When we see crime, we see people who have been treated badly—kicked as puppies until they become mad dogs."

Spence feels that society's selection of attorneys is all wrong. "Lawyers need to be people, not empty intellectual giants who can't hear other people. They have to know what it is to be afraid, to be poor, to be rejected; they should know what pain is, how it is to suffer and to be insecure. All those things make people real, and I don't think you can teach people to be good lawyers by teaching them the niceties of society or cute little intellectual games or how to play golf or a good hand of bridge. Lawyers are useful to people only if they have somehow learned a great deal about themselves first. Too often we select lawyers on the basis of their intellectual acuity when the people who can really speak for others and be convincing are turned away from the legal profession. They're out selling aluminum siding and used cars. We select these sweethearts who know the right bridge clubs to belong to but have never had to work a day in their lives. They know how to smile at the right times and how to play golf. Where are the people from the bowels of the ghettos? They're not in law schools."

Spence insists that law students are taught by the "morticians" of the legal profession. "We have entrusted them to the people who live in ivory towers at the universities who couldn't try a law case if they had to. . . . They begat their own finely tuned intellectuals who haven't been taught to communicate with people." There should be a postgraduate school for trial lawyers, taught by trial lawyers, he says. The National College of Defense conducts a three-week seminar to give young lawyers the opportunity to experience courtroom situations. It's a step in the right direction, Spence concludes, but a complete overhaul of the law school system is needed.

Gerry Spence's trials and tribulations make for interesting reading in his bold autobiography, *Gunning for Justice*. Wyoming's gladiator of the legal arena plans to continue riding roughshod over his courtroom opponents for those fortunate to gain his services.

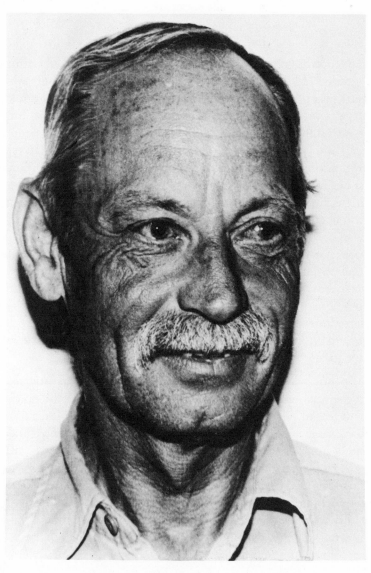

Ed Cantrell, ex-lawman—*author's photo*

ED CANTRELL

"I wish I had never been a police officer"

Throughout history, Wyoming has had its share of notorious gunmen, but none comes to mind more vividly than Ed Cantrell. Despite almost thirty years of dedicated service in the field of law enforcement, Cantrell was branded an executioner although he was acquitted of the shooting of undercover agent Michael Rosa in a Rock Springs police car, July 15, 1978.

Accounts of the shooting incident were reported around the world, but little is known about the lawman's background. He was born in Bloomington, Indiana, in 1928, the son of a Nazarene minister. The sinewy youth excelled in sports and was co-captain of his high school basketball team. He and his older sister attended Van Buren High School in Plainfield, from which he graduated in 1945 with a football and basketball scholarship to Central Normal College in his home state, a teacher's college with an excellent coaching course. Cantrell aspired to be a coach and completed almost three years of school before President Truman ordered the Berlin airlift in 1948, when Russians blocked the divided German city.

The coaching student immediately enlisted in the air force when he thought there was going to be another major "conflict." He was assigned to military police duty and shipped to central Germany where he served not only as an MP, but as a civilian policeman, since German citizens were still under military control. Cantrell spent three years in the "bombed out ruin" south of Frankfurt where displaced persons were processed and civil order was maintained. But when he returned to Camp Kilmer in New Jersey for discharge, the president extended all servicemen for an additional year due to the Korean conflict. The MP spent the next year in a military police company in Indiana and before his discharge, took the examination for Indiana state police. He was accepted, 1 of 25 applicants from 2,500 hopefuls who apply each year. "I've always been proud to have been an Indiana state police officer," he says, adding that the department ranks among the top three in the country.

Cantrell was an honor graduate from the state police academy, as he was from the military police training school five years earlier. He was stationed at the Pendleton barracks northwest of Indianapolis for six months before being transferred to the town of Portland where he met Norma Gleason, a secretary whom he married not long afterward. They were then transferred to Putnamville, his home district in the center of the state.

An avid hunter, fisherman and marksman—the patrolman came to Wyoming in 1956 to hunt in Big Horn County where he met Al Brinkerhoff who was sheriff of Lovell. As a result of meeting the sheriff and a number of other local residents, Cantrell decided to move to Wyoming in 1958, where he served as deputy sheriff with the understanding that he would apply for the state highway patrol when he completed his residency requirement. In 1960, he was eligible to take the patrol exam and was accepted for school in Cheyenne. The patrol assigned him to Rock Springs where he worked until 1967; then he requested transfer to Cody.

Cantrell resigned from the highway patrol in 1971 to lobby for a state police bill for Wyoming. "A little skeleton crew of highway patrolmen and a sheriff's department were understaffed," he says. "We knew that and were trying to look to the future and prepare for it with a bill to create a state police that would broaden the base of the patrol and make it an effective police organization." He resigned during that period because he felt he couldn't, in good conscience, draw a paycheck from the patrol while lobbying "to do away with it." Without income, he spent considerable time making long distance phone calls to ask friends to contact their legislators to favor the bill. Those efforts paid off. The state police bill passed both houses of the legislature "overwhelmingly," but was tabled for interim study by Governor Stan Hathaway. During the next two years, the bill died from political opposition, but Cantrell is "proud" that he had a part in it and served as unofficial spokesman for members of various law enforcement agencies.

The following January he secured a job as range detective in Lusk and describes his job as "deterring crime" — cattle rustling, vandalism, theft, homicide, arson, etc. "People don't think about crime in the country," he says, "but it's there. It's really the agricultural people, the backbone of this country, who are getting ripped off because they're paying huge sums of money for taxes without getting adequate police protection."

Cantrell's job took him all over Wyoming as well as neighboring states, and as far south as Texas in pursuit of rural lawbreakers. "Fugitives can find no better place to hide than a back country Wyoming ranch," he says. The range detective remained in Lusk until March of 1976, when his oldest son was killed in a car accident just after his twenty-first birthday, having passed the exam for the U.S. border patrol. "When that happened, we just kind of folded it up and came back to Rock Springs," he says. Cantrell went to work as undersheriff for Jim Stark because the sheriff had requested his assistance in reorganizing the department. Soon afterward, he turned down an offer to accept the newly created post of safety director; he declined the prestigious job with a $4,000 pay increase because of his promise to Stark. Several months later, when Clyde Kemp had been fired as safety director, he relented and accepted the post, a move that eventually led to his arrest for murder the following summer.

Cantrell found some badly demoralized police officers in the department when he assumed his new post. Turmoil and disorganization "were rampant," he says. "But there was a nucleus of very good police officers who worked overtime without pay for me although they were being blasted by the news media as

317

a bunch of crooks. That got pretty discouraging." The new safety director formed a detective's division from existing officers and appointed Jim Callas as detective sergeant. He then hired Michael Rosa as an undercover agent, unaware that Rosa had been given the option of resigning or being fired by the Lander police department for indiscretions involving women and other forms of misconduct while on duty, according to Police Chief Bill Campbell. Cantrell had little contact with Rosa because the agent reported directly to Callas, and he was surprised when Rosa threatened him at the Rock Springs courthouse after Cantrell admonished him for appearing on the witness stand in an unkempt manner. Cantrell says Rosa asked to meet him at the Holiday Inn on the afternoon of July 14, 1978, and at one point asked his boss, "Where's your gun, old man?" Rosa had incurred a forty-dollar discrepancy on a drug-buying transaction and was also involved in a relationship with a Rock Springs radio dispatcher, two situations that could have led to the married officer's dismissal from the department.

That evening, Cantrell was called at his home by Sergeant Callas who wanted to discuss the forty-dollar discrepancy with his boss at the police station. The two men later drove to the Silver Dollar Bar with police officer Matt Bider to talk to Rosa. "When he came out of the bar he had a wine glass in his hand," Cantrell says, "and when he saw me he was livid. He was so mad that when he walked over to the car, he kicked the asphalt. He didn't want to be fooled with." Rosa got into the car behind the driver, Callas, into the back seat beside Bider. Cantrell was sitting in the front passenger's seat with his head down "thinking" how he could discuss the discrepancy without angering Rosa further, he says.

Callas asked for Rosa's social security number and was writing it down when "something made me look over my [left] shoulder," Cantrell says. "Either my [dead] son told me or it was a sixth sense. Otherwise, I think he would have blown the back of my head off, or the side of my face. He was glaring at me and he said, 'What do you want you mother fucker?' and his hand went like this," he says, pulling his hand back from his lap in the direction of his belt. "I shot him. I didn't have any choice.

I couldn't reach him. If he had been closer, I could have reached him, and I wouldn't have had to kill him. I've often thought that if I had gotten out of the car and talked to him there in the parking lot, maybe it wouldn't have happened." Officer Bider was reportedly looking out of the window when the shooting occurred, and Callas was writing down numbers in the front seat.

Cantrell called in the F.B.I., the state criminal investigation department and the highway patrol to investigate the killing, and he booked himself in jail the following morning, expecting a routine self-defense hearing. Instead, he was sent to Evanston State Mental Hospital for evaluation and confined to a small cell for ten days. Pronounced sane, he was returned to Rock Springs where bail was set at $250,000, which was raised by "friends." Cantrell was told to "get out of town" (but not the state), because local authorities were afraid of more killings, he says.

Cantrell literally owes his life to his lawyer, Gerry Spence, who at first refused to take the case because he was "prejudiced" by news reports that Cantrell was a hired assassin. But Lusk attorney Bob Pfister persuaded Spence to meet with Cantrell before passing judgment. Cantrell talked to Spence at his ranch the day following his release from Evanston and convinced him of his innocence, but it was a year and a half before the case came to trial, an agonizing period for Cantrell and his family. No one would hire him, and he was forced to accept charity from friends. Later, he worked for Spence at the lawyer's ranch and cow camp. He also developed a drinking problem while he was separated from his family.

Found innocent by a jury that deliberated less than two hours, Cantrell soon learned that the verdict had not been accepted by the general public. His safety director's job had been abolished without notice and he finally found work in South Dakota as a range detective before getting a heavy equipment operator's job in Rock Springs, where his family still lived, in January 1981. He then sold cars for five weeks before being sworn in as a Sweetwater County range detective July 1 of that year by Judge Kenneth Hamm, who had set bail after his confinement at Evanston Mental Hospital.

The thin, wrinkled, nervous lawman says, "I wish I had never been a police officer. The thing that hurt me worst is that people insinuated that I'm a crook. I'm honest, you know. And never in my life have I had to go around protesting not only that I'm innocent, but also that I'm honest."

BIBLIOGRAPHY

Cannon, Lou, "Stepping Out of Rumsfeld's Shadow," *The Washington Post*, November 5, 1975.

"Congressional Wives Carve Their Own Careers," *U.S. News and World Report*," September 14, 1981.

Conversation with Lander Police Chief Bill Campbell concerning the employment record of undercover agent Michael Rosa.

Conversations with Merna Anderson and Susan LeMaster concerning Duane Shillinger's youth and the new state penitentiary.

Demarte, Kent, "A Tough and Corrupt Wyoming Mountain Town is Shocked by the Death of a Good Cop," *People Weekly*, August 28, 1978.

"Early Aviatrix Continues to Promote Air Travel," *Airport Services Management*, December 1980.

Eisenhower, John, *The Bitter Woods*, New York: Putnam, 1949.

Farney, Dennis, "A Congressman Views Washington from New Vantage," *Wall Street Journal*, December 21, 1979.

Fine, Sidney, Appraisal of Collections in the Contemporary Field in the American Heritage Center, University of Wyoming, August 30, 1979. (Written report to UW)

Fripp, Bill, "Riverton's Marlboro Man Featured in the Boston Globe," reprint in *Riverton Ranger*, October 1, 1981.

"Getter Has Grown with Needs of Rocky Mountain Empire," *Drivetrain Comments*, July, 1979.

Goedicke, Jean, Christmas letters to friends and relatives, 1955–80.

Golab, Jan, "Career Breakouts! How They Got There: Clyde and Debbie Kemp," *Denver Magazine*, February, 1977.

Jean Goedicke, Watercolorist, advertising pamphlet, 1980.

Larson, T. A., *Essays in Western History*, University of Wyoming Publication, Vol. XXXVLL, Nos. 1, 2, 3, 4, October, 1971.

Leonard, Peg Layton, *Wyoming LaBonte Country 1820–1972*, Cranberry Press, 1973.

McElfresh, Beth, *Chuck Wagon Cookbook*, Swallow Press, 1960.

Medved, Michael, *The Shadow Presidents*, Time Books, 1979.

Miller, Tim, "Wyoming Politics and Government," *Wyoming News*, August–September, 1978.

President's Report, "Happy Birthday, Lucile," *International Aviation Council Newsletter*, August, 1980.

Rae, John B., Report on Aeronautical History Collection, University of Wyoming, August 4, 1979. (Written report to UW)

Rasmussen, Wayne D., The Livestock and Farming Manuscripts in the Western History Research Center of the University of Wyoming, July, 1980. (Written report to UW)

Rather, Dan, Our Town broadcast script, "60 Minutes," September 3, 1978.

Rather, Dan, Our Town broadcast script, "60 Minutes," October 23, 1977.

Reid, T. R., "White House Staff Chief in Love with Governing, Now Runs for Congress," *The Washington Post*, November 5, 1975.

Rice, Ruth Geier, "Ruth," *The Polled Hereford Hub*, Vol. 6, No. 6, December/January, 1981.

Shadow, The, "Trained Staff," *The Monthly Con-versation*, January, 1980.

Sprinkle, Leo, UFO questionnaire form, 1981.

Wataha, Paul J., letter to Dan Rather, pre-airing warning, September 9, 1977.

White, Gerald, Report on Petroleum History and Research Center, University of Wyoming, August 30, 1979. (Written report to UW)

ABOUT THE AUTHOR

Jean Mead is a free lance photojournalist and national publicity director for Western Writers of America. Since 1968 she has worked as a staff writer/photographer/editor for four newspapers in California and Wyoming, including the Casper Star-Tribune. Her free lance articles have appeared in magazines such as *Saga* and the Denver Post's Sunday supplement, *Empire*, as well as western magazines in Norway and West Germany. She has also served as editor of *In Wyoming* magazine and president of Wyoming Writers. Her work has won numerous state and national awards.